UI is Communication

UI is Communication

How to design intuitive, user-centered interfaces by focusing on effective communication

Everett N. McKay

Principal UX Design Edge

AMSTERDAM • BOSTON • HEIDELBERG • LONDON
NEW YORK • OXFORD • PARIS • SAN DIEGO
SAN FRANCISCO • SYDNEY • TOKYO
Morgan Kaufmann is an imprint of Elsevier

Acquiring Editor: Meg Dunkerley
Editorial Project Manager: Heather Scherer
Project Manager: Priya Kumaraguruparan
Designer: Russell Purdy

Morgan Kaufmann is an imprint of Elsevier
225 Wyman Street, Waltham, MA, 02451, USA

Library of Congress Cataloging-in-Publication Data
McKay, Everett N., 1961-
   UI is communication : how to design intuitive, user centered interfaces by focusing on effective communication / Everett N McKay.
      pages cm
   Includes bibliographical references and index.
   ISBN 978-0-12-396980-4
   1. User interfaces (Computer systems) 2. Communication. I. Title.
   QA76.9.U83M443 2013
   005.4'37–dc23
                                        2013004824

British Library Cataloguing-in-Publication Data
A catalogue record for this book is available from the British Library.

For information on all MK publications visit our
website at www.mkp.com

Working together
to grow libraries in
developing countries

ELSEVIER   Book Aid International

www.elsevier.com • www.bookaid.org

To Jan Miksovsky, who taught me that great UI design is ultimately about effective human communication. To the memory of Steve Jobs, who taught everyone the importance of the human side of technology.

And to my family, Marie, Philippe, and Michele, who had to endure the human side of book writing.

Contents

CHAPTER 5   A Communication-Driven Design Process................... 241

CHAPTER 6   UI Design Examples... 293

Acknowledgments

My name is the one on the cover, but writing a book is a surprisingly complex affair that involves the contribution of many people. Without their help, this book wouldn't be what it is—or might not have happened at all.

I must start by acknowledging the people who have influenced my user experience design thinking the most over the years. **Jan Miksovsky** has been the most influential by far. His inductive user interface work at Microsoft is what started me down this long road of communication-focused design. Jan's key insights were that tasks ought to be designed to be self-explanatory and that focusing on the purpose of each step in a task is the best way to make them so. Without Jan's influence, the core principles behind this book would have never occurred to me.

Other UX design influences are **Steve Jobs**, for helping me understand the human side of technology; **Don Norman**, for helping me understand the principles that make designs intuitive; and **Alan Cooper**, for helping me understand user-centered, goal-directed, socially acceptable design. My interaction guidelines work at Microsoft was essential for developing my depth of knowledge in the UI space. Jan, **John Pruitt, Asa Noriega, Tjeerd Hoek, David Vronay, Meredith Regal,** and **Ken Jones** were primarily responsible for giving me that opportunity.

If patience is a virtue, then **Meg Dunkerley**, my acquisitions editor, and **Heather Scherer**, my senior editorial project manager, are the most virtuous people I have ever met. Due to unforeseen business circumstances (way too much of it), I managed to miss every deadline, but Meg and Heather kept everything together to make this book happen. I'm sure less virtuous editors would not have been so forgiving. I feel privileged to have worked with them on this book. I must also thank **Rachel Roumeliotis**, my original acquisitions editor, for fighting to get my proposal accepted.

My reviewers are responsible for the quality of the content through their helpful comments and suggestions. **Paul Hibbitts** and **Barbara Karsch** somehow endured the entire journey, and **Casey McKinnon, Paul Cutsinger,** and **Manuel Clément** provided great help along the way.

Jodi Hersh of Orange Star Design is my top-notch graphic designer who helped me with all the illustrations and many of the screenshots. The book would not look nearly as good if I hadn't had her help. Thanks to **Kevin Cheng**, **Tom Chi**, **Matthew Inman**, and **Scott Adams** for their insightful UI design cartoons. Also, thanks to Paul Hibbitts and **Charles Caldwell** for their help with agile user stories.

This entire project started with an email from **Linda Newman Lior** about starting her book *Writing for Interaction: Crafting the Information Experience for Web and Software Apps.* Without Linda's encouragement, this project would probably still be on my to-do list. I would like to thank **Paul Hibbitts, Barbara Karsch, John Pruitt, Liza Potts, Christian Schormann,** and **Na'ama Shapira** for reviewing drafts of my proposal and providing excellent advice.

Finally, I have been presenting the core material in *UI is Communication* in my *UX Design Essentials* course over the past few years. Everyone who has taken *Essentials* has contributed to the quality of this book in some way. Training is a two-way street, and my students have taught me a great deal. I must thank **Scott Berkun** for accidentally getting me into the training business in the first place.

Everett McKay
Saint Albans, Vermont

About the Author

Everett McKay is Principal of UX Design Edge, a user experience design training and consulting company for mobile, web, and desktop applications based in Vermont. Everett's specialty is UX design training through onsite and public courses for software professionals who aren't experienced designers. He also runs AskAUXExpert.com, a Web-based UX design consulting service.

Previously, Everett was a Senior Program Manager at Microsoft Corporation on the Windows 7, Windows Vista, and Windows Server teams. While at Microsoft he was responsible for writing and consulting on the *Windows User Experience Interaction Guidelines*. He was also responsible for teaching Microsoft's in-house introductory UI design course. Before joining Microsoft, Everett was a programmer, specializing in designing and developing Windows and Macintosh user interfaces. He holds Master of Science and Bachelor of Science degrees in Electrical Engineering and Computer Science from Massachusetts Institute of Technology (MIT).

You can contact Everett at everett@uiiscommunication.com.

Introduction

"The moment a user sees your UI, it communicates where they have arrived, what they can do, and how they should do it. The user receives this message from every aspect of your design: graphical and textual, silent and audible, static and moving, intentional and accidental. Figure out what you want that message to be, then do everything you can to ensure the message your UI sends is as close as possible to the one you intended."

—JAN MIKSOVSKY

FIGURE 0.1
Does it really depend (so often)? OK/Cancel ©2005 Tom Chi and Kevin Cheng. Used by permission.

For me, the least satisfying answer to any user interface design question is an unqualified "It depends." Yet people often give variations of that answer to many design questions.

There are situations where it really does depend: The problem is complex and unfamiliar, there are many factors and tradeoffs in play, it's not clear what our users really want, and you can't really know for sure until you do a lot of brainstorming, prototyping, user testing, and many rounds of iteration.

But if we really understood user interface (UI) design well, shouldn't this labor-intensive approach to decision making be infrequent and reserved for unusual and most important design challenges? Shouldn't we at least be able to address routine design decisions quickly and confidently? After all, no competent engineer ever answers the question, "Will this bridge fall down?" with "Well, it depends." And they don't have to build bridge prototypes and perform user testing to find out. They *know*.

FIGURE 0.2

A competent engineer would never answer "Will this bridge fall down?" with "Well, it depends."

There is a lot at stake here. To users, *the user experience is the product* and the product's success depends on designing the user interface well. Saying "It depends" means more design and development time and effort to find the right answers. User experience (UX) teams can spend enormous amounts of time wrangling over routine design decisions—and still manage to get them wrong. Engineering teams without design talent often just wing those decisions based on personal preference or by copying familiar UIs they know. Either way, the cost of designing a product with a poor user experience and having to fix it later—or even worse, keeping it permanently—is enormous.

Technical managers, who are typically evaluated and rewarded for shipping features on schedule, are reluctant to be distracted by anything that might slow their teams down. Having to invest significant time and money to research, prototype, test, and iterate routine design decisions is a deal breaker for them. As a result, they will talk about having a great user experience, but they won't make the investments required.

Don't get me wrong: The traditional brainstorming, prototyping, user-testing, and refinement process works great—especially when you have no idea what else to do. Can we do better than "It depends" for many design decisions—especially the routine ones? I think we can!

THE *UI IS COMMUNICATION* CONCEPT

The concept behind *UI is Communication* is that a user interface is essentially a conversation between users and a product to perform tasks that achieve users' goals. A UI differs from human conversation primarily in that it uses the language of UI instead of natural language. A well-designed UI boils down to communicating to users in a way that is natural, professional and friendly, easy to understand, and efficient. By contrast, a poorly designed UI is unnatural, technological and mechanical, and requires users to apply thought, experimentation, memorization, and training to translate it into something meaningful. Effective communication is often what makes the difference.

FIGURE 0.3
With Apple's Siri, the user interface actually is a natural, friendly conversation.

From this point of view, user interface design isn't a subjective visual art about pixels and aesthetics but rather a principled objective communication skill to explain tasks to users. By focusing on communication, design decisions that initially appear subjective—such as control selection, icon design, layout, color, and animation—become much more objective. Beauty, style, and fashion are largely subjective, but what constitutes a comprehensible and intuitive task explanation to the target user is not.

Every user interface element can be evaluated by how effectively it communicates. If users need to translate your UI into something meaningful, you should use that translated, meaningful version instead. If your UI has elements that communicate nothing, you should remove them. And if your UI communicates in a way that would be rude or inappropriate in person, it is equally rude or inappropriate in your user interface. Confusing controls, labels, and icons; pages that are hard to read and scan; awkward task flows; and the need for user manuals and training are all forms of communication problems.

This communication-focused approach to UI design allows you to leverage everyday interpersonal communication skills that you have practiced all your life. If you can explain how to perform a complex task in person in a way that's clear and concise, *UI is Communication* will help you map that explanation into the language of UI—both in terms of interaction and visual design—in a way that feels simple, natural, easy to understand, and humane. The outcome of this approach is naturally user- and user-goal centered. If you would explain a task in a certain way in person, why should your UI be any different?

The most important concept to understand now is that UI isn't some completely different form of communication. Good UI is designed to communicate to people, not robots, so it is *human* communication. At the highest level, many UI design problems for well-conceived products that are confusing, hard to use, and unintuitive relate to a failure to communicate.

For example, consider the classic "Should I use radio buttons or a checkbox?" question. Although there are dozens of possible considerations, answering the question "What are you trying to communicate?" drives the decision.

FIGURE 0.4
Should you use radio buttons or a checkbox? To answer, determine what you are trying to communicate.

If you are providing an option that can be turned on or off, a checkbox is the better choice; if you are providing two or more independent states (other than on/off), radio buttons are the better choice. If you can't craft a checkbox label that is meaningful in both states, that is a sure sign that you should use a different control. Other design considerations (such as screen space used), although important, are usually secondary. **Focusing on effective communication gets you to the right decision quickly and confidently.**

☑ Landscape   ○ Portrait
                ◉ Landscape

FIGURE 0.5
Landscape versus portrait mode is a choice between two independent states, making radio buttons the better choice.

By contrast, if you make such decisions based on design by committee, design by copy, personal preference, or gut feel, chances are you are doing it wrong. And it's possible that if you were to prototype and user-test this wrong design, many details like this wouldn't even surface. Design by coding trial and error is a long, rough road.

I'm not saying that subjective design aesthetics aren't important, that visual design doesn't matter to users, or that graphic designers aren't valuable members of the design team. They do, it does, and they are. But all too often, teams make design decisions by battling over subjective personal opinion—what I like versus what you like—and the boss or loudest voice usually wins. Although beauty, style, and taste are very subjective and personal, effective communication is much less so. If a UI isn't comprehensible, little else matters. Confusing is never in style or tasteful.

FIGURE 0.6

Making design decisions by battling over personal opinion usually isn't productive. DILBERT ©2007 Scott Adams. Used by permission of UNIVERSAL UCLICK. All rights reserved.

WHY I WROTE THIS BOOK

Over the years, I have noticed that by far the most common UX design book request has been for that *one book* that will help people new to design get started. This request is so common that I don't recall a significant runner-up.

When asked, I recommend my personal favorites, such as Donald Norman's *The Design of Everyday Things,* Steve Krug's *Don't Make Me Think*, and Alan Cooper's *About Face*. Even though these are all excellent books, none of them really fulfills that "one book" request, because they tell only part of the story. By contrast, Kim Goodwin has done a fantastic job of documenting the UX design process in detail with *Designing for the Digital Age*, but it is too much to recommend to beginners.

The technology world needs a simple UX design book that is sufficiently comprehensive, yet concise and approachable for those new to design. I strongly believe that exploring user interface design from objective human communication-based principles and techniques is the best approach to developing design thinking and taking on this "one book" challenge, especially for technically oriented nondesigners.

WHO THIS BOOK IS FOR

The target readers for *UI is Communication* are entrepreneurs, executives and managers, developers, business analysts, user researchers, testers and quality assurance, user assistance

writers and editors, and other nondesigner software professionals who are working with UI and want to raise their game. There are no prerequisites other than an interest in learning how to design better UIs and general awareness of UI design.

Even though experienced designers aren't my target audience, I am pleasantly reassured when professional designers tell me that the concepts in *UI is Communication* have helped them gain a better understanding of what they have been doing without really understanding why before. If you are an experienced designer, please take a look, too.

Developers who specialize in backend technologies such as databases and API design usually consider themselves off the UI design hook, but my experience indicates otherwise. If your product has awkward task flows, poor performance, isn't responsive, provides poor feedback, has incomprehensible error messages, or presents inscrutable data, chances are your team has backend developers who incorrectly believe that they don't have to worry about UI design. Even application programming interfaces (APIs) are user interfaces that need to be usable, too.

WHAT UI TECHNOLOGIES IS THIS BOOK FOR?

In short, all of them. Thinking about UI in terms of effective human communication applies to all user interfaces, from mobile to desktop apps, from Websites to embedded systems. It even applies to voice-driven UIs. I have used examples from Websites, Web-based apps, mobile apps, and Windows and Macintosh desktop apps to reinforce this technology independence.

That said, there are situations in which designing mobile apps is somewhat different due to limited screen space and touch-based interactions. I have called out such differences when appropriate.

UI VS. UX, AND WHY ISN'T THIS *UX IS* LIKE *COMMUNICATION*?

You might be wondering why I didn't call this book *UX is* Like *Communication*. Or you might be wondering what the difference between UI and UX is in the first place.

A *user interface,* or UI, is what connects users to a product's underlying technology. It is what users see and feel directly when using a product. For a car, the user interface includes the steering wheel; accelerator, brake, and clutch; the dashboard; the various controls; the seats and interior; the keys and remote control; the overall ambiance of the interior, and so on.

By contrast, a *user experience,* or UX, encompasses the entire experience users have with a product. That experience includes the UI, but it also transcends the UI to include the internals that users don't interact with directly, as well as the externals, such as the purchasing process, the initial product experience (often called the "out-of-box" experience), customer and technical support, product branding, and so on. For a car, the user experience includes internals such as the engine, chassis, handling, and reliability, as well as the externals, such as the product showroom, the purchasing and delivery experience, the owner's and repair manuals, the product warranty, and the service department.

User interface design addresses actions users must do, but user experience design also addresses actions users *don't* have to do. For example, a good product might have a well-designed user interface for its initial configuration, but a good *user experience* might make that initial configuration unnecessary in the first place. User experience design is the more encompassing goal and is what most design professionals focus on today. I named my company *UX Design Edge* for a reason.

I named this book *UI is Communication* because the "design as effective human communication" concepts apply mostly to user interface design—what users see and interact with on the screen. For example, by reading this book, you will learn exactly what it means for a UI to be intuitive. While I'm confident that you can apply these concepts to the broader scope of user experience design, that goal is beyond the scope of this book.

Also, I named this book *UI is Communication* instead of *UI is Like Communication* to suggest that this isn't a metaphor or simile, but a definition. UI design *is* a form of human communication.

If you are new to design and aren't familiar with the lingo, please check out the Glossary in the Appendix. Most of the vocabulary you will need is defined there.

WHAT'S IN THE BOOK?

The book is organized into six chapters, each of which presents the *UI is Communication* concept from a different angle.

Chapter 1: *Communication Design Principles* establishes baseline principles of intuitive UI design as a form of effective human communication. It presents the core design principles that support the *UI is Communication* concept and explores effective human communication, what it means for a UI to be intuitive, how consistency is often required to be intuitive, when it makes strategic sense to not be intuitive, how to ask intuitive questions, and a general user model to understand typical user behavior.

Chapter 2: *Interaction Design* establishes the language of UI—essentially, the parts of speech for user interface. It presents interaction design by exploring the language of UI from the perspective of effective communication, including controls, commands, labels, feedback, messages, grouping, tasks, and dynamic elements.

Chapter 3: *Visual Design* **explores visual UI design from the communication perspective.** It covers the importance of good visual design, how to work with designers, layout and designing for scanning, the effective use of visual design elements, and how to demand the user's attention when needed.

Chapter 4: *Communicating to People* **covers the human side of human-computer interaction.** Your target users are emotional, error-prone humans, not robots, so a good software interaction should have the same standards as a good social interaction. This chapter explores how people react to software emotionally, having a good personality and tone, motivating users by providing value, minimizing the user's effort, being forgiving and trustworthy, being smart, and making the experience enjoyable.

Chapter 5: *A Communication-Driven Design Process* **presents a communication-driven design process** for making good design decisions, especially when working within a team. This chapter defines exactly what design is and identifies the classic design mistakes, both of which have profound implications for the design process itself. It then explores specific ways in which having a communication focus affects the design process.

Chapter 6: *UI Design Case Studies* **applies a communication-driven design process to some real design problems.** This chapter covers both desktop and mobile examples. It's the proof of the pudding.

SUMMARY OF THE TOP PRINCIPLES

Here is a summary of the top design principles that you will learn as you read this book:

1. **A user interface is essentially a conversation between users and a product to perform tasks that achieve users' goals.** Start a design by understanding what you need to communicate to users, and then let that communication drive the design process and the UI design itself. At the highest level, many UIs that are confusing, hard to use, and unintuitive relate to a failure to communicate.

2. **Explain tasks clearly and concisely, as you would in person.** The key is to understand that the UI isn't some completely different type of communication. Rather, it's the same communication using a slightly different language.

3. **Every UI element can be evaluated by what it communicates and how effectively it does that job.** The need for effective communication applies to everything, including control selection, layout, icon and other graphic design, color, and animation. If users need to translate your UI into something meaningful before they can use it, you should use that translated, meaningful version instead. If your UI has elements that communicate nothing, you should remove them.

4. **If a UI feels like a natural, professional, friendly conversation, it is probably a good design.** This is a simple yet remarkably effective technique for evaluating a design. If you wouldn't say something in person, why say it in a UI?

5. **Users are humans, not robots.** Humans are emotional. They are in a hurry. They want to enjoy what they are doing. They make small mistakes all the time. They are focused on their work and are easily distracted. Your product should communicate to users on a human level—so, it's not just what you say but how you say it.

6. **Be polite, respectful, and intelligent.** Good software interaction should have the same standards as a good social interaction. If an interaction would be inappropriate, rude, disrespectful, or stupid between people, it is equally inappropriate with software. Software shouldn't get a free pass for rudeness and disrespect. Like people, UIs communicate through their personality, tone, and attitude.

7. **Mechanically enabling tasks is only the first step in great design, not the last. Great UI design transcends mechanical usability** by recognizing that there is an emotional, impatient, error-prone human at the other end of the interaction. User goals, context, and intent often make mechanical solutions a poor choice. We need higher expectations than mechanical usability.

8. **UI form follows communication. At the wireframe level, every visual design element should be justified by what it communicates.** If a UI element doesn't communicate anything, remove it. If it communicates poorly, redesign it. Through the lens of visual communication, many visual design decisions that initially appear subjective, emotional, arbitrary, and aesthetic are actually objective, rational, coordinated, and principled.

9. **People are emotional and react emotionally to a product's visual appearance. Consequently, your product should look the part—it should look like it fulfills its purpose well.** But if instead your product's visual appearance is of questionable quality, users will naturally assume that the rest of the product has the same level of quality. Don't assume that users will see the beauty that lies beneath—they won't.

10. **Use a communication-driven design process to create better designs and make the right decisions quickly and confidently.** During the planning phase, develop value propositions, define personas, and determine your top scenarios to understand who your target users are, what they are likely doing, and why they care. Start the design phase by sketching out what the UI needs to communicate by thinking about how you would explain the task in person. Use scenarios and communication-focused evaluation techniques to refine the design and evaluate it from the target user's point of view.

IS THIS REALLY ALL THERE IS TO UI DESIGN?

No, but I'm not claiming that it is. Rather, I believe that "design as effective human communication" is the best way to build your design thinking, to help you understand the language of UI, learn how to design intuitive user interfaces, and help you make solid design decisions quickly and confidently. And effective communication is a quality that successful modern products must have.

Still, UI design is a very broad subject that requires an equally broad skill set. To list my top 10 personal favorite design skills, ideally you should understand the overall design process, design principles design guidelines, value propositions, scenarios, personas, data-driven decisions, simplicity, prototyping, and team culture. And that's just for interaction design. UI programming, product planning, graphic design, information architecture, user research, branding, and user assistance are completely different fields.

Yes, UI design is a challenging subject, but as Voltaire once said: *The best is the enemy of the good.* **Why make UI design harder than it needs to be?** Let's not overwhelm ourselves. Instead, start with a solid product concept that provides clear value; understand your target users and their goals, tasks, and problems; get the UI communication right; hire a great visual designer, and you are most of the way there. This book will help you get the communication part right.

HOW TO READ THIS BOOK

I hope you have the time to read *UI is Communication* from cover to cover, but I know you are busy and might not have the time available right now. **To help you get started quickly, I have designed this book to be easy to skim. Find the chapters that are most relevant to your current needs and just read the headings, any text in bold, the examples and their captions, and the summary at the end of the chapter, and you will learn the most important information in the chapter.** You can then go back to read entire chapters as needed to get a better understanding of the details. I especially recommend this approach if you are new to design because it will make the material easier to absorb.

Although you probably won't be able to read the entire book on a long plane ride, you will be able to skim the entire book and have time left for a movie.

Each chapter builds on the previous chapters, but the chapters are sufficiently independent to be read in any order without missing too much. Although it would help to read Chapter 1, "Design Principles," first to understand the core communication-related design principles, doing so isn't a requirement.

UI DESIGN IS A TEAM EFFORT

I recommend sharing *UI is Communication* with everyone on your team—or better yet, giving everyone a copy. You are about to learn a nontraditional approach to UI design, and it will have much more impact if everyone on your team has their head in the game and is working from the same page. You will need to collaborate with your team to work these ideas into your current software development process. But ultimately, reading this book will enable your team make better design decisions more quickly and confidently—for the right reason!

Communication Design Principles

"One cannot not communicate. Because every behavior is a kind of communication, people who are aware of each other are constantly communicating. Any perceivable behavior, including the absence of action, has the potential to be interpreted by other people as having some meaning."

—PAUL WATZLAWICK

The concept behind *UI is Communication* is that a *user interface* (UI) is essentially a conversation between users and a product to perform tasks that achieve users' goals. A user interface differs from human conversation primarily in that it uses the language of UI instead of natural language. A well-designed UI boils down to communicating to users in a way that is natural, professional and friendly, easy to understand, and efficient. By contrast, a poorly designed UI is unnatural, is technological and mechanical, and requires users to apply thought, experimentation, memorization, and training to translate it into something meaningful. Effective communication is often what makes the difference.

The goal of this chapter is to establish baseline principles of intuitive UI design as a form of effective human communication, which I will use throughout the book. In doing so, I will present the attributes of intuitive UI for both individual interactions and entire tasks. Many UIs involve asking users questions, so I will present principles for doing this common pattern intuitively. Finally, I will present a model for typical user behavior to help determine how well your designs communicate.

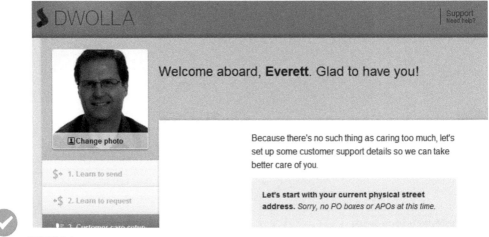

Communicates
well

FIGURE 1.1
A user interface is essentially a conversation between users and a product.

IMAGINE THIS TYPICAL UI DESIGN SITUATION . . .

Imagine this: You are working in a small team developing a new software product, and you realize that having a great user experience is crucial for its success. Everyone on the team is a manager, developer, business analyst, or tester, but unfortunately, nobody on the team has a UI design background or any experience designing "user-friendly" UI. You can't hire any design talent or one of those user experience (UX) design consultants—the budget is too tight—so you are on our own. (If you are like most readers, you shouldn't have to imagine too hard, because this situation is quite typical.)

But not to worry—Bob and Alice are our best developers and have been assigned to the UI design. Although they don't have any UI design experience, they are smart and articulate, they have a strong command of the technology, and everyone on the team loves working with them. They have an excellent track record for getting things done.

You have watched Bob and Alice from a distance for the past few weeks and you are cautiously optimistic. After all, they have taken time to talk to everyone on the team, they have talked to customers and key stakeholders, they even did some site visits, and they have done lots of UI sketching on their white boards. You have heard them constantly use terms like *user experience*, *user friendly*, *usability*, *intuitive*, and *simple*. They frequently talk about having user empathy.

Right now, Bob and Alice are about to present their initial UI design proposal to the team for the first time. What do you expect to happen? I have two questions:

1. How good do you think their initial UI design will be?

2. How well do you think the meeting will go?

Please think these questions through before turning the page. Base your answers on your personal experience.

FIGURE 1.2
Bob and Alice presenting their UI design proposal to the team for the first time.

This is a purely hypothetical situation and there are no right or wrong answers, but here are my expectations based on my experience:

1. **Their initial UI design won't be very good.** Even though Bob and Alice have gone through the motions, they will make the classic mistakes that everyone else makes, such as designing for themselves, considering only one solution, and ultimately focusing on technology and features instead of user goals and tasks. Their page designs will be confusing, overly complicated, and nonstandard. Frankly, the pages will look like they were designed by programmers—because they were.

2. **The meeting itself will go quite well.** Bob and Alice are smart and articulate, they have a strong command of the technology, and everyone on the team loves working with them. Their talent will show up in the meeting. They will do an excellent job of explaining (and defending) the design to the team, and their designs will make much more sense after they explain them. If anyone on the team objects to a questionable design decision, Bob and Alice will have a technology-based defense as to why it has to be that way.

Neither of these likely outcomes should be very surprising. After all, UI design is challenging, and Bob and Alice don't have any training or experience. But they have plenty of experience explaining their ideas in person—a lifetime of experience, in fact—so that skill comes naturally.

What is surprising is that these two results are so different! If Bob and Alice can communicate the tasks to us effectively using English, why can't they communicate those tasks equally well using the language of UI? Aren't they ultimately communicating exactly the same thing—just using a *slightly* different language? During the design review, you might have thought, "If they just put what they said in the meeting directly in the UI, it would all make sense!" Good question—why didn't they?

As humans, we are extraordinarily skilled at communicating to other people, because this is a skill that we have continuously developed throughout human civilization. Communication between people tends to:

- Be natural and friendly and use plain language.

- Be goal-oriented, results-oriented, and very purposeful; we carefully explain why people need to do things.

- Follow the person's mental models and natural workflows (where the mental model is their interpretation of how a program works or how the task should be performed).

- Be very simple, getting right to the point.

When we communicate directly in person, we are totally focused on the person's goals: *What does this person care about now?*

Communicates well

FIGURE 1.3

This UI feels like a natural, friendly conversation between people.

By contrast, communication through technology tends to:

- Be unnatural, using technical language and tone.

- Be technology or mechanically oriented—rarely bothering to explain why.

- Follow the way the code works, revealing the raw data structures.

- Be overly complicated, laboring over unimportant details.

When we communicate through UI, we are focused on the technology and details: *What does the software need now?*

If our ability to communicate in person is so much better, why can't we use the same approach? Why don't we put essentially what we say in person directly on the UI? Simply put, we can and we should! Often, great UI design boils down to eliminating these differences, making the experience simple and natural. The old technical approach is artificial, historical (that is, we have always done it that way), and no longer necessary.

Too often, we design UIs by exposing the underlying technology directly to users—asking users to fill in raw data structures and perform the task the same way as the code does—and expect the results to be usable. We are surprised when this approach leads to poor UI. We shouldn't be. From the point of view of effective communication, there are no surprises here.

FIGURE 1.4
By contrast, this UI feels technical and unnatural, as though the raw data structures are displayed directly on the page.

Designed for robots

> Great UI design often boils down to communicating to users as we do in person: in a way that is simple, natural, friendly, and focused on the user's goals.

CORE PRINCIPLES OF *UI IS COMMUNICATION*

Here are the *UI is Communication* core principles:

Principle #1: UI is Communication. A user interface is essentially a conversation between users and a product to perform tasks that achieve users' goals. Start a design by understanding what you need to communicate to users, then let that communication drive the design process and the UI design itself. At the highest level, many UIs that are confusing, hard to use, and unintuitive relate to a failure to communicate.

Principle #2: Explain tasks clearly and concisely, as you would in person. The key is to understand that the UI isn't some completely different type of communication. Rather, it's the same communication using a *slightly* different language.

Principle #3: Every UI element can be evaluated by what it communicates and how effectively it does that job. The need for effective communication applies to everything, including control selection, layout, icon and other graphic design, color, and animation. Controls even have a "body language," in which their presentation suggests details on how they are used. If users need to translate your UI into something meaningful, you should use that translated, meaningful version instead. If your UI has elements that communicate nothing, you should remove them.

Principle #4: Be polite, respectful, and intelligent. We must have the same standards for human-to-computer interaction as we do for human interaction. If an interaction would be inappropriate, rude, disrespectful, or stupid between people, it is equally inappropriate with software. Software shouldn't get a free pass for rudeness and disrespect. Like people, UIs communicate through their personality, tone, and attitude.

Principle #5: If a UI feels like a natural, professional, friendly conversation, it is probably a good design. This is a simple yet remarkably effective technique for evaluating a design. If someone is explaining a design, compare the explanation to what is on the screen. If you are reviewing your own design, ask yourself: Would I actually say this in person? Either way, any discrepancies reveal problems.

Focusing on effective communication is the simplest way to make designs intuitive and to focus on users and their goals. This is because communication between people tends to be naturally intuitive and user centered.

I will apply these core principles throughout the remainder of the book.

FIGURE 1.5
Some conversations with software are thoughtful. This one is more emotional.

> If a UI feels like a natural, professional, friendly conversation, it is probably a good design. If you wouldn't say something in person, why say it in your program?

EFFECTIVE COMMUNICATION

This communication-focused approach to UI design allows you to leverage everyday interpersonal communication skills that you have practiced all your life. **Clearly I'm assuming that you have developed fantastic interpersonal communication skills. In case you haven't, here's a quick refresher.**

A UI communicates effectively when it has the appropriate combination of these attributes:

- **Useful, relevant, necessary.** The UI provides information that is useful and relevant to the task at hand and that doesn't go without saying. If a completely confused user could readily provide the same information, skip it.

Click the **Add note** button to add a note.

FIGURE 1.6

But I already knew that! This instruction goes without saying.

- **Purposeful.** The UI helps users understand the task, focusing on the objective and tying them to the user's goals and motivation, not the basic mechanics of the interaction. If novice users who understand basic interaction could provide the same information, skip it.

Enter the Snarfbladt name:

FIGURE 1.7

OK, great ... but what's a Snarfbladt and why do I need to provide one? This instruction is focused on the mechanical interaction, not the purpose.

- **Clear and natural.** The UI speaks the user's language—using language users would naturally say in conversation. The text avoids unnecessary jargon, abbreviations, and acronyms, fully spelling out words in plain language whenever possible. It's common advice to avoid jargon, but jargon exists for a reason—it is a specialized language for precise communication between people in a particular profession. Using jargon is fine as long as your target users routinely use it. But if they don't, use plain language instead.

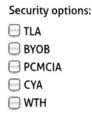

Security options:

☐ TLA
☐ BYOB
☐ PCMCIA
☐ CYA
☐ WTH

FIGURE 1.8
These options need a decoder ring to translate into plain language.

• **Easy to understand.** Even if the information is useful and in plain language, the UI shouldn't require thought, experimentation, documentation, or special knowledge to understand.

> You have interrupted a hard disk restore, which must be run to completion.
> Are you sure that you want to continue?
>
> [Continue] [Cancel]

FIGURE 1.9
Continue … with what, the restoration or the interruption? Not feeling lucky.

• **Specific and explicit—it doesn't undercommunicate.** The UI provides the right level of detail so that users know what to do. For example, error messages should identify the specific object that's encountering a problem, what specifically is wrong, and specifically what to do about it.

> ✖ Invalid address

> Mailing address postal code doesn't match the city. If the postal code is correct, verify the city name or try alternative spellings.

FIGURE 1.10
The bottom example explains specifically what is wrong with the address and what to do about it, whereas the vague top example makes users experiment to figure it out.

- **Concise, efficient—it doesn't overcommunicate.** The UI provides the right level of detail so that users can make informed decisions confidently but without going overboard. It provides the essential information by default but, when appropriate, allows users to get more details when they really need them. By contrast, UIs that overcommunicate explain every detail, no matter how irrelevant, often in large blocks of text that discourage reading.

Create a database replica

What is the purpose of this replica?

- ◉ A personal, offline, editable copy More
- ○ A copy for a remote location to improve performance More
- ○ A read-only copy that can receive updates More
- ○ To make changes to an offline production copy, then publish to a live database More

[Next]

Communicates
well

FIGURE 1.11

Although these options and the technology behind them are complex, the options here focus on the purpose of the replica types without overwhelming the user. If users want more information, all they have to do is ask.

Please log on to the system

Please type your user name in the field below:

[   ]

Please type your password in the field below:

[   ]

Click the Log on button to log in.

[Log on]

Communicates
poorly

FIGURE 1.12

By contrast, this logon screen severely overcommunicates. The extra language only says the obvious and discourages reading.

- **Inspires confidence—it doesn't overwarn.** The UI is encouraging and builds users' confidence that they are doing the right thing. Warnings should be reserved for infrequent issues that require special attention. Minor problems should be presented as minor problems, not disasters. Nothing should ever be described as catastrophic, fatal, critical, a failure, or illegal. Users should never asked to abort, kill, or terminate anything.

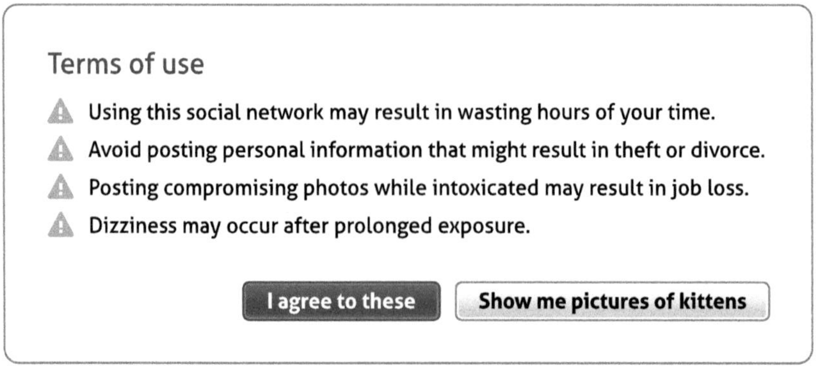

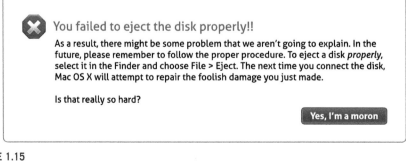

FIGURE 1.13

Using this social network sure feels like a hazard-prone activity.

- **Timely.** The UI provides the information at the right time and in the right context, neither too early nor too late. Information presented too early presumes that users will read something that isn't relevant yet and remember it, whereas information presented too late presumes that users will proceed with the task confidently without it. If the information is important to the task, neither presumption is valid.

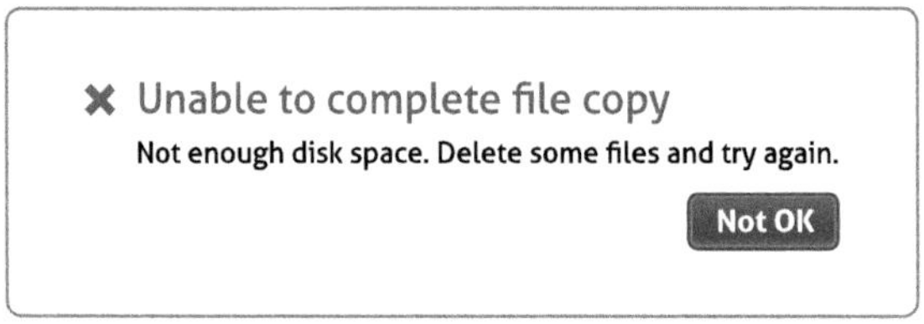

FIGURE 1.14

I would have preferred to know this before I wasted my time.

- **Good personality and tone.** I address personality and tone extensively in Chapter 4, but Alan Cooper's summary is best: "If we want users to like our software, we should design it to behave like a likeable person."

Communicates
poorly

FIGURE 1.15

This error message definitely does not behave like a likeable person.

- **Rarely interrupts.** The UI rarely interrupts and never breaks the user's workflow to ask unnecessary, unimportant questions. Rather, the UI interrupts users only if it has a very good reason to. The UI confirms actions only if there is a good reason not to proceed without asking.

Downloading internet images can expose your address. Continue?

Yes   No

FIGURE 1.16
Although this confirmation raises a valid security concern, after a while it is nothing but an annoying interruption.

These effective communication attributes clearly apply to text, but they apply to all other UI elements as well.

Put some thought into these attributes in your everyday conversations. Think about conversations that are unimportant, hard to understand, overly terse, overly chatty, and rude and when you are constantly interrupted. I'm sure these are not pleasant experiences. The exact same rules for good in-person conversations apply to conversations through software.

INTUITIVE UI

For any software project, it's a sure thing that having an "intuitive UI" is a top goal. For users, describing a UI as intuitive is among the highest praise they can bestow. For marketers, it's a requirement to describe their product's UI as "intuitive and easy to use"—regardless of whether it is.

Given this universal design goal, it's reasonable to ask what it means for a UI to be intuitive. Surprisingly, nobody really knows. Ironically, most people's definition of intuitive is, well, intuitive itself, as they struggle to define the term in a specific, meaningful way. (Try defining it yourself before continuing.) For most people, *intuitive* just means *better*. How can you achieve a project goal if you don't even know what it is?

Intuitive: A definition

Given all the talk about intuitive UI, you would think every UI design book would define and explain the term in detail. Surprisingly, few do. **The world's most confusing UI could be credibly described as intuitive as long as the term isn't defined specifically. So let's define it.**

I struggled to find an existing definition worth repeating, so here is my own definition of intuitive UI:

A UI is intuitive when target users understand its behavior and effect without use of reason, memorization, experimentation, assistance, or training.

In other words, a UI is intuitive when users can quickly figure it out on their own.

> If users can't understand how to use a UI on their own, they can't figure it out with confidence on the first try, or the results are surprising or don't meet their expectations, it's not intuitive—by definition!

No manual required

Well-designed products shouldn't need a user's manual, online help, or training to use. Any task, even an advanced task, can be designed to be sufficiently self-explanatory to make a user's manual, help, or training redundant.

FIGURE 1.17
Well-designed user interfaces shouldn't require a user's manual.

To be clear, many advanced tasks require documentation or training. But the instruction should be focused on learning how to perform the task itself, not how to figure out how to use a confusing UI to perform the task. Although I absolutely want my airline pilots to be thoroughly trained, I sure hope their training is focused on flying the plane safely, not on how to use poorly designed, confusing, unintuitive avionics.

FIGURE 1.18
Oh, so that's what the Water button does! Perhaps I should have checked the manual first.

User's manuals are relics of poor design that document the way confusing UIs should have been designed so that users could understand them. But why should users have to go somewhere else to figure out how to use your product? That's the proper purpose of the user interface itself! If you can explain how to do a task in the manual, you should present the same information in the UI itself.

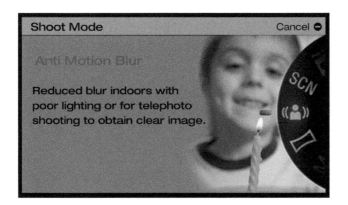

FIGURE 1.19
Note how this shooting mode description is self-explanatory, whereas the icon alone is not. No manual required!

Communicates well

In reviewing a client's product, I often start with the user's manual or training documents because that is a quick way to find the well-known usability problems. I recommend that you do the same.

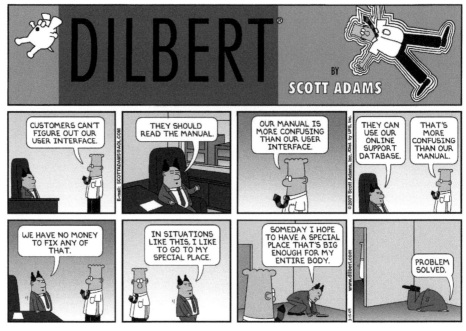

FIGURE 1.20

Never expect users to read the manual. DILBERT ©2009 Scott Adams. Used by permission of UNIVERSAL UCLICK. All rights reserved.

Users, it's not your Fault!

As Donald Norman observed in *The Design of Everyday Things*, when users don't understand a product or make mistakes using it, they have a tendency to blame themselves. They shouldn't, because it's not their fault. Rather, the product is poorly designed. It's not intuitive—by definition.

Every confusing design element or botched interaction, no matter how small, betrays potential for improvement. For every routine botched interaction, there exists a better design that reduces or prevents confusion for its target users. For every confusing design element, there exists an alternative that is self-explanatory. And it's the product designer's responsibility to find them.

Based on this concept, I would like to propose *Everett's Law of Intuitive UI*:

> For every UI design that requires experimentation, assistance, or training to understand, there exists an alternative, self-explanatory design that doesn't.

Attention users: If you can't figure out how to use a product—if its interaction isn't obvious, is overly complex, requires too much effort, or is too error prone—it's not your fault!

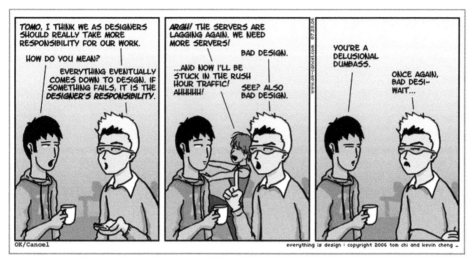

FIGURE 1.21

Everything eventually comes down to design. OK/Cancel ©2006 Tom Chi and Kevin Cheng. Used by permission.

Intuitive attributes

My definition of *intuitive* is a good place to start because it clearly describes the outcome for an intuitive UI. However, that definition doesn't offer any insight into how to achieve that outcome.

What exactly do you need to do to make an interaction intuitive? To think this through, let's review the steps in an interaction life cycle. An interaction starts with a goal—the user thinks, "Now I want to <achieve some goal>..." From there, the user must:

1. Determine a task or set of tasks that will achieve that goal.

2. Find the starting point for the each task and initiate it.

3. For each step in the task:

   - Decide what to do.

   - Determine how to perform the interaction.

   - Perform the interaction.

   - Review the results for acceptability and fix any problems.

   - Determine the next step.

4. Review the overall results for the task.

5. If satisfied, move on to the next task.

Don Norman outlines a similar model that he calls the Seven Stages of Action in *The Design of Everyday Things.*

Based on these steps, a UI is intuitive when it has an appropriate combination of:

- **Discoverability.** Users can easily find the starting point in context—when and where they need it. The command is visible, obviously a command (and not something else), and in an expected location.

- **Understandability.** Users can make an informed decision quickly and confidently. Users don't have to experiment or get assistance to make a choice. Many task steps boil down to making decisions.

- **Affordance.** The UI has visual properties that indicate how to perform an interaction. Users don't have to experiment or deduce how to perform the interaction.

- **Predictability.** Functionally, the UI delivers the expected results with no surprises or confusion. It has natural mapping. Users don't have to experiment or deduce the result of the interaction.

- **Efficiency.** The UI enables users to perform the action with a minimum amount of effort or tweaking. Inefficient and cumbersome interactions do not feel intuitive.

- **Responsive feedback.** The UI gives clear, immediate feedback to indicate that the action is happening. When the user is done, the UI makes it clear whether the action was successful or unsuccessful, providing specific details when needed.

- **Forgiveness.** If users make a mistake, either the right thing happens anyway or they can fix or undo the action with ease. Users make small mistakes all the time, so UIs that punish for such mistakes do not feel intuitive.

- **Explorability.** Users can explore the UI without fear of doing something wrong or getting lost.

Not every attribute listed here is required for every interaction, so the key is to determine the *appropriate* combination, which we will do soon. I address how to achieve these attributes extensively in terms of interaction in Chapter 2 and visually in Chapter 3.

> A UI is intuitive when it has an appropriate combination of discoverability, understandability, affordance, predictability, efficiency, responsiveness, forgiveness, and explorability.

Given that the word *intuitive* is so poorly understood, I recommend against using it in design discussions. Teams often waste enormous amounts of time debating whether a feature is intuitive, without accomplishing anything. Even though I understand the term well, when somebody tells me a UI that I designed isn't intuitive, usually I don't have a clue what they mean. Instead, I recommend using the specific attributes of an intuitive UI when you're giving feedback. When somebody tells me that a control has misleading affordance, I understand exactly what that means and know what to do about it.

FIGURE 1.22

Finding the serial number for a Mac requires clicking on the version number, so it lacks both discoverability and click affordance. That's much more useful than saying it isn't intuitive.

Communicates
poorly

NECESSARY (AND UNNECESSARY) CONSISTENCY

If you review the list of intuitive attributes carefully, you'll notice that discoverability, affordance, and predictability are strongly influenced by users' prior experience. It's worth considering Jakob Nielsen's *Law of the Internet User Experience*:

Users spend most of their time on other sites.

which can be more generally stated as:

Users spend most of their time using software other than yours.

Users' expectations about discoverability, affordance, and predictability are set by their prior experiences with all the other software they have used. If your product is unexpectedly inconsistent with those other experiences, it's *your* product that is unintuitive; users will constantly have to relearn that your product is unexpectedly different.

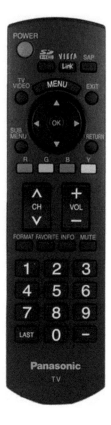

FIGURE 1.23

Communicates
poorly

Many Panasonic television remotes flip the volume and channel controls. This lack of consistency makes their UI unintuitive.

Designers are constantly coming up with new methods for interaction. Such new interactions may work well when they are obviously necessary and users can figure them out with ease. By contrast, unnecessary or accidentally novel interactions are rarely successful, because any small improvements or efficiencies they achieve through inconsistency are easily outweighed by users' lack of familiarity.

For intuitive interaction, start with standard interactions for your environment and consider creating new ones only when you have demonstrated that the standard approach won't meet your objectives. Knowing and applying the UI design guidelines for your environment is a great way to start.

That said, not all consistency is good, and people often make poor UI decisions in the name of consistency. Consistency with respect to interaction is almost always a good idea. By contrast, visual consistency often isn't necessary and may even be harmful. Although nobody would complain that a Ferrari is visually inconsistent with a Yugo, the accelerator and brake pedals on both cars had better be placed consistently and predictably.

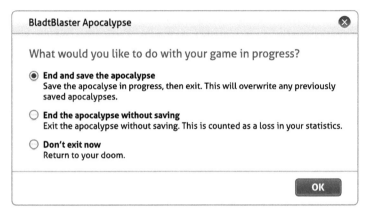

FIGURE 1.24
No doubt, the desire for unnecessary consistency motivated the designer to explain the meaning of "Don't exit." As if you didn't know.

Users' expectations about discoverability, affordance, and predictability are set by their prior experiences with all the other software they have used. For intuitive interaction, be consistent with the UI design guidelines for your environment.

STRATEGICALLY UNINTUITIVE UI

If you were to take a well-designed product that you think is intuitive and apply the attributes from the previous section, you would probably discover that some interactions don't have all the attributes. You might also discover that you don't care that much and you consider the product to be intuitive anyway.

How can this be? In short, not every interaction in a well-designed UI needs to be intuitive. Intuitive UIs have an *appropriate* combination of these attributes—they aren't all always required.

Being intuitive is important, but being intuitive often has a cost, and sometimes those costs aren't worth it. There may be other design objectives, such as simplicity and efficiency, that are more important. Sometimes a small amount of unintuitiveness can be traded for a whole lot of simplicity. Apple's iPhone makes this tradeoff successfully all the time. For example, the Undo command is the shake gesture, which isn't discoverable but is easily remembered and eliminates the need for displaying the command everywhere it's needed.

Here are the costs for some of the intuitive attributes:

- **Costs for discoverability.** Having visible access points for every interaction may result in cluttered pages. For advanced and infrequent commands, it may be better to not have visible access points.

- **Costs for affordance.** Having static affordances for every control results in cluttered pages and a heavy feel. It might be better to display affordances dynamically or sometimes even not at all. I explore the downside to affordances in detail in Chapter 3.

- **Costs for predictability.** Sometimes users might not be able to accurately predict the results of an interaction, but this may be acceptable with trivial deduction or quick experimentation.

- **Costs for forgiveness.** Providing the ability to correct or undo certain actions may not be practical or may harm performance unacceptably.

You should design basic commands that all users must perform to be intuitive, but here are some situations in which being intuitive isn't required:

- **Shortcuts and gestures.** The nature of shortcuts and gestures—streamlined interactions that require memorization—is to not be readily discoverable or have any affordance. Yes, shortcuts and gestures aren't intuitive, but that is by design. But for basic commands, there must be an intuitive, less efficient alternative.

- **Inevitable discoverability.** If the discoverability of an interaction is inevitable, it doesn't have to be visible. For example, playing a full-screen video hides all commands and their affordances (sometimes called *lights-out mode*), but this is acceptable if any interaction displays them. For another example, the iOS and Android keyboards insert a period at the end of a sentence when users type two spaces. There are no clues that this will happen, but users will inevitably discover it.

FIGURE 1.25

A full-screen video player's controls aren't visible, but they are displayed when users do any interaction.

- **Advanced, infrequent commands.** Making advanced, infrequent commands discoverable and giving them affordances might not be worth the visual clutter or the development cost required to make them intuitive. Given their usage, it is acceptable if users have to do a quick experiment to figure them out.

FIGURE 1.26
You can select multiple slides in PowerPoint for moving and deleting. But this action is so infrequent that the undiscoverable Ctrl+click and Shift+click command selection is a better choice than displaying a checkbox affordance on each slide.

- **Delighters.** Some interactions are unintuitive by design so that expert users are delighted and rewarded when finding them. Such unintuitive interactions are often used in games, where players are rewarded for finding them. As the Google Design Principles state: Engage beginners, attract experts.

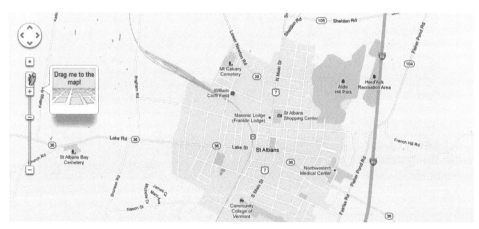

FIGURE 1.27
In rare cases, interactions are unintuitive on purpose so that advanced users are delighted when they discover them. Here the yellow tilting man, although discoverable, lacks any standard affordance. Still, it's delightful to discover that dragging him will show Street View in Google Maps.

• **Advanced modes.** Advanced modes, like programming modes, benefit from being unintuitive so that users don't enter them accidentally. Many products use a push and hold (sometimes a very long hold) to enter a programming mode, which requires documentation or assistance to discover.

FIGURE 1.28
iOS uses press and hold to enter a special mode to rearrange apps on the Home screen.

Strategically trading off intuitiveness for power and simplicity for advanced, infre-quently used features is a great way to engage beginners and attract experts—without overwhelming either group.

But being unintuitive works well only when it is deliberately and strategically designed rather than accidental. Having to figure out poorly designed, unintuitive UIs is never delightful.

> Being intuitive is important, but its attributes have a cost and it sometimes isn't worth it. There may be other design objectives, such as simplicity or efficiency, that are more important.

LEVELS OF INTUITIVENESS

A good general approach is to make all basic commands intuitive, and for the rest, make strategic compromises when necessary to achieve other goals. Figure 1.29 shows the levels of intuitiveness, which I find helpful when making these strategic compromises. Note that by *standard*, I refer to interactions that are used consistently in a product's environment, so experienced users may be familiar with them and expect them.

	DESIGN ATTRIBUTES	USABILITY OUTCOME
INTUITIVE	Automatic—nothing for users to do. Has all appropriate intuitive attributes.	**Fully intuitive** because users can achieve their desired outcome without experimentation, assistance, or training.
USABLE	Lacks discoverability or affordance, but in a standard way.	**Sensible** because it makes sense even though it requires trivial deduction or prior experience. Users will "get it" after trying it once and the mechanics are natural so they will easily remember the interaction.
	Lacks other intuitive attributes (such as predictability and clear feedback), but in a standard or consistent way.	**Learnable** because it requires quick thought or experimentation for users to figure out on their own. Users will "get it" after trying it a few times and its consistency will make it easy to remember.
	Lacks other intuitive attributes in a non-standard way, but otherwise is well presented.	**Guessable** because it is still usable with trial and error. But because it is inconsistent or nonstandard, users often have to relearn the interaction later but may often guess the interaction correctly.
	Lacks other intuitive attributes in a non-standard way, and isn't well presented.	**Trainable** because it is good enough to muddle through, and users will eventually learn it through experience, documentation, and training.
UNUSABLE	Has intuitive attributes, but they are contradictory.	**Confusing.** Design might appear intuitive but it isn't because the attributes are contradictory and misleading, resulting in many mistakes.
	Lacks most intuitive attributes, is non-standard and poorly presented.	**Unusable.** Even documentation and training aren't enough, so it requires assistance or technical support to use. The mechanics aren't natural so users often forget the interaction.

FIGURE 1.29

Use these levels of intuitiveness to evaluate your design strategy.

To work through some examples, suppose you are designing a walkup kiosk where users can check in for an airline flight. Such users are in a hurry, aren't likely to be familiar with the kiosk UI, don't have prior experience that you can leverage, and will consider the need for external assistance to be a design failure. In this case, all kiosk interactions should be *fully intuitive*. Intuitive but nonstandard interactions might work (as long as they don't confuse experienced users) because the target users are unlikely to know standard kiosk interactions anyway.

Now suppose you are designing keyboard shortcuts or gestures for advanced users. A level of *sensible* is the right target because shortcuts and gestures aren't discoverable and don't have affordances. Well-designed gestures should make sense based on real-world physics, behaviors, and natural mapping, so they will make sense to users after they try them once.

Now suppose you are designing an advanced feature that has significant value but will be rarely used, and making it *fully intuitive* would be too costly. Here, a design that is *learnable* or *guessable* would be the right target level.

Finally, let's look at a real example. Here is a digital shower control used in a hotel room. Does it have the right level of intuitiveness?

FIGURE 1.30
Is this digital shower control used in a hotel well designed?

Unfortunately, it's not. Like the kiosk user, a hotel guest needs a shower control to be fully intuitive. The affordance of a push button is to push, yet as the sticker indicates, to increase the temperature users must *push and hold*—which is unexpected. Note how the hotel tried to compensate for this confusion by adding a "Push & Hold" sticker—guessable and perhaps learnable information, but not intuitive or even sensible. The difference: Because this task is not intuitive, most users will fail on the first few tries—until they notice the sticker.

An interesting question: Does intuitive UI change over time? Yes, because users' expectations for discoverability, affordance, and predictability change over time. For example, users' expectations for touch-based interactions have changed significantly recently, so users now expect UIs to be touchable whereas they wouldn't have before. Still, if I were designing a touch-based kiosk where touch might not be expected, the first screen would prominently say "Touch to continue" somewhere.

INDUCTIVE UI

The previous intuitive attributes apply at the individual interaction level—find the right control, interact with it, and interaction does what you expect. But these attributes are too low level to make entire tasks intuitive. Designing intuitive task flows is also very important, so let's explore that now.

Presentation Zen

Presentation Zen is an approach to designing slide presentations developed by Garr Reynolds in his book of the same name. Instead of the traditional titles and bullets, slides using the Presentation Zen approach have a strong image with a minimum amount of text—a quotation, sentence, phrase, or even no text at all. Such slides make a stronger, more emotional, more memorable impact on viewers.

FIGURE 1.31
A visually powerful slide, but what does it mean? The presenter will have to explain it because the slide itself isn't saying.

Many UI tasks are like this—not because they are visually impactful but because they aren't self-explanatory. Consider the example shown in Figure 1.32.

FIGURE 1.32
Can you feel the Zen here?

Communicates
poorly

What does this UI do? How do you interact with it? What does this UI accomplish in a task? Please take a moment to think about these questions before continuing.
OK, got it?

How do you interact with this UI? You click Add. But how do you know that? You scan the page, you determine that the Properties title and the Objects instruction don't really tell you anything, that Remove and Details are disabled and therefore not useful, that OK and Cancel are enabled but clicking them first will accomplish nothing, so you click Add because there is nothing else to do.

What does this UI do? What does this UI accomplish in a task? As a user, you don't have a clue. Your best hope is to click Add and see what happens next. You might then have to experiment to figure out what is going on. Another UI puzzle to figure out.

You might not be aware of it, but what you are doing is the process of elimination plus a bit of experimentation, both of which are forms of deductive logic. You have to *deduce* what to do because the UI itself isn't telling you. Unfortunately, such deductive, unintuitive task flows are all too common. Not exactly Zen-like.

To design products that don't require training, you need to design task flows that are self-explanatory. My friend Jan Miksovsky coined the term *inductive UI* to describe self-explanatory task flows because they lead users through the task. With *Presentation Zen*, there is a presenter in the room who explains the meaning of the slides to the audience. Deductive UIs need a presenter, too, but for software that person is called a *trainer*.

Inductive UIs make task flows self-explanatory.

Inductive UI

The core principle behind inductive UI is that an easily explainable UI is an easily understandable UI. Simply put, if you can't easily explain the steps to perform in a UI you are designing, there's little chance that users are going to easily figure them out themselves. Thus, it's important for task steps to be easily explainable.

The key is to break multistep tasks down into individual steps and describe each step with a clear, concise explanation. Let's call these explanations *main instructions,* to distinguish them from ordinary instructions. A good main instruction should be what you would actually say to users to explain the page, so this instruction should be long and complicated only if what you would say in person would be long and complicated. (And most likely it wouldn't be—so keep it short, simple, and purposeful.)

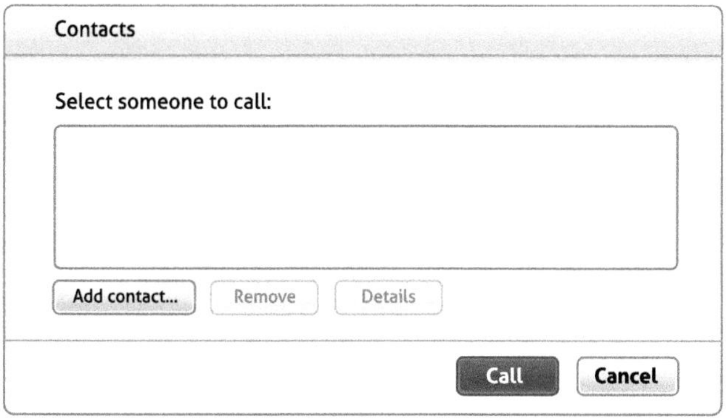

FIGURE 1.33

OK, now I get it! Why? Because the UI tells me what to do.

Communicates
well

The main instruction answers the first question users have with an unfamiliar UI: What am I supposed to do here? Although it's possible that users could answer this question on their own, why *force* them to? If a main instruction is something that you would say in person in explaining the step, say it explicitly in the UI as well instead of forcing users to figure it out on their own.

Another important goal is that the design of the page should accurately reflect its main instruction. If a UI element isn't clearly related to the instruction, it shouldn't be on the page. If a UI element is crucial to performing the step, it should be on the page. As you will see in Chapter 5, a communication-driven design process starts by identifying and optimizing these main instructions and designing pages to support them.

By doing so, all UI elements are on the page because they belong, not because they fit physically. You aren't playing a game of UI Tetris.

Inductive UIs explain each task step with a clear and concise main instruction that answers the first question users have: What am I supposed to do here? Everything on the page then accurately reflects that main instruction.

Effective main instructions (and therefore well-designed pages!)

The quality of the main instruction is an excellent leading indicator of the quality of the page. If you can't explain the purpose of a page clearly and concisely, the page lacks focus, cohesion, and integrity. Main instructions with vague verbs like *manage* or *maintain* are a bad sign, too—it is rarely a real user goal to manage or maintain stuff, and just about any action falls under these umbrella verbs—so try to design pages around instructions with more specific verbs.

Often designers and developers don't worry about UI text much because technically it can be changed at any time before release. Although this is technically true (ignoring

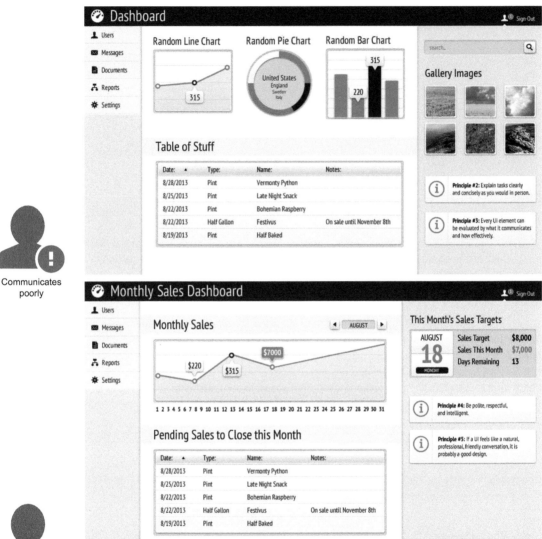

Communicates
poorly

Communicates
well

FIGURE 1.34

What is the purpose of dashboards generally? What is the purpose of these dashboards? Which one is more obvious? What factor makes the difference?

localization concerns), if UI is ultimately communicating to users, then not thinking about these instructions early in the design process is a huge missed opportunity.

If the main instruction sounds like what you would actually say to users in person, it is probably a good instruction. Most likely what we would say in person will have a specific verb—we rarely give instructions without verbs in person, and weak verbs (like *manage*) are more confusing than specific verbs (like *back up*).

Here are some instruction types to give you a better idea of instruction quality (best first):

- The instruction explains what users need to do conceptually, explaining the purpose if helpful:

Select your photos to share

- The instruction vaguely hints at what users need to do:

Your photo album

- The instruction explains how to perform the step mechanically, but without explaining the purpose:

Click to select photos

- The instruction gives the step name, often from the code's point of view:

Photo selection

- The instruction provides information that isn't helpful or relevant and that could mean anything:

Photo management

Of these, only the first main instruction is desirable; the remaining aren't very helpful. Note that a main instruction may be a question.

Note how a page named *Select your photos to share* is likely to have a very focused, easy-to-understand design. By contrast, a page named *Photo management* could have just about anything related to photos on it.

> The quality of this main instruction is an excellent leading indicator of the quality of the page. Not thinking about these instructions early in the design process is a huge missed opportunity.

STRATEGICALLY DEDUCTIVE UI

Not every UI needs a main instruction, and many don't have them. The key: If a user were to ask you what to do in person, would you bother to say the instruction? If not, the page is better off without it. In such cases, the main instruction is so obvious or the deduction required to use the page is so trivial that giving the instruction is more annoying than helpful.

If you choose not to provide a main instruction, make sure it's because of the high quality of the page design, not the low quality of the instruction itself. In my experience, main instructions for complex or unfamiliar tasks don't go without saying.

Communicates
well

FIGURE 1.35

Although this main instruction might seem obvious to the developer, it's not obvious to most users.

> Don't display main instructions that go without saying. Main instructions for complex or unfamiliar tasks usually don't go without saying.

You might have noticed that most mobile app screens don't have a main instruction. Here's why:

- Mobile apps are focused on doing "one thing" well.

- Apps screens are focused on a single clear step. Often the step is explained visually.

- Given the context of performing a specific step on a focused screen within a focused app, the purpose of a screen is usually obvious in context by quick inspection.

- Mobile apps are optimized for small displays, and the top of the screen is especially valuable real estate.

Putting all these factors together results in a higher bar for explicitly showing the main instruction. The context of mobile apps is often so specific that users can accurately predict what to do on a screen without looking at it at all. Even so, main instructions are sometimes used to keep users oriented.

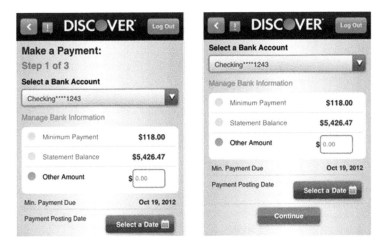

FIGURE 1.36

The focused nature of mobile apps makes explicit main instructions less important. Still, this screen works better with the *Make a Payment* instruction than without it.

Even if you don't display the main instructions, you can still design better, more intuitive mobile task flows by breaking them down into individual steps, describing each step with a clear, concise instruction, and designing the screens to accurately reflect that instruction. In fact, not having explicit instructions makes this technique even more important because users must figure out the screens on their own. This part always works—even for mobile apps.

> Mobile apps benefit from inductive UI design, even if the main instruction isn't displayed.

ASKING INTUITIVE QUESTIONS

Many task steps involve asking users questions, and questions are a common type of main instruction. What's surprising is how often those questions are unnecessary or poorly presented. There's an art to asking well-presented, easy-to-answer questions. The following section explains that art.

Don't ask if you don't have to

Many questions are unnecessary and result from the lack of design courage. Not sure about something? It's better just to ask, right? Why take a chance? The problem is that always asking the user is the easy way out and results in a cumbersome, annoying, and even frustrating experience.

Suppose you have a question, and there's an 80% chance you know the answer. Do you ask anyway? What if you are 95% sure? What if you are 99% sure? Apparently many designers don't like those odds. Consider this example: I'm physically in Vermont (which my IP address would indicate) and I search for Berlin, VT. Is the question in Figure 1.37 really necessary? In *About Face: The Essentials of Interaction Design*, Alan Cooper refers to this as "stopping the proceedings with idiocy."

FIGURE 1.37
Just wanted to make sure … I might be planning a vacation in Viterbo, Italy.

Given my current physical location, I suppose there is a 0.00001% chance that I really meant Viangchan Kampheng Nakhon, but why not play the odds and make me refine my search if that's what I really wanted?

Here are some ways that you can avoid asking questions in your UI:

- **Don't ask if the user doesn't care.** Users don't care if they always choose the default option or the question has no consequence because users don't do or think differently as a result. It's surprising how many questions just aren't worth asking.

Untitled
You are closing a message that has not been sent.
To save the message, click Save as Draft. The message will be saved in your Drafts folder.
Discard Changes
Continue Writing
Save as Draft
Cc:
Bcc:
Subject:

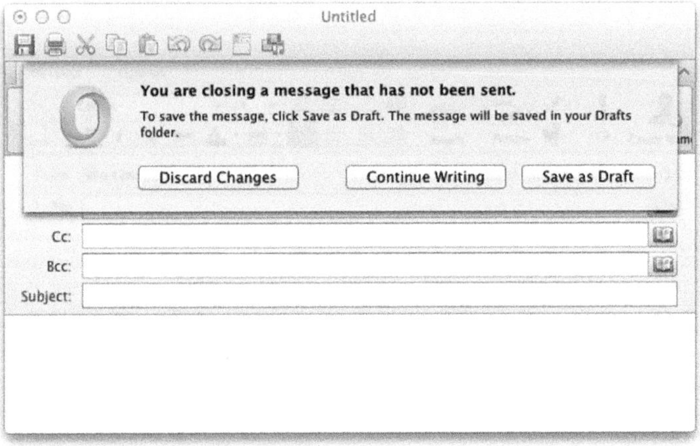

FIGURE 1.38

Why ask me if I want to save an empty email? I don't care.

- **Don't ask if you already know the answer.** Often you can determine the answer based on the task, the context, or best practices. Many questions can be answered simply by remembering the user's previous input.

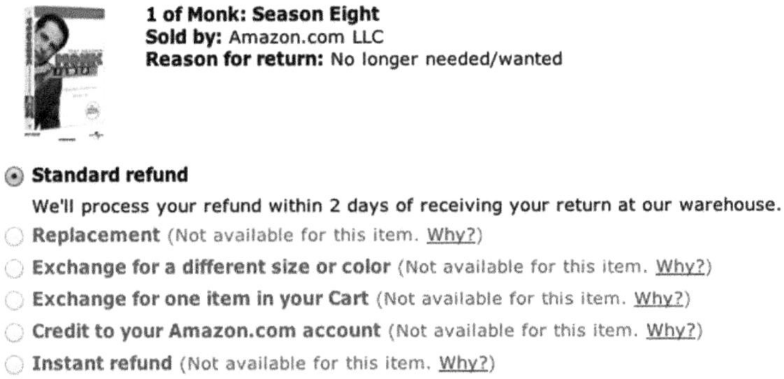

1 of Monk: Season Eight
Sold by: Amazon.com LLC
Reason for return: No longer needed/wanted
Standard refund
We'll process your refund within 2 days of receiving your return at our warehouse.
Replacement (Not available for this item. Why?)
Exchange for a different size or color (Not available for this item. Why?)
Exchange for one item in your Cart (Not available for this item. Why?)
Credit to your Amazon.com account (Not available for this item. Why?)
Instant refund (Not available for this item. Why?)

FIGURE 1.39

I love how Amazon makes it clear why the other return options aren't available, but there's no choice here. Why ask?

- **Don't ask if you probably know the answer.** If there's an 80% chance that you know the answer, just do it without asking. Raise the bar significantly if there is a consequence for being wrong. Slide that bar down significantly if the user's effort required to answer the question is on par with the effort to fix any mistakes.

Designed for robots

FIGURE 1.40

I just searched for the Great Wall of China (a lot of typing on a touch keyboard) mere seconds ago, but I made a small mistake. I clicked Back to fix the mistake—only to return to a blank form. Guess what I want to search for now?

Communicates well

FIGURE 1.41

For a good example, I gave this reminder after midnight. Siri recognizes that "tomorrow" is ambiguous and asks for a clarification.

- **Don't ask if users can't possibly answer intelligently.** If users can't make an informed decision, why ask—unless your goal is to shift liability?

FIGURE 1.42
Where's the I Haven't a Clue button?

> Don't ask questions unless you really need to. There are many questions that you
> don't have to ask—with a little thought, effort, and courage.

Ask the real question directly

**Many questions are poorly phrased—often dancing around the question rather than asking
it directly and not providing specific information.** The better the phrasing of the question,
the better the answer users will give.

FIGURE 1.43
The Windows Vista User Account Control dialog box (left) hints at a question, whereas the Windows 7
version (right) asks it directly.

Sometimes questions (such as "What is your password?") are better phrased as
instructions (such as "Please type your password") or even as ordinary labels (just "Password" in a form). As always, interpersonal communication provides insight here: we often
give instructions instead of asking explicit questions when questions would be tedious or
chatty.

Add a new meeting

What type of meeting would you like to create? | Status meeting ▾ |

When would you like to have the meeting? | 01/01/2013 📅 | Start | 9:00AM ⇕ | End | 10:00AM ⇕ |

Who would you like to attend? | <Select attendees> ▾ |

What is the meeting about? | |

What outcoming would you like to achieve? | |

| Add meeting to your calendar now |

Communicates
poorly

New meeting

Meeting type: | Status meeting ▾ |

Date and time: | 01/01/2013 📅 | Start | 9:00AM ⇕ | End | 10:00AM ⇕ |

Attendees: | <Select attendees> ▾ |

Meeting purpose: | |

Meeting objective: | |

| Add to calendar |

Communicates
well

FIGURE 1.44

Consider phrasing questions as instructions or ordinary labels when questions would be tedious or chatty. Although the question format feels friendly, it is also quite tedious. All the extra language doesn't improve the conversation or add clarity.

Ask once

If you must ask a question, ask it once. Sometimes programs ask the same question multiple times because they don't bother to remember a prior answer. Sometimes they ask partial questions instead of one complete one. At other times programs ask multiple questions because different layers in the technology stack aren't aware that the question has already been asked.

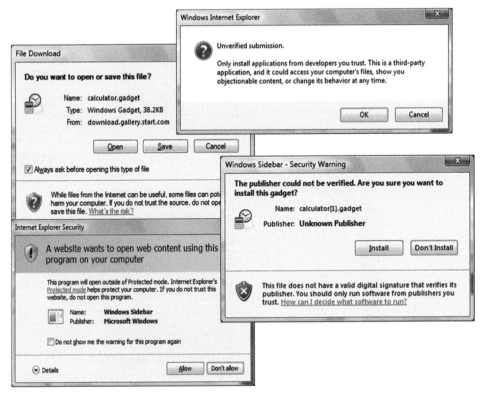

FIGURE 1.45

Although it's an extreme example, here are four variations of "Do you really want to install this untrusted program?" that you are asked when you install a gadget in Windows 7. Final answer?

Communicates poorly

Set Your Location

You only have to enter it once, we'll save it.

Please enter the location for the area where you plan to use your phone the most so we can give you accurate information about wireless pricing, coverage, customer service, and offers near you.

Enter Your Zip Code:

[   ] [Set Location]

☑ Remember my location What's this ❓

or Select State:

[Select State ⬦]

FIGURE 1.46

By contrast, Staples asks you to set your location and goes out of its way to let you know that it will ask only once. Very considerate!

Communicates well

Provide enough information to answer intelligently

Even if the question is necessary and well phrased, the responses might be confusing and poorly presented—making it difficult for users to make an intelligent, informed decision. Here are the attributes of intuitive question responses:

- **There's enough information to understand the response.** Too often responses are tersely listed, requiring help to understand what they mean. Instead, present responses that can be easily understood on their own and selected with confidence.

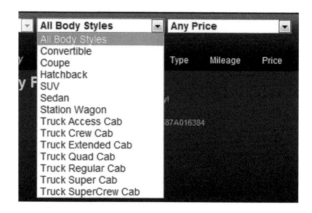

FIGURE 1.47

What do all these different types of trucks mean? What if I want to see all the trucks?

- **There's enough information to choose the response with confidence.** It's not enough to understand what responses mean; users also need enough information to make an informed decision.

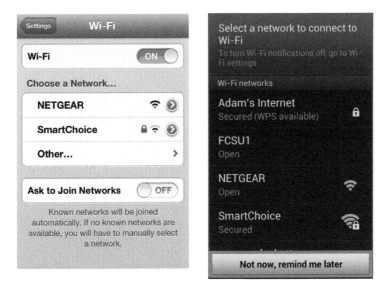

FIGURE 1.48
I'm in a restaurant looking for a Wi-Fi hotspot. The iPhone provides the minimum information, whereas Android provides enough information to help me choose confidently.

SHIPPING AND PAYMENT INFO
Enter Your Payment Details

Items shipping from South Bend, Indiana

	Shipping Method	Estimated Delivery Date	Cost
●	UPS Ground	01/09/2013	$154.95
○	FedEx 3Day Express Saver	01/08/2013	$158.94
○	FedEx 2DAY	01/07/2013	$192.45
○	UPS 2nd Day Air	01/07/2013	$271.58

*Normally scheduled deliveries are made Monday through Friday.
*Saturday delivery is only available on orders placed by phone. Please call 888-541-1777 during our normal business hours. There is an extra charge for Saturday delivery.

Communicates well

FIGURE 1.49
TireRack gives me all the information I need to choose the shipping method confidently.

- **But there isn't too much information, either.** If there is too much information, there's a good chance users won't read the descriptions at all. Consider using progressive disclosure if options really need more information than can be easily read.

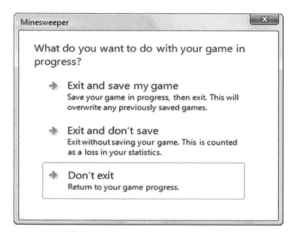

FIGURE 1.50

Reads like a spec … I'm choosing a response, not writing the code.

- **The responses are presented in order of likelihood (more or less).** As Steve Krug points out in *Don't Make Me Think!*, users don't optimize, they satisfice. So, instead of reading the entire list of options, users scan until they find an option that sounds promising. Presenting the options in order of likelihood helps ensure that the promising option is the right one.

FIGURE 1.51

As someone who does most of my business in the United States and Canada, I appreciate not having to scroll this long list past Uganda to find the United States.

- **The responses are presented in a usable order.** Short lists can be presented in logical order, but longer lists should be alphabetized.

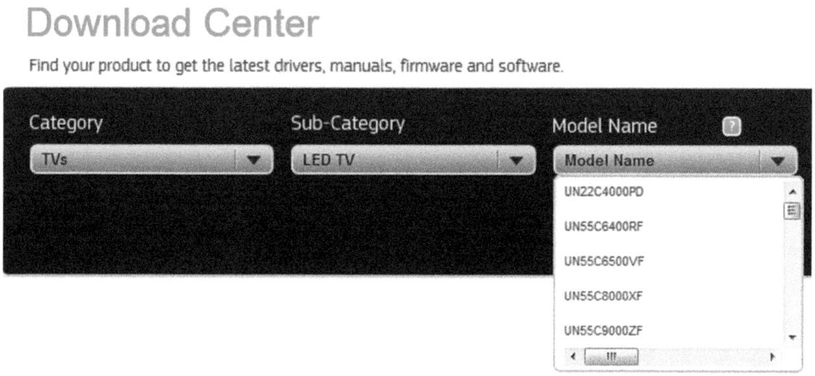

FIGURE 1.52
This long list isn't sorted. It looks like I'm going to have to browse the entire list to find my TV.

- **The recommended responses are clearly identified.** Having recommendations helps users choose with confidence.

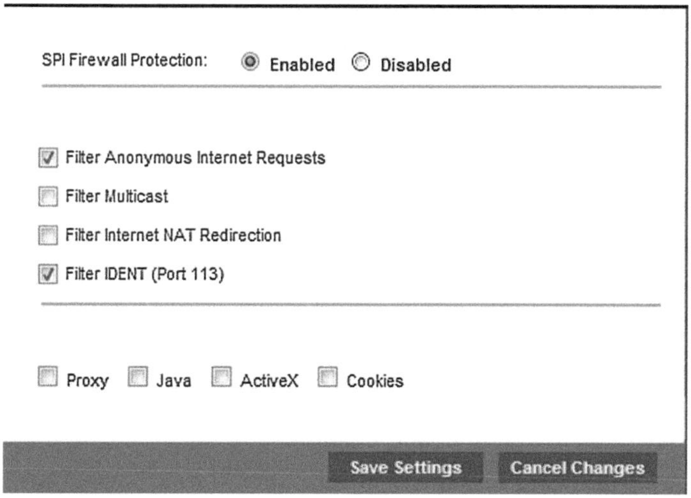

FIGURE 1.53
These options are very technical. Although I might not understand them, having recommendations helps me choose with confidence.

Ask at the right time and in the right place

Finally, even if a question and its responses are well presented, an intuitive question needs to be asked at the right time and in the right place. Here are some problems to look out for:

- **Don't ask too early.** If you ask a question too early, users either aren't fully engaged or won't know how to answer yet.

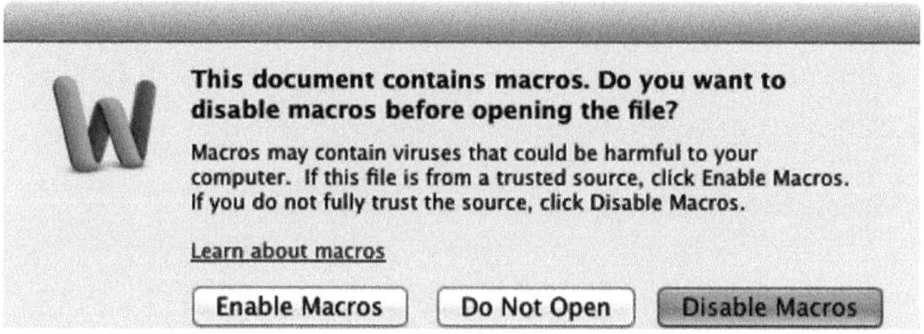

FIGURE 1.54

I don't know yet. Better to open the document securely without asking and let me enable macros once I need them.

- **Don't ask too late.** If you ask an important question too late, users might not have confidence that they are doing the task correctly and may abandon the task before getting there.

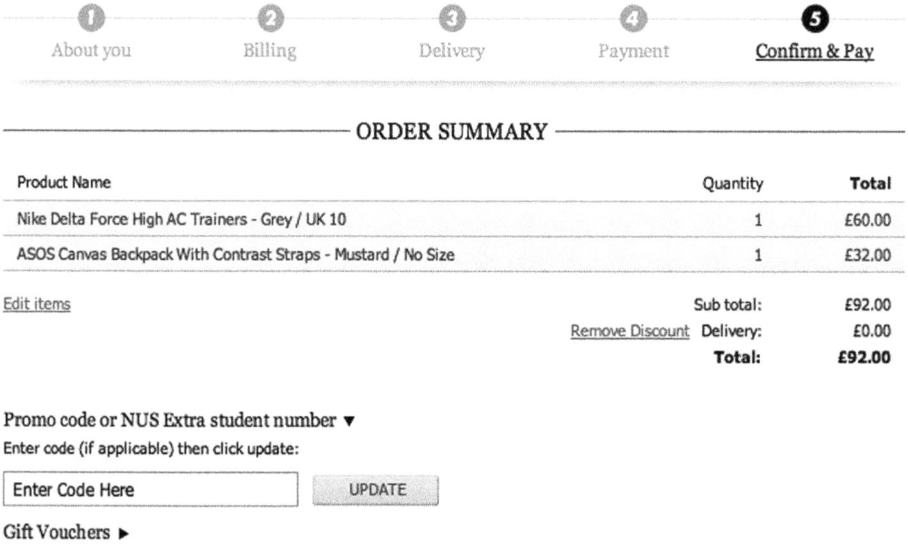

FIGURE 1.55

I wanted to use a discount code and was just about to give up.

- **Ask in context.** By asking questions when they are relevant, users can make more informed decisions. Contextual questions are often much easier to answer with a non-modal UI.

FIGURE 1.56
It's much easier to think about accessories in the context of buying a product, and it's more convenient, too.

FIGURE 1.57
Having the request in context, plus the explanation of why the sensitive information is necessary, really helps.

Communicates well

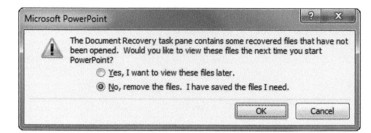

Communicates
poorly

FIGURE 1.58

In contrast, I can't possibly answer without seeing the files in question.

> Unintuitive UIs often ask questions or present choices that are unnecessary or poorly presented. Well-designed UIs ask the right question once, at the right time and place, and provide enough information for users to answer intelligently and confidently.

A MODEL FOR USERS

You need to understand your target users with enough detail so that you can make good design decisions on their behalf. Ideally, your team will do plenty of user research and create models, called *personas,* for your target users; I describe these in detail in Chapter 5. Unfortunately, it isn't always practical to build these models based on research. Many teams don't have the time, budget, research talent, or even customer access.

   In this section, I will build a general model for users, to give you a better understanding of how real users are likely to behave. Understanding this model will help you design for that behavior. Yes, all target users are different and have different knowledge, needs, and preferences. But instead of focusing on their differences, let's now focus on their similarities. These user attributes are fairly safe bets. Your target users' characteristics might be different from what I have outlined here, but unless your research shows otherwise, don't bet on it.

What users know

- Users know their goals but not how to achieve them. They know the task destination but not the starting point or the steps to get there.

- Users know what to choose at a high level but not necessarily the specific details. Assume that they know only the most essential data from memory and need help with everything else.

- Without prior knowledge or experience, users don't know what your program does, what tasks it performs, how it works, or that they can trust it. They have questions and concerns that you take for granted.

- Users are smart, but they might be focused on other things. "Dumbing down" your program is disrespectful and not likely to solve any real problems.

- Unless they have been trained or already know what to do based on prior experience, users know only what your program tells them. If your program fails to communicate important information, users will have to discover the information through experimentation, research, or training.

- Unless you are designing features clearly targeted at experts or novices, assume that your target users are efficient beginners in terms of computer experience, domain knowledge, and vocabulary. That is, they know the basics and want to work efficiently, but they don't have much experience and have very little memorized.

- Unless they use your product frequently, assume that your target users will routinely forget their username (unless it is their email address), account number, and password. They might not even remember whether they have an account and may sign up for a new one unnecessarily.

Bottom line: Make it clear what your program does, how to do its tasks, and what the options are. Don't assume that users have anything beyond the essentials memorized. Don't take users' trust for granted; show that your program will achieve their goals. Make it easy for users to sign in and recover forgotten account information.

User motivation

- Users are motivated by value—where the benefit of a task clearly exceeds the time and effort required. If that is not the case, nothing else matters, because users won't be sufficiently motivated to perform or complete the task.

- Different target users have different levels of motivation:

  - If users have high motivation, they will do whatever it takes to get the task done. Users are likely to be highly motivated if a task is required for their job or there is financial incentive to complete the task.

  - If users have low motivation, they will make a modest effort to perform the task but abandon it if they can't figure it out easily and they don't believe it is worth continuing.

- Unless you have research data to the contrary, assume that your target users have low motivation for most tasks.

Bottom line: Users are motivated by value, so always take the user's motivation into account. Make using your UI worth the time and effort.

Top questions users have when looking at a UI

- What does this UI do? Am I even in the right place?

- What am I supposed to do here?

- Is this going to do what I want? Will it meet my needs? Can I trust it?

- What is the difference between these options? Which one should I select?

Bottom line: Design your UIs so that users can easily answer these questions quickly and confidently.

How users figure things out

- Users will assume that your program has design patterns and interactions that are standard for its environment.

- If users are familiar with a similar task from another feature or other program, users will assume that the current feature has a similar interaction.

- Unless they perform a task frequently, users won't remember exactly how to perform it from memory and will have to relearn it each time. If your UI is well designed, that re-learning will be trivial and hardly noticeable. If the UI is nonstandard or inconsistent, users won't remember the next time and will have to relearn it.

- If an action is discoverable, looks relevant, and has a clear affordance, users will try it right away.

- If an action doesn't have affordance, users will try it only after eliminating all obvious alternatives first.

- If an action isn't discoverable, novice users won't find it.

- If users discover an unusual interaction or control, they will form a hypothesis as to how it works and perform a quick experiment to confirm. If their hypothesis is correct, they will consider interaction intuitive (and will be delighted that they figured it out). If not, they will consider the interaction unintuitive and poorly designed.

- Only the most motivated users bother with online help and only after exhausting all other possibilities first.

Bottom line: Simple, standard, intuitive, self-explanatory, and consistent works best. Good help can't save a poor UI.

What users will and won't do

- As Steve Krug points out in *Don't Make Me Think!*, users don't read, they scan. That is, they don't read UIs completely for comprehension; rather, they scan to find what they are looking for quickly.

- Users don't read large blocks of text or long instructions. They do read control labels for clicking on them.

- Users don't optimize, they satisfice (again, from Krug). That is, given many options, users act on the first promising option they find.

- Users will scroll long pages, but only if they have a reason to. (Mobile UIs are an exception because users are used to scrolling them.) Users won't scroll to see if there is anything worth scrolling for—so the motivation to scroll needs to be visible without scrolling.

- Users won't memorize anything.

- Users don't learn how things work, they muddle through. (Another one from Krug.)

- Users won't reveal sensitive information without a good reason. Nor should they. They are likely to abandon a task if sensitive information is required without a clear justification.

- Users won't register, create an account, or sign in unless they are really, really motivated. This is doubly true when users are typing on a touch keyboard.

Bottom line: Users are focused on their work, not on learning how to use your UI. They are in a hurry and don't want to take the time to learn, memorize, or perform unnecessary steps.

What users dislike doing

- Creating accounts, signing in, and retyping CAPTCHAs.

- Waiting or other forms of wasting time.

- Unnecessary typing or other interaction.

- Reentering previously entered information.

- Providing apparently unnecessary information, especially if sensitive.

- Unnecessary repetition.

- Having to start completely over.

- Making easily preventable mistakes.

Bottom line: Users' time and effort is precious, so don't waste it—especially on mobile devices.

How users lose confidence

- Users need to gain confidence as they perform a task and are reluctant to proceed with a task or make commitments without building sufficient confidence. Without confidence, users may restart a task or look for alternatives.

- Users need to know where they are at each step in a task. They need clues to confirm that they are in the right place.

- Users need to know how to make the next step confidently. The likely next step should always be obvious.

- Users lose confidence if:
  - They can't find what they are looking for.
  - They don't understand the instructions, options, or other UI text.
  - They aren't clearly making progress toward their goals.
  - The results don't meet their expectations.
  - They feel like they are being taken advantage of, such as with poorly chosen defaults and opt-out options, along with unreasonable costs (shipping and handling or "convenience" fees).
- After performing an interaction, users need clear feedback that the action was successful or unsuccessful.

Bottom line: Users won't complete a task if they lack confidence. Don't take users' confidence for granted; instead, make sure your UI builds it.

Again, these are pretty safe bets for most users. It's surprising how often user research boils down to discovering these basic observations about users.

Use this general model as a starting point to evaluate your assumptions about your target users—whether explicit or implicit. Any discrepancies suggest a problem.

SUMMARY

If you remember only 13 things:

1. **UI is Communication.** A user interface is essentially a conversation between users and a product to perform tasks that achieve users' goals. Start a design by understanding what you need to communicate to users, then let that communication drive the design process and the UI design itself. Great UI design often boils down to communicating to users as we do in person: in a way that is simple, natural, friendly, and focused on the user's goals.

2. **Explain tasks clearly and concisely, as you would in person.** The key is to understand that the UI isn't some completely different type of communication. Rather, it's the same communication using a *slightly* different language.

3. **Every UI element can be evaluated by what it communicates and how effectively it does that job.** The need for effective communication applies to everything, including control selection, layout, icon and other graphic design, color, and animation. Controls even have a "body language," whereby their presentation suggests details on how they are used. If users need to translate your UI into something meaningful, you should use that translated, meaningful version instead. If your UI has elements that communicate nothing, you should remove them.

4. **Be polite, respectful, and intelligent.** We must have the same standards for human/computer interaction as we do for human interaction. If an interaction would be inappropriate, rude, disrespectful, or stupid between people, it is equally inappropriate with software. Software shouldn't get a free pass for rudeness and disrespect. Like people, UIs communicate through their personality, tone, and attitude.

5. **If a UI feels like a natural, professional, friendly conversation, it is probably a good design.** This is a simple yet remarkably effective technique for evaluating a design. If someone is explaining a design, compare the explanation to what is on the screen. If you are reviewing your own design, ask yourself: Would I actually say this in person? Either way, any discrepancies reveal problems.

6. **Too often we design UIs by exposing the underlying technology directly to users—** asking users fill in raw data structures and perform the task the same way the code does—and expect the results to be usable. We shouldn't be surprised when this approach leads to poor UI.

7. **Effective communication is useful, relevant, necessary, clear, natural, purposeful, specific, explicit, concise, efficient, and timely.** It neither overcommunicates nor undercommunicates. It has a pleasant personality and tone and inspires the user's confidence.

8. **A UI is intuitive when it has an appropriate combination of discoverability, understandability, affordance, predictability, efficiency, responsiveness, forgiveness, and explorability.** Users spend most of their time using software other than yours, so what users consider intuitive is often based on their prior experiences with other software.

9. **Although you want your UIs to be intuitive, being intuitive often has a cost, and sometimes those costs aren't worth it.** There may be other design objectives, such as simplicity and efficiency, that are more important. A good general approach is to make all basic commands intuitive and strategically downplay discoverability and affordances when necessary for advanced commands and shortcuts.

10. **Inductive UIs are intuitive at the task level. You can make multistep tasks inductive by breaking them down into individual steps and describe each step with a clear, concise explanation.** Furthermore, each page should accurately reflect its explanation. The core principle behind inductive UI is that an easily explainable UI is an easily understandable UI. If you can't easily explain the steps a user is to perform, there's little chance that users are going to easily figure the steps out themselves.

11. **Not every UI needs a main instruction, and many don't have them. The key: If a user were to ask you what to do in person, would you bother to give the instruction?** If not, the main instruction is so obvious or the deduction required to use the page is so trivial that giving the instruction is more annoying than helpful. If you choose not to provide a main instruction, make sure it is because of the high quality of the page design, not the low quality of the instruction itself.

12. **Unintuitive UIs often ask questions that are unnecessary or poorly presented.** Well-designed UIs ask the real question once, at the right time and place, and provide enough information for users to answer intelligently and confidently.

13. **When making design decisions, have a model for how your target users think and behave as well as what motivates them.** This chapter presents a general model that most users share. It's a smart idea to do user research to see how your actual users differ.

EXERCISES

To improve your ability to design intuitive user interfaces through effective communication, try the following exercises. *Assume that anything is possible. Don't let concerns about development costs or current technology limitations inhibit your thinking.*

1. **Understanding intuitive UI.** Find an unfamiliar product that you have never used before (a coffee maker, for example), examine it carefully, and predict how to perform its top tasks without experimenting with it, reading the user's manual, or anything else. Now try to use the device and see if you can perform the task successfully on the first try without making any mistakes. If you can, explain how you were able to figure it out. If you can't, explain what led you astray.

2. **Eliminating user's manuals.** Find a product that has a user's manual. Carefully examine each instruction in the manual. For each instruction, determine a design that could eliminate the need for instruction. Could a better design make the manual unnecessary?

3. **Explaining a task to a friend.** Find a product that is unintuitive and confusing but that you understand how to use. Ask a friend to perform the top task with it and see what happens without any coaching. Now walk your friend through the task, this time explaining each step in plain language. Hopefully your friend is more successful. Now compare your in-person explanation to how the product's design explains itself and see what is different. Do those differences help you understand how to improve the UI?

4. **Natural, friendly conversation.** Find an example of a UI that does not reflect what you would naturally say in person. Now redesign the UI to reflect what you would actually say. Is your redesign better?

5. **Understanding unintuitive UI.** Find a product that is unintuitive and confusing. Evaluate the design for each of the intuitive attributes (discoverability, affordance, etc.) and look for weaknesses. Do those weaknesses explain why the product is unintuitive or is there more to it? Now redesign the UI to make it intuitive. Characterize the changes.

6. **Consistency.** Find a variety of products that more or less have the same purpose but have radically different designs (consider reviewing apps in the same category in an app store). Evaluate each design for intuitiveness. Now evaluate each design for consistency with the most standard design. Did you find a correlation between intuitiveness and consistency?

7. **Intuitive with poor communication.** Find an example of a product that you believe is intuitive (demonstrate why by evaluating the intuitive attributes) yet communicates its purpose rather poorly. Were you able to find such an example?

8. **Strategically unintuitive UI.** Find an example of a well-designed UI that has elements that appear to be unintuitive on purpose. Are there other design objectives (such as simplicity or efficiency) that are more important than intuitiveness? Or were these elements design mistakes?

9. **Inductive UI.** Find an example of an unfamiliar complex, multistep task that you have never done before. Perform the task and make a note of how easy each step was to perform. Now go back and see if each step has a clear, concise explanation. Is there a correlation between the ease of use of each step and its explanation?

10. **Poorly presented questions.** Find examples of poorly presented questions in UIs. Characterize why each question is poorly presented. Now redesign each question to be easier to understand and respond to.

11. **Designing a user settings UI, part 1.** Choose an everyday product that has a variety of user settings and that has a UI with buttons and a small display. Design a UI that enables users to modify the settings by enabling a mode (if necessary), choosing a specific setting, selecting a value, making the change, moving on to the next setting, and leaving the mode (if necessary). Strive for a design that uses three or four buttons. Determine the function of each button, design a good label, and determine what the display needs to show in each state. For the labels, try both icons and text. Determine the level of intuitiveness based on Figure 1.29.

12. **Designing a user settings UI, part 2.** Continuing with the previous exercise, try adding more buttons to your design to make it more intuitive, efficient, and forgiving. For example, if you have a three-button design, trying adding a fourth, then a fifth, and then a sixth or more buttons. Determine the function of each button, design a good label, and determine what the display needs to show in each state. What does each extra button buy you? Is there a correlation between the ease of explaining each button and the ease of using each button?

    Now go in the opposite direction and try removing buttons from your original design while maintaining functionality. Try a one- and two-button design. What does removing each button cost in terms of intuitiveness, efficiency, and forgiveness? Once done, choose the optimal design for first-time users.

Interaction Design

"Everything is best for something and worst for something else. The trick is knowing for what, when, for whom, and why."

—BILL BUXTON

The concept behind *UI is Communication* is that a *user interface* is essentially a conversation between users and a product to perform tasks that achieve users' goals. A user interface differs from human conversation primarily in that it uses the language of UI instead of natural language.

The goal of this chapter is to establish and help readers understand the language of UI—essentially the parts of speech for user interfaces. In doing so, the chapter presents the traditional UI elements—controls, labels, feedback, pages, dialog boxes, error messages, and so on—and focuses on how to choose and use them effectively based on what they communicate. My goal is to help you make the right decisions quickly and confidently, for the right reasons.

To help you visualize this language analogy, Figure 2.1 shows how common UI elements map to the parts of speech and other elements of communication. This chapter is organized around those elements, starting with words and working up to conversations.

Conversation — Log In

FIGURE 2.1
The language of UI maps well to the parts of natural speech and other elements of communication.

As you will see in this chapter, although there are many factors, effective communication often drives decisions in UI design. I have observed that designers sometimes develop a set of UI elements that they like and others that they avoid. This approach is fundamentally wrong. There are no good or bad UI elements—rather, there are appropriate and inappropriate ones based on what you need to communicate. As Bill Buxton observed, "Everything is best for something and worst for something else. The trick is knowing for what, when, for whom, and why."

FIGURE 2.2
That flashing icon on the taskbar is very distracting and makes it hard to concentrate. It's great choice for something that really requires attention; otherwise, it interferes with getting work done.

INTERACTIONS

A typical UI element can be broken down into these constituent parts:

- **Purpose.** The purpose of the element; what it does. For example, the purpose of a textbox is to allow users to input unconstrained text.

- **Affordance.** Visual clues that indicate how to perform an interaction. For example, a box around text indicates that the text is editable. Poorly designed UI elements require labeling to explain how to perform the interaction. For example, labels like "Click here to type" should go without saying.

- **Body language.** The details of an element's presentation that provide additional information beyond its purpose and affordance. For example, the size of a textbox suggests the size of the expected input.

- **Interaction.** The specific user action to perform an interaction. For example, users interact with textboxes by clicking or tapping and typing.

- **Labeling.** Text labels, placeholders, icons, or tooltips that explain the meaning or effect of an element. For example, nearly all textboxes need a label to explain their meaning.

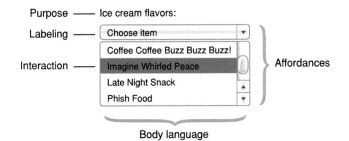

FIGURE 2.3
UI elements can be decomposed into purpose, body language, affordance, interaction, and labeling. In this case, the body language is the width of the control.

We will explore purpose, body language, and labeling in detail later and affordances in Chapter 3, so let's start by reviewing the different types of interactions used by most UI elements. **Here are the common mouse interactions used by desktop UI:**

Left-click	Activate or select an object. For text, set the insertion point.
Double-(left) click	Select an object and perform its default command, such as opening. For text, select a word.
Hover	Show tooltips or secondary affordances. (Not supported by touch screens.)
Right-click	Select an object and display its context menu.
Left-click+drag	Slide, move, resize, split, or drag an object. (Exact effect is indicated by the mouse pointer.)
Triple-click	For text, select a paragraph.
Control+left-click	Toggles a list item selection.
Shift+left-click	Extend a list selection contiguously.
Shift+left-click+drag	A constrained left-click+drag. For example, constrains resizing an oval or a rectangle to the existing aspect ratio.

This list is presented roughly in order of discoverability. (The ⌘ key is the equivalent of Control on Macintosh.) It's safe to assume that all users know about left-clicking and that most users know about double-clicking, hovering, and right-clicking. The remaining interactions are less discoverable and therefore more advanced.

Many users are confused by the difference between single click and a double click and may double-click objects when only a single click is required. As a rule, double-clicking is required to invoke a selectable object (such as items in a list, where the first click selects, and the second click invokes or opens), whereas nonselectable objects (items not in a list, such as command buttons, links, and checkboxes) are invoked on the first click, and any second click should have no effect. Other combinations such as double right-click are nonstandard and should not be used.

Here are the common keyboard interactions used by desktop UI:

Shortcut keys	Advanced keystrokes primarily for efficiency, known mostly to advanced users. In Windows, usually assigned to Function keys or Control keys; on a Mac, usually assigned to Control, Option, and ⌘ keys. Shortcut keys are memorized and therefore must be assigned consistently within a platform.
Access keys	Keyboard access to controls primarily for accessibility. In Windows, usually assigned to Alt keys. They cannot be assigned consistently, so they are documented within the UI. Access keys are not used on Macs.

Shortcut keys or access keys are secondary interactions, so they shouldn't be the only way to perform a command. For desktop UI, there should be a mouse-based alternative.

Here are some common interactions and gestures for touch-based UI:

Tap	Activate or select an object. For text, set the insertion point. Stop a scroll.
Double-tap	If in the center of the screen, zoom in and center the content or zoom out if already zoomed in. If at the top or bottom, scroll up or down a half page (iOS only). For text, makes selection.
Touch and hold	Display a magnified view for insertion point position. Display the context menu or additional commands. Change of modes (for example, edit mode).
Drag	Drag an object, reorder a list, pan or scroll a screen.
Pinch or spread	Spread two fingers apart to zoom in, pinch fingers together to zoom out.
Rotate	Rotate an object.
Flick	Pan or scroll a screen quickly.
Drag from top	When already at the top, dragging down reveals a search box or refreshes the content.
Swipe	Swipe across to reveal a Delete button for a list item. Swipe from top of screen to reveal notifications, timely information, important settings. Navigate between views such as items in a list (Android only).
Shake	Initiate an Undo or Redo command (iOS only). Refresh time-sensitive information (Android only).

Again, this list is presented roughly in order of discoverability. It's safe to assume that all users know about tapping and that many users know about double-tapping, touching and holding, dragging, and pinching. The remaining interactions are less discoverable and therefore more advanced.

Use standard interactions for your software's platform. Don't be creative here because consistent interaction is required for intuitive UI. For basic commands, avoid using advanced interactions with which your target users aren't likely to be familiar. Make sure that shortcuts (which require special knowledge) aren't the only way to perform a basic command.

CONTROLS (WORDS)

Controls are the words of expression in the language of UI. In this section, my goal is to help you have a clear understand of the purpose of each type of control and how to use controls effectively.

In human communication, there is what you say—the meaning of the words—as well has how you say it—the "body language." In human communication, body language is a form of nonverbal communication that subtly suggests how to interpret the meaning.

Controls are similar. Each type of control has a certain meaning, but the control's presentation also communicates subtle clues about how to interpret the control. Here are the most common forms of control "body language":

- **Size of expected input.** The physical control size suggests the size of the expected input or data. Example: A textbox width and height indicate the expected input size.

- **Number of items.** The physical size suggests the number of items. Example: A list box height suggests the length of the list, whereas longer lists usually are displayed in longer controls.

- **Screen space required.** The physical size required to display the control. Example: A set of checkboxes requires screen space to display each option, whereas a scrollable checkbox list does not.

- **Immediate versus delayed effect.** When the interaction takes effect—some controls are immediate, but not all. Example: Command buttons and sliders usually have an immediate effect, whereas checkboxes and drop-down lists usually have a delayed effect.

- **Default values.** The value a control has when it is initially displayed. Example: Most radio button groups have a default value, but to prevent bias, radio buttons used in surveys don't.

- **Required input.** Controls without default values are often marked to indicate that user input is required. Example: Forms often indicate required fields with a red asterisk.

- **Encourage change.** Open, easy-to-change controls encourage users to make selections, whereas closed, harder-to-change controls do not. Example: Sliders encourage users to try different values.

- **Presentation, order.** Whether a control enables users to change its presentation. Example: List views enable users to sort and filter list items.

- **Level of commitment.** Whether an action can be easily undone. Example: A button labeled Next does not imply commitment, whereas a button labeled Purchase does.

- **Forgiveness.** Whether user mistakes are prevented or easy to correct. Example: Some multiple-selection lists are unforgiving; if users make a small selection mistake, they have to start completely over.

- **Complexity.** The overall complexity of the control and its presentation. Example: Hierarchical tree controls are more complex than flat lists.

- **Discoverability.** How noticeable the control is. Example: Command buttons are more discoverable than links, making command buttons appropriate for primary commands and links a possible choice for secondary commands.

FIGURE 2.4

In this case, an open list of Wi-Fi connections encourages selection, making it a better choice than a drop-down list.

Usually, control choice is driven by purpose first and body language issues second, but sometimes body language is important enough to make the decision.

Common controls

Here are the most common input controls, organized by their purpose.

- **Textboxes:**

  Purpose: *Purpose of required field:

  `For unconstrained text|`   `For unconstrained text|`

  - Purpose: Used to input unconstrained text, such as names and addresses. Because they are unconstrained, textboxes require more knowledge and are more error-prone than other controls.

  - Body language: Control width suggests maximum input size. Control height suggests maximum numbers of lines of text. Red asterisk indicates a required field.

- **Numeric textboxes (with optional spin buttons):**

  - Purpose: Used to input unconstrained numeric values. Spin buttons can be used for convenience if the default value is close to the expected value.

  - Body language: Control width suggests maximum input size. Red asterisk indicates required field.

- **Sliders:**

  Purpose

  Low   High

  - Purpose: Used to select a value from a range of values where the desired value isn't known exactly or the exact value isn't meaningful, so users need to experiment to choose. For example, the numeric value of a volume slider usually isn't meaningful.

  - Body language: Needs immediate effect because feedback helps users select the desired value. Encourages change and experimentation.

- **Radio buttons:**
  - ◉ Option 1
  - ○ Option 2

  - Purpose: Used to select an exclusive choice from a small number of choices (say, eight or fewer).

  - Body language: Needs screen space to display all the choices.

- **Checkboxes:**
  - ☑ Option 1
  - ☐ Option 2

  - Purpose: Used to enable or disable an option or small number of options (say, eight or fewer).

  - Body language: Needs screen space to display all the choices.

- **Drop-down lists:**   `Selected option ▾`   `[Select an option] ▾`

- Purpose: Used to select an exclusive choice from a possibly large number of choices (up to several hundred).

- Body language: Needs a fixed amount of screen space. Closed presentation discourages change, but default values such as "[Select an option]" require change.

- **Combo boxes:** | For unconstrained text| ▼ |

  - Purpose: Used to input unconstrained text, but most likely selections are in the drop-down lists. Drop-down list values may be fixed or based on previous user input.

  - Body language: Needs a fixed amount of screen space.

- **Single-selection list boxes:**

  Select an ice cream:

  | Coffee Coffee Buzz Buzz! |
  | Imagine Whirled Peace |
  | Late Night Snack |
  | Phish Food |

  - Purpose: Used to select an exclusive choice from a possibly large number of choices (hundreds or even thousands).

  - Body language: List height is roughly proportional to the number of items in a list, where larger lists are usually displayed in larger boxes. In contrast to drop-down lists, open presentation encourages change.

- **Multiple-selection list boxes:**

  Select ice cream(s):

  | Coffee Coffee Buzz Buzz! |
  | Imagine Whirled Peace |
  | Late Night Snack |
  | Phish Food |

  - Purpose: Used to select independent choices from a possibly large number of choices (hundreds or even thousands).

  - Body language: Multiple-selection capability (through Shift+ and Control+click) is invisible, so it is either suggested by the label or deduced by users through experimentation. Also, very unforgiving, because any selection mistake will result in all previous selections being cleared. List height is roughly proportional to the number of items in the list, where larger lists are usually displayed in larger boxes.

- **Checkbox lists:**

  - Purpose: Used to select independent choices from a possibly large number of choices (hundreds or even thousands).

  - Body language: Multiple selection capability is clearly visible through the checkboxes. Forgiving compared to multiple-selection list boxes because selection mistakes affect only the current item. List height is roughly proportional to the number of items in the list, where larger lists are usually displayed in larger boxes.

- **Tabs:**

  - Purpose: Used to display different information or different views of the same information.

  - Body language: Needs screen space to display all the tabs.

Commands

- **Command buttons:** Submit   Print...

  - Purpose: Used to initiate an action.

  - Body language: Normally immediate. Ellipses are used to indicate that more input is required before the command can be performed. Can be used for any command, but their easy discoverability makes them especially suitable for primary commands (used to invoke the purpose of a page.)

- **Links:** Contact us   Cancel

  - Purpose: Used to initiate an action or navigate to another page or window.

  - Body language: For navigation, always immediate. For commands, normally immediate, but ellipses may be used to indicate that more input is required. Their reduced discoverability compared to command buttons make them suitable for secondary commands. (Secondary commands aren't directly related to the purpose of a page.)

Data controls

Flavor	Rating ⬍	Calories ⬍
Coffee Coffee Buzz Buzz!	★★★★★	230
Imagine Whirled Peace	★★★★★	240
Late Night Snack	★★★★★	250
Phish Food	★★★★	250

- **Tables:**

- Purpose: Used to display and interact with a list or table of data in either a flat organization or organized by groups.

- Body language: Typically users may sort table data by clicking column headings or filter by choosing various filters.

- **Trees:**

  [+] Low calorie
  [−] It tastes good for a reason
  Coffee Coffee Buzz Buzz Buzz!
  Imagine Whirled Peace
  Late Night Snack
  Phish Food
  [+] Frozen yogurt

- Purpose: Used to display and interact with data using a multilevel hierarchical structure. Works best when that hierarchy is unique and well known by users.

- Body language: Users can expand and collapse tree nodes but not change the order or filter as with list views. A very complex control to use and understand, making list views a better choice unless a multilevel hierarchy is required.

Mobile controls

Here are the additional mobile controls, organized by their purpose:

• **Table views and grids:**

A Simple Label
⊕ Add and sub-menu   ❯
⊖ Delete (Cancel)
Two Labels, and a comma   yup
✓ A Checkmark   ◉
● A Bullet   ☰
Space for an icon
Space for a big icon
On button   ON
Off button   OFF
✓ An empty row   (above)

• Purpose: Used to present data in a grid (a single-column grid for iOS table views).

• Body language: Used to gather input, show settings, and make choices.

• **Pickers:**

• Purpose: Used to select an exclusive choice from a moderate number of choices (moderate because users may need to flick through the entire list). Date and time pickers are used to select dates and times.

• Body language: Flicking has momentum, making it easy for users to choose from a moderate range of values. More physical and engaging, and less error prone than typing. Table views are more efficient for selecting from a large list.

- **Switches:** ON ON
  - Purpose: Used to turn an option on or off.
  - Body language: Like checkboxes but more touchable.
- **Segmented controls (iOS only):** | Item | Item | Item |
  - Purpose: Used to show exclusive views (up to about five) and which one is currently selected.
  - Body language: Direct, labeled, and exclusive.
- **Page indicators:** ○ ○ ● ○ ○
  - Purpose: Used to show the number of views open (up to a maximum of 20) and which one is currently visible.
  - Body language: Sequential and unlabeled, so may require users to browse many views to find what they are looking for.

- **Spinners (Android only):**

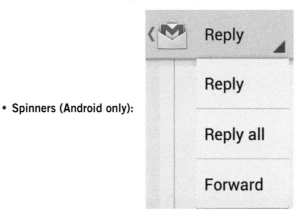

  - Purpose: Used to display a list of options, either in a drop-down or pop-up menu.
  - Body language: Needs a fixed amount of screen space. Closed presentation discourages change (compared to the alternatives).

Removing, disabling, or giving an error message

What should you do if a setting or command doesn't apply in the current context? Here are your choices:

- **Remove the control.** Remove controls that don't apply. This approach simplifies the UI at the potential cost of confusing users who expect to find the control.
- **Disable the control.** Disable controls that don't apply. If users expect the control, they will find it (instead of continuing to look elsewhere), but disabled controls add clutter, and the reason they are disabled isn't always obvious.

- **Give an error message.** Leave the control enabled, but give an error message when users invoke it.

   Although giving an error message might seem like a poor option, it depends on how helpful the error message is. Consider providing an error message if doing so eliminates confusion or the need for experimentation or help. (But to clarify: By "error message," I am referring to the general UI pattern of giving feedback in response to a problem. It doesn't have to look or feel like an error or draw unnecessary attention to the user's mistake.)

Departing Flight

> **1**   From PLATTSBURGH, NY (PBG) to LAS VEGAS, NV (LAS)

Departing flights for Monday Feb 25

Depart	Arrive	Flight	Price *	
11:15 am PLATTSBURGH, NY (PBG)	1:50 pm LAS VEGAS, NV (LAS)	569 Nonstop	$79.⁹⁹	○

Returning Flight

> **2**   From LAS VEGAS, NV (LAS) to PLATTSBURGH, NY (PBG)

Returning flights for Sunday Mar 3

Depart	Arrive	Flight	Price *	
2:30 pm LAS VEGAS, NV (LAS)	10:20 pm PLATTSBURGH, NY (PBG)	568 Nonstop	$174.⁹⁹	○

> Continue

FIGURE 2.5

Is it completely clear why the Continue button is disabled? Better to leave it enabled and give a helpful error message. Communicates poorly

   When in doubt, here is how to decide:

- Start by writing the error message you might give. If it provides useful information that doesn't go without saying and avoids confusion, leave the control enabled and give the error message.

- Determine whether users will be confused if the control is removed. If they won't, remove it.

- For mobile apps, bias the decision more toward removal, to maintain simplicity on small displays.

Control choice is driven by meaning first and body language issues second, but sometimes body language is important enough to make the decision. Generally the simplest, lightest-weight, most constrained, least error-prone control is the best choice.

COMMANDS (VERBS)

We just looked at controls generally. Controls have three purposes:

- To perform commands (verbs)

- To show and change user input, settings, and options (nouns, adjectives, adverbs)

- To navigate between steps

Let's focus on commands now. Commands have a special design challenge: There are often many commands, where do you put them all? Worse, command presentation often has conflicting goals:

- **Discoverability.** For intuitiveness, users need to find the command they are looking for quickly and easily.

- **Directness.** Commands are easier to find and more efficient to use if they are directly visible on the screen (as opposed to being in a drop-down menu).

- **Consolidation.** Commands are easier to find if there is only one place to look. Users shouldn't have to go on a "command safari" to hunt down exotic commands.

- **Context.** Commands are displayed in or next to the objects they affect, rather than out of context.

- **Simplicity.** The cumulative effective of the commanding shouldn't be overwhelming, which is likely if you have many direct commands piled in one place.

- **Space efficiency.** Your app's content is the reason users are there, so it needs to be the star of the show. A poorly designed app shows mostly commands and navigation and very little content.

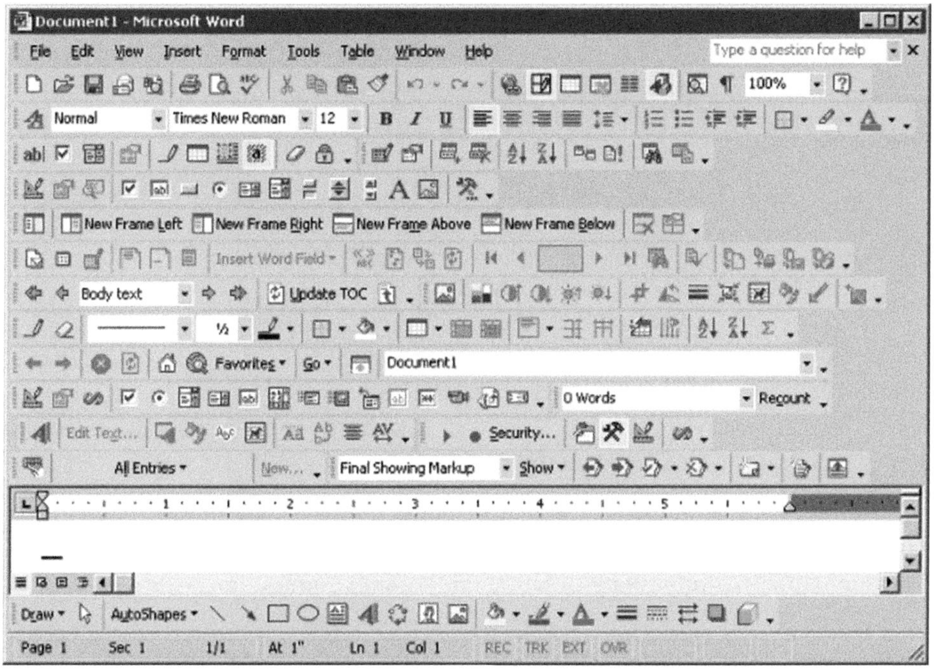

FIGURE 2.6
Discoverability, directness, and consolidation are good, but they have downsides, too.

Communicates
poorly

No one solution to these tradeoffs works best for all situations; hence the need for different ways to present commands. Let's review the most common commanding patterns.

In-place commands

In-place commands are command buttons and links (for secondary commands) placed directly on the UI surface. This approach works well when there are only a few commands used all the time.

- **Pros:** For a few commands, very discoverable, direct, and simple. A great choice for mobile apps.

- **Cons:** Breaks down quickly if there are many commands.

FIGURE 2.7
Calculators are the classic example of in-place commanding.

Sometimes in-place commanding can be eliminated by giving actions immediate effect.

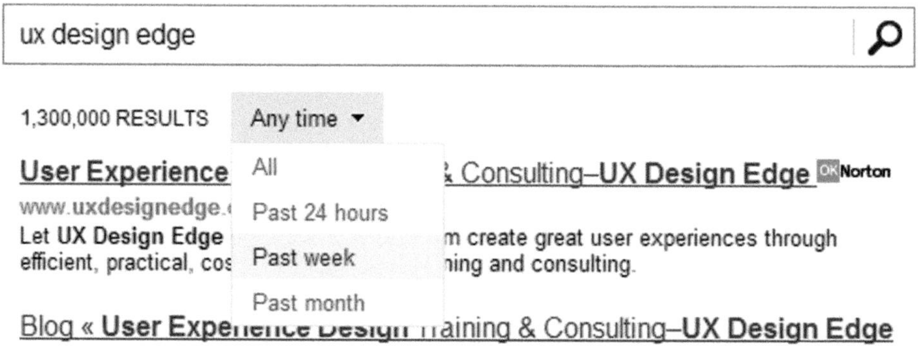

| ux design edge | 🔍 |

1,300,000 RESULTS   Any time ▾

User Experience   All   **Consulting–UX Design Edge** ⊙Norton
www.uxdesignedge.   Past 24 hours
Let **UX Design Edge**   m create great user experiences through
efficient, practical, cos   Past week   iing and consulting.

Past month

Blog « **User Expe**~~rience Design T~~raining & Consulting–**UX Design Edge**

FIGURE 2.8
"Adornments" change the appearance of their associated list. They often have immediate effect, making an explicit command button unnecessary.

Pop-up menus

Pop-up menus are menus displayed contextually by clicking a button. They may pop up, drop down, or slide out in some way. These menus are called action sheets on the iOS and pop-ups on Android. They use screen space effectively, making them a great choice for mobile apps.

- **Pros:** For a few clearly related commands, pop-ups are very discoverable and simple and provide one place to look for related commands.

- **Cons:** Break down quickly if frequently used, if there are many commands, or if they aren't clearly related.

FIGURE 2.9

Pop-up menus are simple and yet still have a contextual feel. These menus are called *action sheets* in iOS.

Menu bars

Menu bars display a comprehensive list of all the commands available in an app. They are indirect because users must interact to do anything. They are typically displayed at the top of a window, although Macintosh displays its menu at the top of the main display. They are labeled primarily with text.

- **Pros:** A great way to summarize all the commands available in one place.

- **Cons:** Not direct or contextual and therefore often inefficient compared to the alternatives.

Given the cons, menu bars are traditionally combined with toolbars for both comprehensiveness and efficiency. With this combination, the toolbar is used to access frequently used commands and the menu bar is used to find infrequently used ones—often the ones that *aren't* in the toolbar.

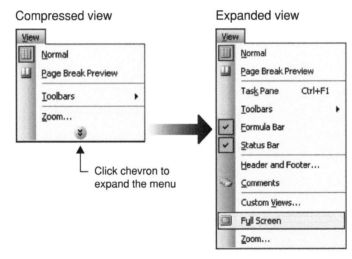

Communicates
poorly

FIGURE 2.10
Office 2000 introduced Personalized Menus to simplify menu bars by hiding infrequently used commands. But finding those infrequently used commands is the primary reason for using the menu bar. Now you know why you didn't like them!

Toolbars

Toolbars display the most frequently used commands directly, making them quick and easy to access. Toolbar commands are labeled with icons or text.

- **Pros:** Very discoverable and direct. Simple, at least compared to ribbons. Perfect for a small set of frequently used commands.

- **Cons:** Not contextual (unless displayed dynamically). Not simple if there are many commands.

Toolbars are strong where menu bars are weak, so the two are often combined. Unfortunately, some toolbars have the exact same commands as their associated menu bars, defeating their purpose of optimizing for the most frequently used commands.

FIGURE 2.11
A typical toolbar with the most frequently used commands.

FIGURE 2.12
A dynamic toolbar shown when an Adobe .pdf file is displayed in Google Chrome.

Communicates well

Ribbons

Ribbons organize commands into grouped tabs. Most ribbon commands are labeled with both a text label and an icon.

- **Pros:** Discoverable, direct, and one place to look. A great choice for complex apps with many commands. Space efficient, at least when compared to piles of toolbars.

- **Cons:** Large and very heavy. Not contextual or simple. Having to frequently change tabs can be a productivity killer.

FIGURE 2.13
Ribbons are a great way to consolidate a large set of commands into a single place. But those tabs!

Communicates well

Context menus

Context menus display the most frequently used commands for a specific object or context. They are called edit menus on the iOS and pop-ups on Android.

- **Pros:** Very contextual. Discoverable, at least for advanced users. One place to look for commands related to a specific object.

- **Cons:** Break down quickly if there are many commands. Must be used only for contextual commands, not global ones.

Communicates
well

FIGURE 2.14

Context menus are a great way to show only the commands that apply to the context at hand.

Palettes

Palettes display the most frequently used commands for a specific task on a user-movable surface. Palette commands are usually labeled with icons.

- **Pros:** Very discoverable, direct, and contextual. More efficient than the alternatives when doing detailed work in a specific area. Perfect for a small set of frequently used commands in a specific context.

- **Cons:** Because they are movable, they require users to move them where they're needed or out of the way when they're not. Introduces another place to look for commands.

Communicates
well

FIGURE 2.15

Palettes are an efficient way to show commands in the exact context where they are needed.

The challenge in displaying commands is to present them in a way that is discoverable, direct, easy to find, contextual, simple, and space efficient. These are tradeoffs, so you need to choose the commanding UI that strikes the right balance.

Command-labeling patterns

We will look at labeling generally in the next section, but let's now look at the common command-labeling patterns.

Commands are labeled with some combination of text labels and icons:

- **Text-only labels.** Self-explanatory but not easy to scan and recognize. Traditionally used in menus but now used in toolbars as well.

FIGURE 2.16
Toolbars can have text-only labels. Note how most of the commands on the Windows Explorer toolbar in Windows 7 don't have icons.

- **Icon-only labels (plus tooltips).** Compact, easy to scan and recognize, but not self-explanatory. Commands are verbs, and verbs are hard to show with symbols, which are nouns. So, except for the most well-known icons, icon-only labels depend on tooltips to explain them—which makes them harder to use than text labels. One benefit to icon-only labels is that they don't require translation, but of course tooltips do. Touch screens don't support hovering, making unlabeled nonstandard icons a poor choice.

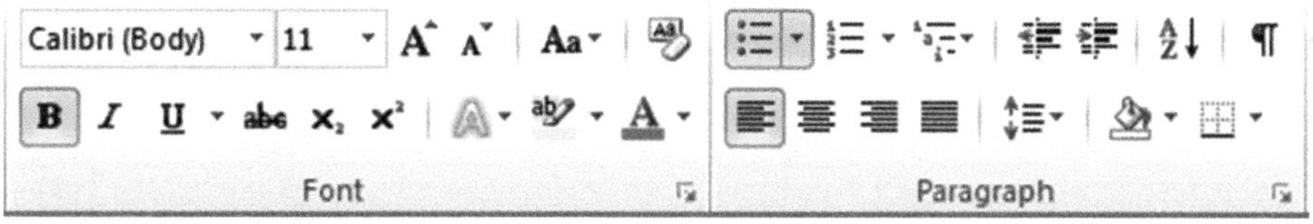

FIGURE 2.17
These icons are well known, so the commands are clear, even without labels.

Communicates
poorly

FIGURE 2.18

By contrast, the meaning and differences between these commands aren't entirely clear. They require tooltips to help users understand them.

- **Icon and text labels.** Both self-explanatory and scannable but at the cost of being larger than the alternatives.

Communicates
well

FIGURE 2.19

iOS apps often label commands with both icons and text.

Not all commands require icons. Modern, intuitive UI designs tend to favor text labels (often without icons) to be self-explanatory without depending on tooltips. Modern, simple designs with few commands benefit less from using icons to help scanning than from classic UIs with dozens.

Commands don't require icons, so don't feel obligated to provide them. Icons work well without text labels only when they are well known. If they're not, provide a text label; avoid relying on tooltips.

LABELS AND INSTRUCTIONS

Labels refer to text or icons directly on controls or associated with controls, whereas instructions refer to additional explanations beyond the labels. This section focuses on the label and instruction text. We will explore label layout in Chapter 3.

FIGURE 2.20
Examples of labels and instructions.

Most controls need a label for users to understand their purpose and effect. On rare occasions, some controls (like a playback control in a media player) don't need labels, but they are the exception rather than the rule.

FIGURE 2.21
Most controls need a text or icon label. Controls that don't—like this playback control—are the exception.

Main instructions are large text instructions at the top of a page that explain the purpose of the page. A good main instruction should be what you would actually say to users to explain the page. Designing good main instructions and pages to accurately reflect those instructions leads to better, more intuitive task flows—even if you don't explicitly display the instruction, which is often the case in mobile UI. Main instructions were covered in detail in Chapter 1.

Ordinary (not main) instructions should rarely be needed. Use ordinary instructions when concise, self-explanatory labels aren't possible or when users need information beyond the individual control labels.

FIGURE 2.22

Communicates well

Design controls so that further instructions usually aren't needed. Here the Speaking Rate slider requires no further instructions, but the Speak Selection and Highlight Words options do.

An important contrast between labels and instructions is that users rarely interact with controls without reading their labels first, but users frequently skip over instructions without reading them at all. Moral: If there is text that users must read, try to put it directly on a control label.

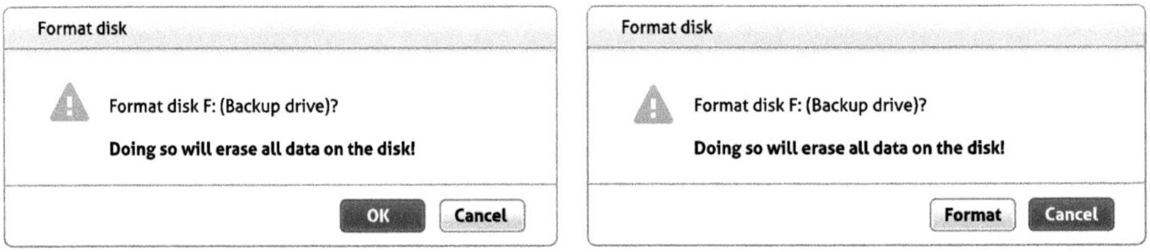

FIGURE 2.23

Very few users will click on Format without reading the button label, but many users will click OK without reading the warning.

Concise vs. self-explanatory: Getting the right balance

Imagine a conversation with someone in which all her responses were limited to a single word—usually OK or Cancel. You could engage in such a conversation, but it wouldn't be effective and it would feel very tedious. Yet many UI "conversations" are like this.

FIGURE 2.24
Fortunately, humans rarely communicate this way.

There is a tradeoff between concise and self-explanatory labels. Traditionally, control labels were very concise, often using a single word such as OK, Cancel, Submit, Close, Done, or Save. These single-word labels were originally motivated by small, low-resolution displays and poor typography. Although we still have small displays for smartphones, for desktop UI and tablets we have high-resolution displays and excellent typography.

By contrast, modern UI tends to make the tradeoff in favor of being self-explanatory. Being self-explanatory occasionally results in having more text, but that isn't always the case. In fact, my experience is that it usually results in less but much *better* text—without repetition. Say it well, yet concisely, once instead of many times poorly, and add an extra word or two as needed to add clarity. You have permission to do this now—we have the technology!

Item condition: **New other (see details)**

Quantity: 1   5 available / 60 sold

US $12.95   Buy another

Add to cart 🛒

Add to Watch list ▾

Communicates well

FIGURE 2.25

Modern UI labeling is self-explanatory but less redundant—using more words but ultimately much less text. This example uses very little text, but it communicates quite clearly.

In *The Elements of Style*, William Strunk Jr. famously admonished, "Omit needless words!" My additional advice: "Add needed words!" The alternative is having users rely on experimentation, documentation, and training—clear signs of an unintuitive UI.

Attributes of effective labels and instructions

As I explained in Chapter 1, effective labels and instructions should reflect what you would actually say to someone in person. If a UI feels like a natural, professional, friendly conversation, it is probably a good design. If it feels unnatural, technical, or robotic, it probably isn't.

Chapter 1 presented the attributes of effective communication in detail. **Here is a summary of the attributes most relevant to labels and instructions:**

- **Useful, relevant, necessary.** The label provides information that is useful and relevant to the task at hand and doesn't go without saying. If a completely confused user could readily provide the same information, skip it.

- **Purposeful.** The label helps users understand the UI element, focusing on the objectives and tying them to the users' goals and motivation, not the basic mechanics of the interaction. If novice users who understand basic interaction could provide the same information, skip it.

- **Clear and natural.** The label speaks the users' language—using language users would naturally say in conversation. The text avoids unnecessary jargon, abbreviations, and acronyms, fully spelling out words in plain language whenever possible.

- **Easy to understand.** The label doesn't require thought, experimentation, or special knowledge to understand.

- **Specific and explicit—it doesn't undercommunicate.** The label provides the right level of detail so that users know what to do.

- **Concise and efficient—it doesn't overcommunicate.** The label provides the right level of detail so that users can make informed decisions confidently but without going overboard.

- **Good personality and tone.** The text has a good personality and tone—like a likeable person. If saying what is on the label would be inappropriate, rude, disrespectful, or stupid between people, it should be considered equally inappropriate with software.

Label and instruction details

When crafting label and instruction text, here are some details to get right:

- **Placeholders.** Placeholders are textbox labels placed temporarily inside the control. They disappear once users activate the control. Placeholders can simplify the appearance of a UI and work well with small screens but disappear when users potentially need them most. For that reason, reserve placeholders for simple forms where it's obvious what to do.

| *User name* |
| *Password* |

FIGURE 2.26
Placeholders work great for simple forms where users already know what they should enter.

- **Ellipses.** Use on command labels only to indicate that more input is required to perform the command. Ellipses are a constant source of confusion on desktop UI. (Note that ellipses aren't used for this purpose in mobile UI.) Commands normally have immediate effect, whereby the command is executed immediately after an interaction. Ellipses are added to labels to indicate when a command isn't immediate—when more input is required. Many people mistakenly believe that ellipses indicate that the command displays a window or dialog box. The difference: If the purpose of a command is to display a window or dialog box, ellipses aren't needed.

FIGURE 2.27
Print... indicates that more input is required to print the document (by displaying Print Options). By contrast, a command that displays Options doesn't have an ellipsis.

- **Capitalization.** Follow your platform's guidelines, but generally use title capitalization for titles, sentence capitalization for everything else. In classic UI, title capitalization (where pretty much all words are capitalized except articles, conjunctions, and prepositions) is used for commands. Title capitalization made the commands more legible with poor typography, but it makes the text feel overly formal and awkward with multiword labels. By contrast, sentence capitalization (where only the first word of a new sentence is capitalized) feels friendly and is more flexible.

Choose your shipping options
Choose Your Shipping Options

FIGURE 2.28

Sentence caps are friendlier and work better with longer labels.

- **Periods.** Don't use periods at the end of labels, links, or main instructions. However, use periods at the end of ordinary instructions presented as complete sentences.

Choose the quantity.

I would like to buy:

○ One copy of UI is Communication.

○ 10 copies of UI is Communication.

◉ 100 copies of UI is Communication.

FIGURE 2.29

Unnecessary periods look awkward.

- **Underlining.** Don't underline any text that isn't a link; use italics if necessary for emphasis. Most links don't need underlines, either. Use them only when text isn't clearly a link based on its context.

| Forgot your password | Contact us | Better be a link and not colored text |
| Forgot your password | Contact us | Better be a link and not colored text |

FIGURE 2.30

We get it … it's a link. No underline required. But colored text must be a link.

> Modern UI uses more self-explanatory labels and instructions than classic UI. However, the goal isn't to have more text but rather to have less but much *better* text. Usually this boils down to using more useful, relevant, purposeful text, adding a word or two as needed to add clarity and removing unhelpful, mechanical text and repetition.

FEEDBACK

Feedback **indicates that the action is happening and was either successful or unsuccessful, providing specific details when needed.** Effective feedback communicates status, keeps users oriented, and builds their confidence in a task. Although you can communicate feedback using a heavy modal dialog box, it is usually better to keep it simple, lightweight, and engaging.

FIGURE 2.31

Feedback is an excellent opportunity to be engaging. Why be dull? Here, without using a heavy UI, MailChimp vividly lets you know when you have stretched your email too wide.

Communicates well

Effective feedback is responsive. When users perform an action, they expect to see feedback within 200 ms before they start to wonder what is going on and perhaps retry the action. No response is always poor feedback; there should be some visual clue that the action is happening.

Here are the most common forms of feedback, least intrusive first:

- **Progressive rendering.** Shows progress by rendering as it happens. More informative than other forms of feedback because it is the actual progress instead of an indirect indicator. The best first step in the rendering is to make the content and its layout stable so that users can interact right away with confidence.

FIGURE 2.32

Progressive rendering shows the actual progress as it happens. Note that the first step is to make the new items stable.

Communicates well

- **Animations.** Animations visually show that an interaction has happened, the relationship between an action and its effect, or the outcome or side effect of an action.

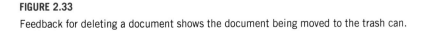

FIGURE 2.33

Feedback for deleting a document shows the document being moved to the trash can.

Communicates well

- **Activity indicators.** Spinners and indeterminate progress bars show that work is getting done but without indicating progress toward completion. Spinners work well for actions that take only a few seconds, but they are uninformative after that.

FIGURE 2.34
Spinners show activity but not progress.

- **Progress feedback.** Determinate progress bars show an approximate percentage of completion. Progress bars provide useful feedback for actions that take longer than a few seconds. The value of a progress bar is undermined if progress stalls or—worse— the bar resets to the beginning. Resetting turns a progress bar into an activity indicator.

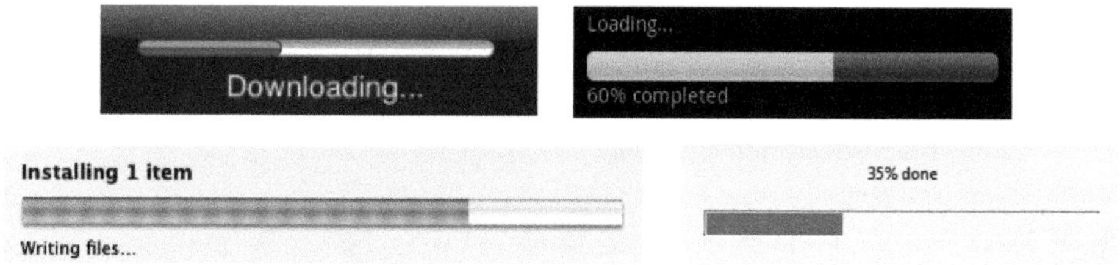

FIGURE 2.35
This progress bar shows that the task is almost complete.

- **Modal dialog boxes.** Show feedback primarily through text, using a presentation that users must respond to. Can be a good choice to show complex results for a long-running task but not so good for other forms of feedback.

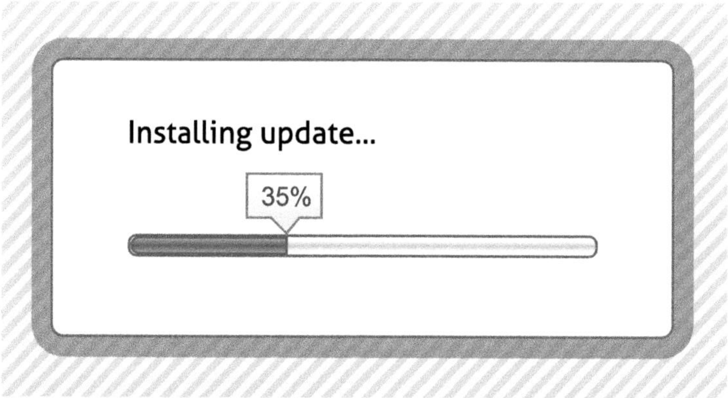

FIGURE 2.36
Modal feedback for a long-running task.

- **Flashing or bouncing.** An attention-demanding, often intrusive animation to indicate that something requires the user's immediate attention. For flashing, the frequency indicates the urgency and seriousness of the issue. Use another form of feedback if the user's immediate, undivided attention isn't required.

FIGURE 2.37
Bouncing demands the user's immediate attention. It had better be worth the interruption!.

- **Beeping.** An attention-demanding, often intrusive way to indicate that something requires the user's immediate attention. The volume, frequency, and dissonance of the beeps indicate the urgency and seriousness of the issue. Not only is beeping annoying, but the meaning and source of the beep are often unclear.

FIGURE 2.38
This beeping device appears to have some problem that I can't figure out. I can't get it to stop! Where is my hammer?.

Use feedback to indicate that an action is happening and was either successful or unsuccessful. Provide feedback responsively so that users remain confident and know what is going on. There are many ways to provide feedback, so choose the least intrusive form that communicates well.

Grouping (sentences)

Grouping shows relationships between controls visually within a page and makes pages easier to scan and parse.

FIGURE 2.39

Without clear grouping (left), control relationships are hard to parse.

Group boxes

Group boxes **are labeled rectangular frames that surround a set of related controls.** Group boxes have been around forever. Although they're simple conceptually, they are visually heavy and distracting, inflexible, and often overused.

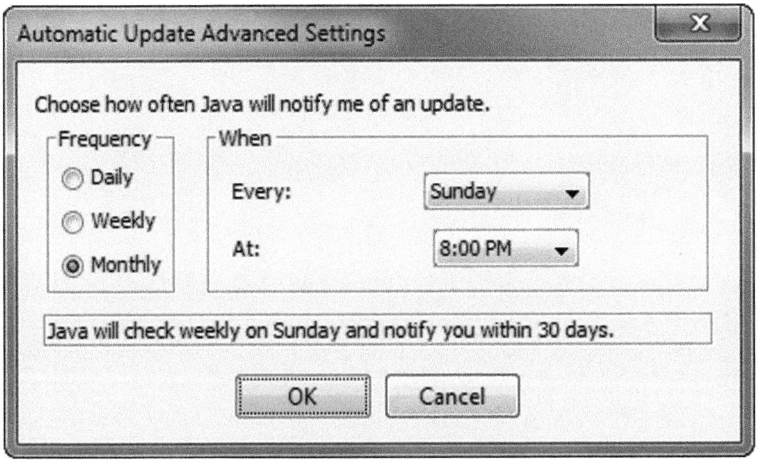

FIGURE 2.40

Even though there is no doubt about the control relationships, all I see are boxes.

On the iOS, group boxes within table views and forms are the most common form of grouping. Group boxes' visual style makes them look like an integral part of a screen, so they don't feel as heavy or distracting.

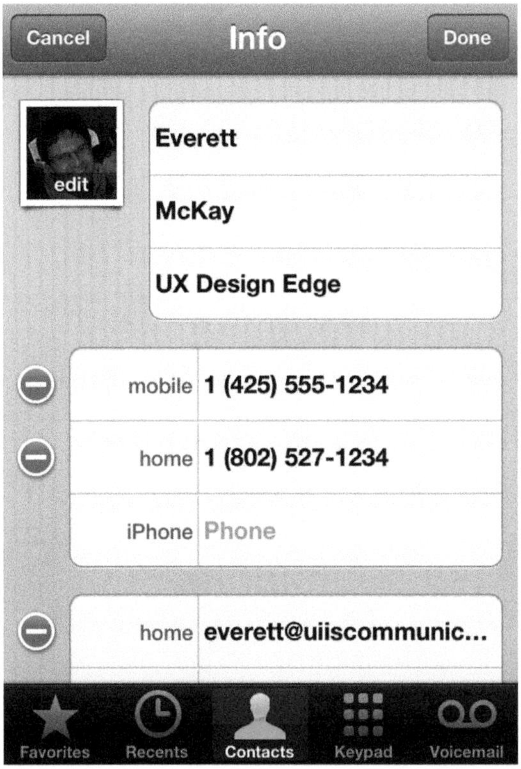

FIGURE 2.41
Group boxes are commonly used on the iOS.

Separators or heading banners

Separators and *heading banners* are essentially group boxes without the box—using labeled lines or banners to separate groups of related controls. Although they are a better choice than group boxes, using rich headings (which we'll talk about in a moment) is a cleaner, more modern approach. There is a phenomenon known as *banner blindness* (explained in Chapter 3), so for heading banners I recommend black text on a light background instead of white text on a color background—which looks somewhat like an advertisement, so users tend to ignore it.

| Name | First: [ ] | Last: [ ] | Phone numbers | Home: [ ] | Work: [ ] | Cell: [ ] |

FIGURE 2.42

Some example separators and heading banners. But watch out for banner blindness!

Rich headings and layout

You can use layout alone to show relationships between controls. And instead of using separators to identify sections, you can use rich headings. (By "rich," I mean that the UI text uses a variety of fonts instead of a single font, so headings would be larger and bolder than plain UI text.) Group boxes and separators are sometimes helpful, but rich headings and layout are lighter weight, more flexible, and more modern.

Settings

Sign in

Signed in as everettm@comcast.net. Manage your synced data on Google Dashboard.

[Disconnect your Google Account...] [Advanced sync settings...]

On startup

- ○ Open the New Tab page
- ● Continue where I left off Learn more
- ○ Open a specific page or set of pages. Set pages

Communicates well

FIGURE 2.43

Google Chrome uses rich headings and layout to indicate groups.

Progressive disclosure

Progressive disclosure, in which additional information is displayed on demand, is a way to group dynamically. The information being displayed dynamically can be shown in place, in a pop-up, or in a flyout.

FIGURE 2.44

Progressive disclosure is a dynamic way to group and simplify content.

Sentence-style grouping

Sentence-style grouping shows the relationship between controls by composing them into complete thoughts—much like a sentence. One approach is to make a grammatically correct sentence. Although there might be situations in which this is a good approach, a significant downside is that it can be extremely hard to localize given that sentence structures vary greatly across languages.

FIGURE 2.45

Controls can be composed to form a complete thought—like a sentence.

Communicates well

A more practical approach (that is, no localization worries) is to present an entire thought without making an actual sentence. For example, classic UI often presents settings as *control + label* pairs. Modern and mobile UI often use richer *label + current setting + control to change setting* triplets that form a more complete thought.

Settings
Reminders
Sync
Reminders 1 Month Back
Default List
Reminders
New reminders created outside of a specific list will default to this list.

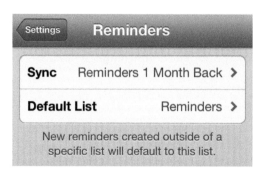

FIGURE 2.46

Some mobile settings read like complete thoughts.

> Use grouping to show relationships visually between controls within a page and to make pages easier to scan and parse. Prefer modern, lighter-weight styles such as rich headings, layout, progressive disclosure, and sentence styles over classic styles such as group boxes.

TASK STEPS (PARAGRAPHS, MONOLOGUES, AND DIALOGUES)

Imagine reading a book that was presented as a single paragraph. No matter the size, content, or writing style, such a book would be excruciatingly tedious to read. Many UIs feel like that.

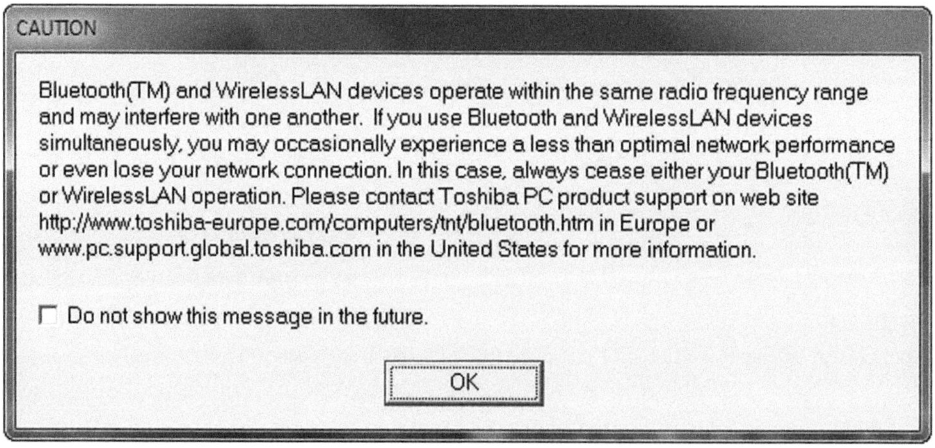

CAUTION
Bluetooth(TM) and WirelessLAN devices operate within the same radio frequency range and may interfere with one another. If you use Bluetooth and WirelessLAN devices simultaneously, you may occasionally experience a less than optimal network performance or even lose your network connection. In this case, always cease either your Bluetooth(TM) or WirelessLAN operation. Please contact Toshiba PC product support on web site http://www.toshiba-europe.com/computers/tnt/bluetooth.htm in Europe or www.pc.support.global.toshiba.com in the United States for more information.
Do not show this message in the future.
OK

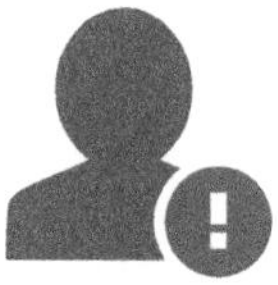

Communicates poorly

FIGURE 2.47

Regardless of the content, reading a book consisting of one paragraph would be excruciatingly tedious. Like this UI.

People often ask me how much information is appropriate to display on a single page. Without looking, I know that a concise response would be, "Much less than you have now." Inexperienced designers have a tendency to put way too much information on their pages—their motivation being that it is easier to develop and that having fewer pages somehow sounds better.

How much information should you have on a page? A safe bet: probably much less than you have now.

But to be courteous and helpful, the response I usually give is: "Think about the conversation you would have in person. The right UI pattern will reflect the nature of that conversation."
Here are some conversation patterns to consider:

- **A speech.** In this pattern, the UI effectively delivers a speech—where all the user does is passively listen. The communication is one way and there is no interaction. In practice, such a UI might answer a user question by providing a .pdf document.

- **A monologue.** In this pattern, the communication is still one way. The user listens, but unlike the speech pattern, the user can control how the information is delivered. In practice, such a UI might present an interactive brochure.

- **App-driven dialogue.** Here the UI displays the information and controls the flow of the conversation. Unlike a monologue, there is plenty of interaction, but the user has little control over it. Such a UI is often called a *wizard*.

- **User-driven dialogue.** In this pattern, users have control over the conversation. The app presents the minimum to get the task done, but users can choose to see or do more and determine the direction of the conversation; they just have to ask.

- **A form.** Here users ask for something and the app responds by having the user fill out a form. This pattern has a bureaucratic feel, but it works well if the form feels simple and its fields are clearly necessary.

Many complex, hard-to-use UIs use heavy monologues or app-driven dialogues when they should be using simple user-driven dialogues. There's nothing wrong with giving a speech—as long as it's the right conversation pattern. It just rarely is. Better to let the user drive the conversation.

FIGURE 2.48
Monologues are often boring.

Here are the common techniques to present dialogues that are simpler and more user driven:

- **Present less stuff.** Though this concept is seemingly obvious, it doesn't go without saying. When evaluating your UIs, take a highlighter and highlight the useful stuff, then take a step back and reevaluate what you didn't highlight. We tend to overcommunicate, so chances are that you should simply remove most of what isn't highlighted.

- **Better organization and a visual hierarchy.** Having better organization and a visual hierarchy presents the same amount of information but in a way that is easier to scan and understand. It doesn't feel like a big pile of stuff.

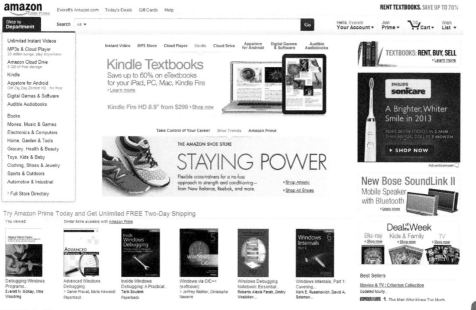

FIGURE 2.49

Even though the Amazon homepage is packed with information, it has a good organization and a clear hierarchy, making things easy to find.

- **Progressive disclosure.** We already looked at progressive disclosure, but it is a great way to let users control how much information they see.

- **Modes.** Although it's a design principle to avoid modes, a more enlightened approach is to avoid unnecessary modes. They are necessary modes and they work well—so don't avoid these. For example, a common pattern is to display information that users might occasionally need to change. Rather than display everything required for both viewing and editing, start in a simple view mode and let users ask to edit.

- **Tabs.** Tabs display related information on demand. Tabs are a great way to display different information or different views of the same information. However, don't use tabs for other purposes, such as presenting steps in a task flow or general commands; users don't expect to find these in tabs.

- **Pages.** Of course, you don't have to display everything on a single page. You can use more than one page—it works great! Though that's an obvious solution, it's not hard to find pages that ought to be split up.

Communicates
well

FIGURE 2.50

My shipping schedule is quite simple, but changing it is much more complex. Better to have an Edit mode than to display the editing UI all the time.

FIGURE 2.51

Google uses tabs to display its various destinations. Works great!

Communicates
poorly

FIGURE 2.52

Where's Checkout? There it is ... What is a command doing on a tab?

In designing the presentation of your content, think about the conversation you would have in person. The right UI pattern will reflect the nature of that conversation. There are many conversation patterns, but long speeches are rarely the best choice. Better to present your content in smaller conversational units and, when practical, let users drive the conversation.

TASK NAVIGATION

A great way to simplify a complex task and let the user drive the conversation is to break a task down into simple steps. But to do that, we have to provide a way for users to navigate between the steps.

A helpful way to think about task navigation is to think about how you find your way around in an unfamiliar city as a tourist. Often you start a journey from "home" (your hotel) by knowing where you want to go, but without necessarily knowing how to get there. As you go, you use navigation aids such as maps, landmarks, street signs, and pointers to specific attractions. You won't consider yourself lost as long as you know roughly where you are and can take the next step with confidence. If you get lost, you might backtrack to the last place where you knew you were and restart from there. If you ask for help, it's likely to be the last thing you try—doubly true if the last time you asked for help wasn't helpful. Navigating through an unfamiliar task in software is much the same kind of process.

There are many possible navigation models, but some variation of Web navigation is often the best choice. By *Web navigation*, I mean a navigation model that:

- Has clear means to advance to the next step

- Offers a consistent way to go back to the previous step when needed

- Has a consistent way to get home or cancel the task

- If helpful, has a consistent way to search

Regardless of the navigation model you choose, keeping navigation simple and consistent across your app will help users get tasks done more efficiently by leveraging their previous experience.

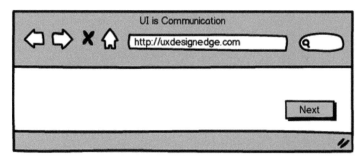

FIGURE 2.53

Browsers support the key elements of the Web navigation model, which works well because it is simple, familiar, and forgiving.

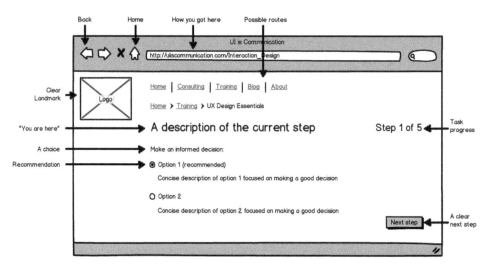

FIGURE 2.54

A typical Web page with navigation elements.

Beyond the basic Web navigation elements, Figure 2.38 shows additional useful components of task navigation:

- **Clear landmarks.** The page header, consistent navigation elements across pages to keep you oriented.

- **Possible routes.** Buttons or links to take you to the top tasks.

- **"You are here" marks.** The main instruction, the address bar.

- **How you got here.** A "breadcrumb" bar that shows your path.

- **Task progress.** A progress bar or step indicator to show you where you are and give you confidence that you are making progress.

- **A choice.** The user needs to make a decision, and the page has enough information to make an informed decision confidently.

- **Recommendations.** Defaults and recommendations to make decisions quickly and confidently based on what is most likely.

- **A clear next step.** This action should be visually obvious. Users should never be surprised to discover that they made a commitment. Commitments should always be obvious.

- **Go back to the last step.** A simple way to recover from small mistakes without having to start completely over.

- **Home.** A simple way to go back to the known starting point.

> Use a simple, consistent navigation model in your app. A Web navigation approach—with consistent Back, Home, and Search—is a good approach. Be sure your page design has all the necessary navigation elements so that users can proceed with the task with confidence yet easily recover from mistakes. Make sure that it's obvious when users make a commitment.

SURFACES (DOCUMENTS)

The final UI elements that I would like to explore are documents—the UI surfaces that we can use to present content to users. Surfaces have these characteristics:

- **Weight.** Some surfaces are lightweight; others are heavy.

- **Floating versus fixed.** Floating surfaces can be moved by users; others are fixed.

- **Modality.** Some surfaces are modal (so users must interact and dismiss before they can do anything else) and others are modeless.

Here are the common UI surfaces, starting from the lightest to the heaviest:

- **Pages.** Lightweight, fixed, and modeless. Fills the entire window, minus any panes or bars. Called *screens* in mobile UI because pages fill the entire screen.

  - **Pros:** A great way to provide a primary work area.

  - **Cons:** Can only display one page at a time.

- **Panes and bars.** Lightweight, fixed, and modeless. Bars are narrow and used to present commands and status, whereas panes are larger and can be used to present anything.

  - **Pros:** A great way to provide an alternative work area or give quick feedback.

  - **Cons:** Doesn't scale well. Use two at the most, if you please.

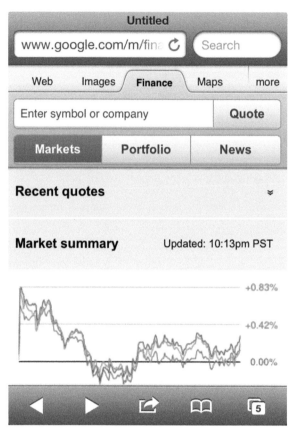

Communicates
poorly

FIGURE 2.55

Nothing but bars. Two bars is a good maximum.

- **Dialog boxes.** Heavy and floating. Can be modeless, but are usually modal. Lightboxes are typically used instead for Web UI to avoid pop-up blockers.
  - **Pros:** Demands the user's attention. Maintains context.
  - **Cons:** Often used to demand the user's attention when it isn't warranted.
- **Properties.** Complex settings presented in a pane or dialog box.
  - **Pros:** Works well for presenting object properties (hence the name).
  - **Cons:** Way too much for things that aren't properties.
- **Windows.** Heavy, floating, and independent.
  - **Pros:** The best surface for an independent application. Very flexible.
  - **Cons:** Having windows means having window management.

Modern UI tends to favor lightweight, fixed, and modeless, whereas classic UI often used heavy, floating, and modal. That said, there's nothing wrong with using heavy UIs such as modal dialog boxes—as long as you are presenting something that users *must* respond to immediately.

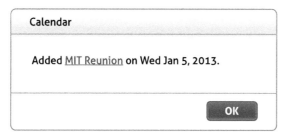

FIGURE 2.56

This information isn't something that users must respond to, so a modal dialog box is too heavy.

Communicates
poorly

Added MIT Reunion on Wed Jun 5, 2013.

FIGURE 2.57

Users get the same information, but they don't have to respond. Much better!

Communicates
well

Choose the right UI surface based on its purpose and the user's need to interact with it. Prefer lightweight, fixed, and modeless surfaces.

ERRORS, WARNINGS, CONFIRMATIONS, AND NOTIFICATIONS (INTERRUPTIONS)

As with real-world interruptions, some UI situations must demand the user's attention:

- **Errors.** Alert users to a problem that has already occurred.

- **Warnings.** Alert users to exceptional conditions that might cause a problem in the future.

- **Confirmations.** Verify that the user wants to proceed with an action.

- **Notifications.** Show timely information that is useful and relevant but not critical.

All these message types are potentially annoying, so reserve them for situations in which they are really needed. Also, try to say what you need to with a single message instead of many. Unfortunately, abusing these messages is all too common.

FIGURE 2.58

Communicates
poorly

Yes, I get it already! I need Internet connectivity to check my mail. One message would have been better.

For errors:

- **Don't give an error message unless users are likely to do something differently.** If users won't do anything differently, don't bother.

- **Clearly state a specific problem with a user-centered explanation.** Say what is wrong from the user's point of view, not the code's. Avoid vague wording, such as *illegal operation.* Provide specific names and values of the objects involved. If helpful, explain the cause as well.

- **Whenever possible, propose helpful solutions that are likely to fix the problem.** Assume that saying "Contact technical support" isn't helpful.

- **Don't blame the user.** Avoid using *you* and *your* in the phrasing. Use the passive voice when the user is the subject.

- **Don't use the following words:**

  - Error, failure (use *problem* instead)

  - Failed to (use *unable to* instead)

  - Illegal, invalid, bad (use *incorrect* or *not valid* instead)

  - Abort, kill, terminate (use *stop* instead)

  - Catastrophic, fatal (use *serious* instead)

Such language is unnecessarily harsh and has a poor personality.

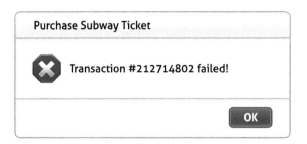

FIGURE 2.59

I tried to buy a subway ticket with my credit card. What is the problem? The kiosk knows, but it's not telling. Should I try again? Is there an insufficient balance on my card? Do I really want to make the trip? Being specific can save the user a lot of time and frustration.

Communicates
poorly

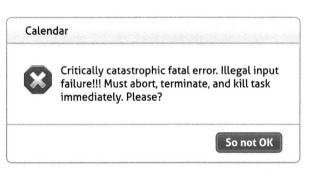

FIGURE 2.60

I made a typo. Sounds pretty bad.

Communicates
poorly

For warnings:

- **Use warnings to describe exceptional conditions that might cause a problem in the future.** Warnings aren't questions, so don't phrase routine questions as warnings, even if they are important.

- **Don't give a warning unless users are likely to do something differently.** If users aren't likely to do anything differently, don't bother.

- **Clearly state a specific condition, the potential problem and its consequences, and what the user needs to do about it.** If users can't do anything but get stressed, that's a clear assessment of the warning's value.

- **Don't overwarn.** Present *exceptional* conditions that involve infrequent, immediate risk, not trivial possibilities. Once users see several inconsequential warnings, they stop paying attention (a phenomenon called *habituation*). All overwarning accomplishes is that it makes your product feel hazard prone—and like it was designed by lawyers.

FIGURE 2.61

Communicates
poorly

Unnecessary warnings (where users don't do anything differently as a result) make your app feel like a hazard-prone one. This program looks like it was designed by lawyers.

FIGURE 2.62

Communicates
well

A low-battery warning presents an exception condition that might cause a problem in the future. The modal dialog box rightly demands the user's attention.

For confirmations:

- **Use confirmations only for risky actions or to alert users to significant, unintended consequences.** Confirmations to prevent the mere possibility of a mistake only serve to annoy. For desktop UI, assume that users are really, really sure. For mobile UI, design destructive actions to be deliberate (with multiple steps or a precise gesture, such as a swipe).

- **Effective confirmations present users a good, unobvious reason *not* to proceed—and a reasonable chance that sometimes users won't.** Effective confirmations make users stop and think rather than immediately dismissing them to get back to work.

- **Use either completely self-explanatory responses or Yes or No responses to confirmations.** Although there is no way to force users to read confirmation instructions, users generally read what they are saying Yes or No to before they click. By contrast, users routinely click on generic responses like OK without giving them any thought at all.

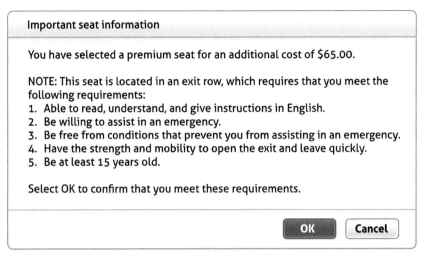

FIGURE 2.63

This confirmation gives a good reason not to proceed, but will users read it first? And notice how the real issue isn't obvious.

Communicates
poorly

Important seat information

You have chosen an Exit Row seat

This is a premium seat that costs an additional cost of $65.00.

To sit in an exist row, you must meet the following requirements:
1. Able to read, understand, and give instructions in English.
2. Be willing to assist in an emergency.
3. Be free from conditions that prevent you from assisting in an emergency.
4. Have the strength and mobility to open the exit and leave quickly.
5. Be at least 15 years old.

| I meet these requirements | I will take a regular seat |

FIGURE 2.64

By contrast, this confirmation focuses on the real issue, gives a good reason not to proceed, and has a presentation that encourages users to actually read it.

Communicates
well

And for notifications:

- **Use notifications to keep users informed about timely, important events unrelated to the current activity that are useful and relevant but not critical enough to interrupt users' workflow.** Examples include new chat messages and calendar events.

- **Notifications are potentially annoying, so make them rare.** Be respectful of users' time, focus, and attention.

- **Don't try to force users to see notifications.** Nothing bad should happen if users don't see notifications or if they ignore them. If users must see the information or take an action, use another UI.

A text (XML) representation of your data has been copied to your clipboard. You can now paste it or import it into a new mockup, save it to a text file, email it to someone...

FIGURE 2.65
This notification presents important but not critical information.

For general guidelines on how to write message text, be sure to review the "Effective Communication" section in Chapter 1.

> Design errors, warnings, confirmations, and notifications carefully by making sure that they are necessary, specific, and actionable. Focus the presentation of each type of message on what users really need to know. Otherwise, these messages are more likely to be annoying than helpful.

DYNAMIC ELEMENTS

In classic UI, nearly all elements are displayed statically on the screen, whereas modern UI has many dynamic elements. To prevent yourself from getting overwhelmed, it's best to start with static designs first, then look for opportunities to add dynamic behaviors. Most dynamic elements fall into one of these categories:

- Progressive disclosure
- Dynamic resizing
- Dynamic secondary commands and affordances
- Direct manipulation

Chapter 1 presented the attributes of an intuitive UI, and discoverability and affordance were at the top of the list. **And there lies the challenge: How can a UI be dynamic (and therefore not always visible) while also being easily discoverable and have good affordance?**

If done right, dynamic elements are a great way to balance power and simplicity. But if done poorly, they are a great way to turn your UIs into unfathomable puzzles that frustrate your users. Unless it's an advanced command for expert users, even beginning users should know that these dynamic UI elements are there.

Your dynamic UI shouldn't feel like a video game where users have to click around to discover secret passageways. To help assure that it doesn't, here is my rule for dynamic behaviors:

> Any dynamic interactions that aren't inevitably discoverable must be redundant, advanced, or infrequently used.

Unintuitive UIs work well only when they are deliberately and strategically designed rather than accidental—as we explored in detail in Chapter 1. Figuring out poorly designed, unintuitive UI is never delightful.

> Well-designed, dynamic UI elements are a great way to balance power and simplicity. Dynamic UIs are initially invisible, but there are many techniques to facilitate easy discoverability.

Progressive disclosure

With *progressive disclosure*, the most commonly used controls and information is displayed by default, but users can display more on demand. This approach works well because the progressive disclosure controls provide discoverability and affordance.

FIGURE 2.66
Common progressive disclosure controls, which all involving clicking on a button or link to see more information, provide discoverability and affordance.

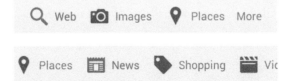

FIGURE 2.67
Using progressive disclosure, you can simplify a UI by displaying only the basic commands by default. Here Android Voice Search displays the basic commands by default. Tapping More and swiping reveals others.

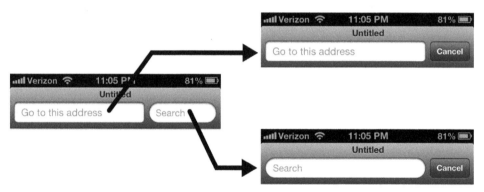

FIGURE 2.68

Communicates
well

Wufoo uses progressive disclosure to reveal form commands. Instead of using a progressive disclosure control, the commands are revealed on hover.

Dynamic resizing

With *dynamic sizing*, **the controls are visible statically (and therefore discoverable), but their sizes change dynamically based on the current context.** Typically, controls that users click on become larger and easier to use, and controls not relevant in the context become smaller or are temporarily removed. This is a great solution when you're working with small mobile screens.

FIGURE 2.69

With Safari on the iPhone, both the address box and the search box are visible, but tapping on the address box makes it larger while hiding the search box, and vice versa.

Dynamic secondary commands and affordances

Dynamic secondary UI elements are normally hidden but displayed automatically when users click on or hover over a control or perform an action to make them relevant. These secondary elements are usually controls, affordances, or additional information and may be displayed in place or in a tooltip or flyout. Unlike progressive disclosure, users don't do this interaction explicitly; rather, these secondary elements are displayed as a side effect of doing something else.

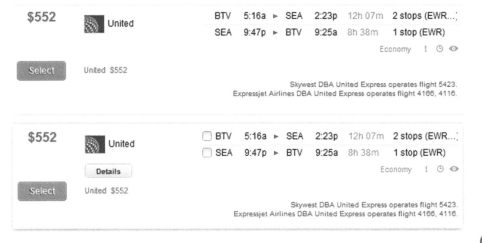

FIGURE 2.70

Kayak displays the list items selection rectangle, a flight Details button, and flight segment checkboxes on hover or click.

Communicates
well

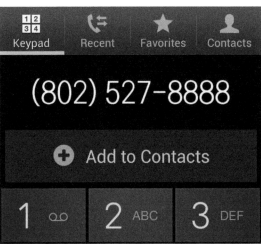
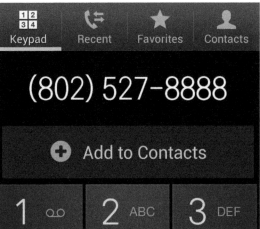

FIGURE 2.71

Android dynamically displays an Add to Contacts command when you enter an unfamiliar phone number.

Communicates
well

Although tooltips can be helpful, they are often abused as usability "duct tape"—and can be annoying as well. Avoid relying on them. And remember that hovering isn't supported by touch screens.

FIGURE 2.72
Users shouldn't have to depend on tooltips to make sense of your program. Any clue what these commands do?

Displaying these secondary elements dynamically reduces the overall heaviness of the static UI, while displaying the primary affordances statically makes it clear what to do. This approach works well because users inevitably discover these secondary elements through normal interaction.

By contrast, hiding primary affordances risks turning your program into a puzzle because users won't know what to do and will have no reason—other than desperation—to click or hover. The key to success is to have a clear understanding of what is primary versus secondary.

FIGURE 2.73

Communicates poorly

Displaying primary commands and affordances dynamically isn't a good idea. What are you supposed to do here? It doesn't look interactive.

That said, inevitable discovery can work for primary controls if everything is removed from the static UI, as is common with video players.

FIGURE 2.74
You can display primary commands dynamically if *any* interaction reveals them.

Direct manipulation

With *direct manipulation*, users move, edit, transform, or perform commands by directly interacting with an object instead of going through an intermediary UI, such as dialog boxes and menus. For example, users can open, move, rename, copy, and throw away files by interacting directly with their icons. Using gestures, users can display, zoom, browse, crop, and fix redeye on photos.

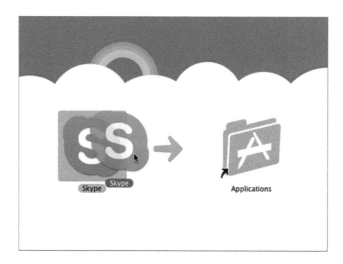

FIGURE 2.75

Users can interact directly with files instead of using dialog boxes, menus, or other intermediaries. On Macintosh, users install programs by dragging them onto the Applications folder.

Direct manipulation has the advantage of being direct, engaging, and modern as well as simple and efficient. With direct manipulation, your program's content can be the user interface! But because direct manipulation often lacks visibility and affordance, it has the potential for being undiscoverable and unexpected. Another potential downside is accessibility, because users lacking fine motor skills might not be able to perform certain manipulations.

Your first plan of attack is to design frequently used or unexpected direct manipulations to be easily discoverable. Here are the typical approaches—listed in order of discoverability for novice users:

- **Explicit instructions.** If users need to drag objects to an area, that area can state that it is a drop target.

This folder is empty

Add your files using the desktop application or the web uploader.

FIGURE 2.76

Dropbox uses a placeholder to indicate that users can drop files.

Communicates
well

- **Contextual commands.** On selection or hover, an object reveals commands that indicate users can do direct manipulation.

Manipulate

FIGURE 2.77

On hover, SketchBook shows contextual commands using marking menus

Communicates
well

FIGURE 2.78

Selecting a form field in Wufoo dynamically reveals everything you can do with it.

Communicates
well

- **Manipulation affordances.** When selected, an object reveals affordances that indicate that users can do direct manipulation.

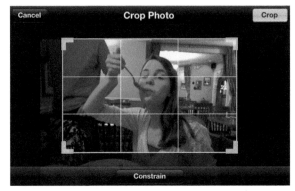

Communicates well

FIGURE 2.79

The iOS photo Crop command reveals its manipulation affordances.

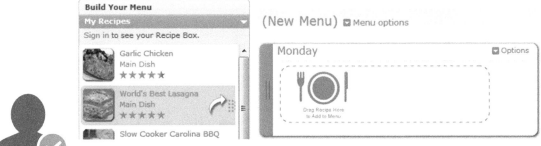

Communicates well

FIGURE 2.80

The AllRecipes Menu Planner reveals a drag affordance for the recipes on hover as well as giving instructions for the drop targets.

- **Hand cursors.** Showing a hand cursor on hover indicates that an object is movable or pannable. This approach works well if users are likely to hover over an object in the first place; it works poorly otherwise.

FIGURE 2.81
Google Maps indicates that a map can be panned with a hand cursor.

- **Experimentation.** In this case, there is poor discoverability, so users must experiment to determine whether direct manipulation is possible. This approach isn't intuitive by definition, but it might work well if users expect the manipulation (so their experiments are usually successful) or the need is infrequent enough that having affordances results in unnecessary clutter.

FIGURE 2.82
The Macintosh Dock has no drag affordance, but users expect to be able to move items, and a quick experiment confirms this ability.

Using these approaches, it's possible to design direct manipulation to be discoverable, but it's fair to say that in practice most aren't. The problem only gets worse when you consider the need for accessibility.

Fortunately, the solution to the discoverability problem is simple: Use less discoverable direct manipulation as a redundant, efficient shortcut for advanced users. Novice users need easily discoverable, perhaps less efficient alternatives to get started, and they can discover direct manipulation through experimentation when they are ready.

FIGURE 2.83

Communicates well

Although users can move and copy files using direct manipulation, the good ol' Copy and Paste commands should still be available.

> Use hard-to-discover direct manipulation as a redundant, efficient shortcut for advanced users. Basic commands should always be easy to find.

SUMMARY

If you remember only 12 things:

1. **Use standard interactions for your software's platform.** Don't be creative here, because consistent interaction is required for intuitive UI. For basic commands, avoid using advanced interactions with which your target users aren't likely to be familiar. Make sure that shortcuts (which require special knowledge) aren't the only way to perform an action.

2. **Generally the simplest, lightest-weight, most constrained, least error-prone alternative is the best choice.** Purpose and body language usually determine which control is best.

3. **The challenge to commands is presenting them in a way that is discoverable, direct, easy to find, contextual, simple, and space efficient.** These are tradeoffs, so you need to choose the commanding UI that strikes the right balance.

4. **Commands don't require icons, so don't feel obligated to provide them.** Unlabeled icons work well only when they are well known. If they're not, provide a text label; avoid relying on tooltips.

5. **Modern UI uses more self-explanatory labels and instructions than classic UI.** However, the goal isn't to have more text but rather to have less but much *better* text. Usually this boils down to using more useful, relevant, purposeful text, adding a word or two as needed to add clarity, and removing unhelpful, mechanical text and repetition.

6. **Use feedback to indicate that an action is happening and was either successful or unsuccessful.** Provide feedback responsively so that users remain confident and know what is going on. There are many ways to provide feedback, so choose the least intrusive form that communicates well.

7. **Use grouping to show relationships visually between controls within a page and to make pages easier to scan and parse.** Prefer modern, lighter-weight styles such as rich headings, layout, progressive disclosure, and sentence styles over classic styles such as group boxes.

8. **In designing the presentation of your content, think about the conversation you would have in person.** The right UI pattern will reflect the nature of that conversation. Although there are many conversation patterns, long speeches are rarely the best choice. Better to present your content in smaller conversational units and, when practical, let users drive the conversation.

9. **Use a simple, consistent navigation model in your app.** A Web navigation approach—with consistent Back, Home, and Search—is a good approach. Be sure your page design has all the necessary navigation elements so that users can proceed with the task with confidence yet easily recover from mistakes. Make sure that it's obvious when users make a commitment.

10. **Choose the right UI surface based on its purpose and the user's need to interact with it.** Prefer lightweight, fixed, and modeless surfaces.

11. **Design errors, warnings, and confirmations carefully by making sure that they are necessary, specific, and actionable.** Focus the presentation of each type of message on what users really need to know. Otherwise, these messages are more likely to be annoying than helpful.

12. **Well-designed dynamic elements are a great way to balance power and simplicity.** Although dynamic UIs are initially invisible, there are many techniques to facilitate easy discoverability. Use direct manipulation as a redundant, efficient shortcut for advanced users. Basic commands should never require hard-to-discover direct manipulation.

EXERCISES

To improve your interaction design skills, try the following exercises. *Assume that anything is possible. Don't let concerns about development costs or current technology limitations inhibit your thinking.*

1. **Misleading or missing affordances.** Find an example of a control that has a misleading or missing affordance. What is misleading or missing about the affordance? What problems did the affordance cause? What can you do to fix the problem?

2. **Using the right control.** Find an example of a UI that uses the wrong controls. What problems did using the wrong controls cause? Fix the problems by determining the right controls and justifying your choices.

3. **Designing list controls.** Design a list optimized for 10 or fewer items. Now design lists optimized for 50, 100, 1,000, and 10,000 items. Consider ease of use and performance. What extra features did you need to introduce to handle the larger scales?

4. **Unlabeled controls.** Find as many examples of unlabeled controls as you can. (Here text and icon labels count; tooltips don't.) Review the list and determine which controls really needed a label and which controls didn't. Now characterize them. What makes the difference?

5. **Instructions.** Review mobile apps to find examples of explicit, contextual instructions. Review the list and determine whether the instructions were really necessary. Now characterize them—what made the difference? When are instructions necessary (and when are control labels not enough)?

6. **Feedback.** Find an example of a UI with poor feedback—where feedback isn't given, is given too late, is too intrusive, or doesn't communicate effectively. Determine the specific problem and redesign the feedback.

7. **Task navigation.** Find an example of a multistep task in which you got seriously lost. (It doesn't have to be a software task.) Review what happened. Where did you get lost? Why? Design an alternative navigation that might have prevented the problem or made it simple to correct.

8. **Modal dialog boxes.** Find several examples of modal dialog boxes. Is the information worthy of stopping users and requiring interaction? If it's not, design a better, modeless alternative.

9. **Error messages.** Find five error messages that aren't effective or unnecessary. For each, what is the specific problem with the error message? Redesign the messages to be effective.

10. **Direct manipulation.** Find as many examples of drag and drop as you can. Characterize them. If they are discoverable, what make them so? If they're not, what does the UI do to prevent this from being a problem?

11. **Sound.** Find as many examples of sound in UI as you can. Characterize them. What is the purpose of each sound? Is the sound ambient, intrusive, annoying, or embarrassing? Is each sound really necessary?

Visual Design

3

"What makes good visual design? Visual design, unlike art, should not be subjective. It has to accomplish a particular purpose such as solving problems, educating, or explaining a new feature. Good visual design communicates in a way that produces its intended result."

—JODI HERSH

People often confuse user interface design with graphic design and therefore assume that UI design is a subjective art that requires extensive training and talent. Nearly all points in this misconception are true: Visual design is an important part of UI design. Graphic designers have extensive training and talent in visual communication. Certainly part of graphic design is a subjective art—and unless you have substantial training and experience, it's an art that you can't do well.

What's misleading about this misconception is that it implies that most of UI design is graphic design. Not true! Even though visual design is a crucial element of UI design, most of your design effort should focus on interaction design—the subject of the previous chapter.

This statement also implies that visual design is mostly a subjective art. Also not true! The subjective, artistic part of visual design is crucial, but for user interface design most of your visual design effort should focus on what it communicates visually.

Through the lens of communication, many visual design decisions that initially appear subjective, emotional, arbitrary, and aesthetic are actually objective, rational, coordinated, and principled. At the wireframe level, every visual design element should be justified by what it communicates. A *wireframe* is a prototype with content and functionality represented by rough controls, rectangles, lines, text, and simple glyphs. Layout and element sizes are rough, and details such as colors, backgrounds, fonts, graphics, and icons are often omitted.

Here is what common visual design elements should communicate:

- **Layout.** Should draw users' attention to a page's focal point, present a clear path for the eye to follow, have a clear termination point that advances to the next step, and draw proper emphasis to the UI elements along the way. Additionally, a well-designed layout appears simple, orderly, easy to scan, and aesthetically pleasing.

- **Typography.** Should ensure that the UI text is attractive, legible, and readable in its target environment.

- **Icons and glyphs.** Should give controls understandable visual labels to either supplement or replace text labels.

- **Affordances.** Should indicate how to interact with controls as well as suggest the effect of interactions.

- **Graphics.** Should supplement layout to give a page visual structure and show relationships between UI elements.

- **Color.** Should be used to communicate status, meaning, and importance visually.

- **Animations and transitions.** Should give feedback, show relationships, draw attention to change, or explain tasks visually.

When we're evaluating a wireframe, if a UI element doesn't communicate anything, it should be removed. If it communicates poorly, it should be redesigned. With only rare exceptions, given a choice between a design with effective visual communication and one that is aesthetically pleasing, the design that communicates more effectively is the better choice.

Communicates
poorly

Create a new Channel Mixer adjustment layer

FIGURE 3.1

What does this icon mean? I don't know either, but it's clear when labeled. If the icon design doesn't communicate anything, why is it there? We should improve the icon or give it a static label.

Form may follow function in industrial design, but in UI good design form follows communication. From the communication point of view, each visual design choice isn't independent or arbitrary. For effective communication, each element should be communicating a different aspect of the same consistent story. That story needs to be coordinated and harmonious. Any inconsistencies reveal design problems.

FIGURE 3.2
The length of this numeric text box suggests long input (like a part number), but the spin buttons (the arrows on the right side) suggests that the default value is close to the right value (so, not like a part number). This inconsistency reveals a design problem.

The goal of this chapter is to explore visual UI design from the communication point of view. I'm not assuming that you have any visual design knowledge or experience. My goal isn't to turn you into a graphic designer, because that's not realistic. Rather, my goal is to help you develop your visual "design thinking," primarily by understanding that visual design is mostly about visual communication. Once you understand and focus on the communication angle, you can make better visual design decisions more quickly and confidently at the wireframe level.

Although you should work with professional graphic designers when designing at the pixel level, the information in this chapter will help you work together more effectively by having a more objective basis for making decisions. By contrast, making design decisions based on personal opinion is a notoriously poor way to work with a visual designer.

If you are designing for a platform that has a visual style guide, give that precedence. I will present visual design techniques that communicate well generally, but always do your best to follow your platform's visual style guidelines.

> At the wireframe level, every visual design element should be justified by what it communicates. If a UI element doesn't communicate anything, it should be removed. If it communicates poorly, it should be redesigned.

THE IMPORTANCE OF EFFECTIVE VISUAL DESIGN

Your users will definitely notice if your product isn't visually appealing—regardless of the power and flexibility of its underlying technology. In my work as a user experience design consultant and trainer, I specialize in helping teams of software professionals who lack design resources improve their product's user experience design. Often their products are unattractive. In their defense, these teams say things like, "Our product might not be a beauty, but it sure does the job!"—implying that the visual appearance is a superficial detail that users will overlook as long as the required functionality is there.

People are emotional and they react emotionally to a product's visual appearance. Your product should look the part—it should look like it fulfills its purpose well. But if instead your product's visual appearance is of questionable quality, users will naturally assume that the rest of the product has the same level of quality. Users assume that attractive products are better designed and more usable (this is known as the *aesthetic-usability effect*). Don't assume that users will see the beauty that lies beneath; they won't.

FIGURE 3.3
People perceive that beautiful products work better. This must be an excellent phone.

Visual appearance is essential to our perception of quality. As rational technologists, we are reluctant to accept this idea. We really want customers to see our product's inner beauty and we want to believe that the quality of the functionality and internal design is what matters—the quality of the system architecture, its performance, robustness, reliability, scalability, and flexibility. These technology details do matter, but only as experienced by users. As Steve Jobs once said:

> Design is not just what it looks like and feels like. Design is how it works.

From the user's point of view, the user experience is the product. And if the user experience is poor, nothing else matters!

Returning to the communication angle, good visual design is important functionally. Users need to be spatially oriented and know where to look, how to scan a page, and how to find what they are looking for quickly—without being overwhelmed. The text needs to be readable and legible and have a clear visual hierarchy. Users need to understand what icons and graphics mean. They need animations and transitions to keep them oriented, give feedback, and show relationships—without being distracted. Ultimately, a good visual design enables users to get their work done efficiently and without distraction.

WORKING WITH GRAPHIC DESIGNERS

If you want a beautiful product, my best advice is to hire a graphic designer. Graphic designers are highly trained professionals who will help take your product to a level that your team of nondesigners couldn't possibly achieve on its own. Hiring a graphic designer is the best, simplest thing you can do to make your UI look great.

But if you work for a small company or have a very tight budget ... still, seriously, hire a graphic designer. Hiring a good designer will help you get the visual design right more efficiently and ultimately save you time and money, no matter how tight your budget. I work with a graphic designer for all my visual design work and I'm sure my budget is tighter than yours.

At this point, you might be wondering: **"If I really should work with a professional graphic designer, why should I bother reading this chapter?"** Here are four excellent reasons:

1. **These are important UI design skills.** Even if your graphic designers do all your visual design work, this chapter will help you understand what they are doing. But chances are you won't have designers do everything; few teams have the required design resources for that luxury.

2. **You can design the basics more efficiently at the wireframe level and have your graphic designers focus their talent where it is needed most.** This is especially important if you are on a tight schedule and budget.

3. **Understanding visual design will help ensure that important design details are faithfully executed during development.** Important design details often get lost in translation when developers don't "get it."

4. **These skills will help you work with your designers more effectively and productively.** You will work together to make better decisions for the right reasons.

The last reason is the most important. Nondesigners do not have an impressive track record for effective, productive relationships with their graphic designers. Quite the opposite. Reading this chapter will help you get on the same page as your designers.

FIGURE 3.4

Louis, I think this is the beginning of a disastrous collaboration. From TheOatmeal.com ©Matthew Inman. Used by permission.

Here are some additional tips for working with graphic designers:

- **Hire the best graphic designers you can and trust them to do their job.** Most of the horror stories I hear from graphic designers stem from their managers lacking trust. If you hire a top graphic designer, assume that that person understands visual design a thousand times better than you—so it would be foolish not to trust him or her.

- **Hire graphic designers early in the process, when they can have the most impact.** If you hire designers after all the code is already written, it's probably too late for getting the most impact from designers. All they can do is fix minor details.

- **Designers' worst nightmare is having nondesigners tell them how to do their job**— so don't do this! Perhaps it's better to keep your color theory to yourself.

- **Focus on your high-level project vision, goals, requirements, direction, and branding guidelines.** To be happy with your designers' work, you must communicate what you want but avoid telling your designers the details—it's their job to figure out those details.

- **Provide constructive feedback and give the designer the benefit of any doubt.** The most diplomatic way to give feedback is by asking questions instead of making demands and assertions. For example, instead of saying, "I don't like this color scheme!" and putting the designer on the defensive, a better approach is to ask: "Interesting ... why did you choose this color scheme?" Once you understand the reason behind a design choice, you are in a better position to give constructive feedback and help make improvements.

- **Don't trivialize designers' contributions.** For graphic designers, "pretty" is a dirty word. It implies that their work is trivial and superficial and that you have already done all the *real* work.

FIGURE 3.5

Normally this feedback technique works well. DILBERT ©2012 Scott Adams. Used by permission of UNIVERSAL UCLICK. All rights reserved.

LAYOUT

Layout **is the placement, sizing, spacing, and emphasis of UI elements and content within a page.** Effective layout is crucial in helping users find what they are looking for quickly as well as making the page's appearance visually appealing. Layout is the visual design skill that nondesigners find most challenging, so let's start here—but without worrying about the traditional artistic details such as golden ratios, rule of thirds, or symmetry.

   The biggest problem nondesigners have with layout is that they are focused on the mechanical layout—getting stuff to fit—without putting much thought into what the layout communicates. Controls are placed because they fit, not because they belong, as though they are playing a game of UI Tetris.

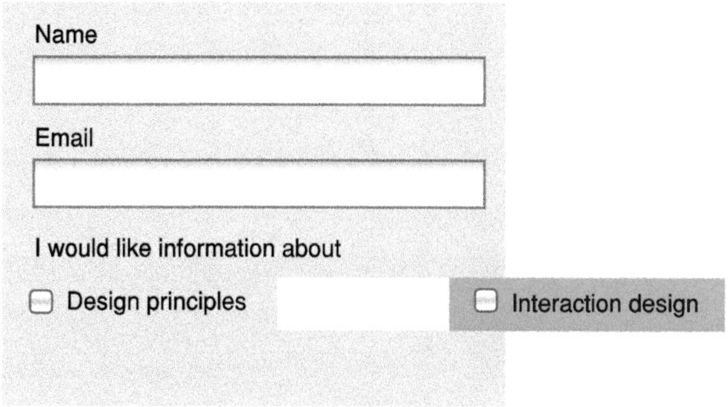

FIGURE 3.6
Nondesigners often lay out pages as though they are playing a game of UI Tetris. Fun!

   This approach works fine for simple UIs, but it breaks down badly with more complex pages or as features are added over time.

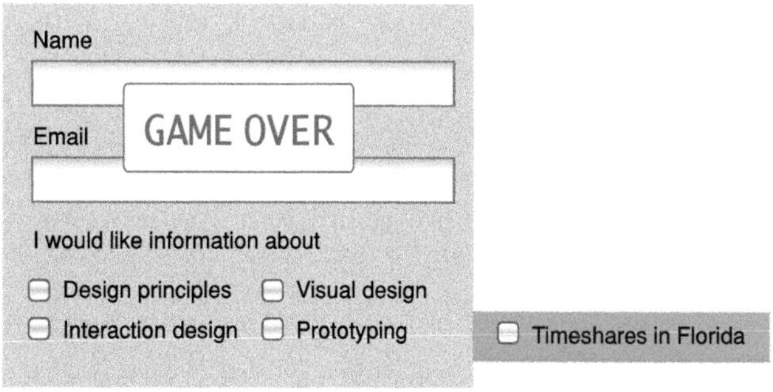

FIGURE 3.7
The UI Tetris approach to layout gets harder over time. Game over?

Communicates
poorly

A page's layout communicates the purpose of the page, how to scan and read the page, and the order in which to use the elements on the page. Additionally, a well-designed layout appears simple, orderly, easy to scan, efficient, and aesthetically pleasing.

There are two modes of reading: immersive reading and scanning. The goal of immersive reading is comprehension, whereas the goal of scanning is to find things quickly. Well-designed layouts need to accommodate both modes well. Let's start with designing for comprehensive reading and address scanning in detail in the next section.

Layout design principles
Reading patterns

Users read immersively in a left-to-right, top-to-bottom order (in Western cultures), following the layout of the page. During immersive reading, users read most of the words and most of the content, but they may skip over content that doesn't appear relevant or that requires too much effort to read.

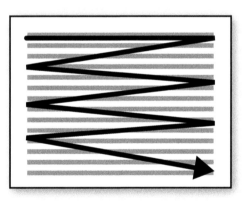

FIGURE 3.8
An immersive reading pattern—for comprehension.

By contrast, users often scan a page using an arching pattern, starting in the upper-left corner and ending in the lower right. Along the way, they might notice the upper-right corner (called the *strong fallow area*). They see the lower-left corner (called the *weak fallow area*) last—if they see it at all. This scanning path is formally known as the *Gutenberg diagram*.

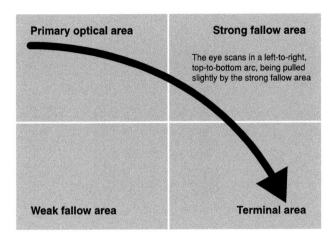

FIGURE 3.9
A scanning pattern for finding things quickly.

Users follow these patterns generally, but the patterns change when there is content that attracts or repulses attention. Users recognize that interactive controls are likely the more relevant ones, so these interactive controls get the user's immediate attention.

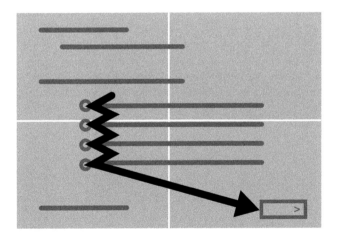

FIGURE 3.10
Interactive controls get the user's immediate attention.

Small screens found on smartphones have a different scanning pattern. Users scan small screens starting in the upper-left corner and going straight down. They can take in the width of the screen without scanning across.

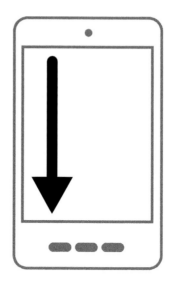

FIGURE 3.11
The scan path for small screens is straight down.

Conversation patterns

Reading patterns indicate how users view the content of a page physically, but they don't tell us how to structure the content. To help you choose the right presentation model, let's look at some conversation patterns—a concept introduced in Chapter 2. For the sake of argument, let's assume that the page has a significant amount of information that we need to lay out. Laying out a simple page is pretty easy, after all.

Start by thinking about the conversation you would have with the target users in person to explain what to do on the page. Naturally you would present the steps in a smooth, logical order instead of an out-of-sequence jumble. You wouldn't explain out of sequence just because it takes less space.

FIGURE 3.12
Logical order versus out-of-sequence.

Would this conversation be a monologue, where you explain *everything* **to anticipate every question, without involving the user?** If so, a document would be a good conversation pattern. This isn't a rhetorical question; a document might be the right choice, but there are other—often better—options.

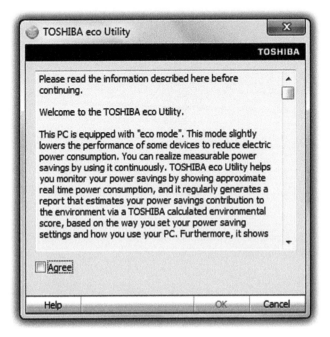

FIGURE 3.13
This agreement is like a monologue. And note how poorly the visual presentation of the OK and Cancel buttons communicates their purpose.

Or would the conversation be like a brief summary of the essentials, followed by Q&A? If so, a summary followed by progressive disclosure of optional content would be a good choice. This approach works well with the *inverted pyramid* presentation style, where the most important information is placed first and details follow according to their importance. Using this style, users can stop reading at any time once they have the information they need.

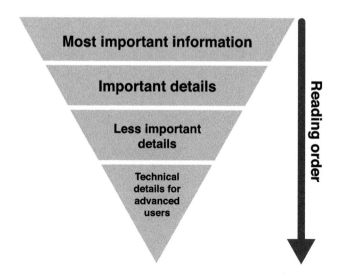

FIGURE 3.14

The inverted pyramid presentation style allows users to stop reading once they have the information they need.

Advantages to this approach are that it's easier for users to find the information they care about, plus once users click to see more information, they are actually motivated to read it.

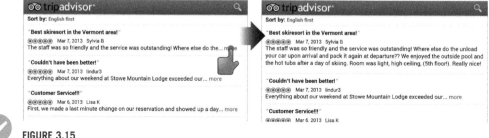

Communicates well

FIGURE 3.15

Progressive disclosure is like a dialogue between people in which the user drives the conversation by asking for more information.

Attributes of an effective layout

Here are the attributes of an effective layout to help users quickly find what they are looking for and quickly figure out what to do and to make the appearance visually appealing:

- **Focus.** Indicates where users are supposed to look first, usually in the upper-left corner or top center of the page.

- **Flow.** Provides a clear scan path for the user's eye to follow smoothly and naturally across the page.

- **Termination.** Indicates where the scan path should end, often with a UI element to go to the next step or complete the task.

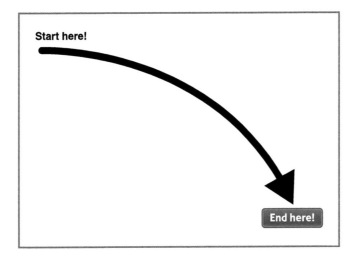

FIGURE 3.16
The eye starts at the focal point, scans across the page, and ends at the termination point.

- **Order.** The UI elements are presented in a logical, task-flow order. The most important information is placed "above the fold." Generally, users won't scroll unless they have a reason to, so that reason needs to be obvious without scrolling. Furthermore, the most important content on the page—the primary reason the user is on the page—stands out from everything else.

- **Control sizing and spacing.** Controls are sized appropriately based on their purpose and need for emphasis. The controls are also spaced appropriately to show their relationships and have adequate space to avoid appearing overwhelming.

- **Emphasis.** UI elements are emphasized based on their importance to give a visual hierarchy. Pages are harder to scan and read if all UI elements appear uniformly. The type of control, font, size, placement, and background all affect emphasis.

Important text 1

Important text 2

| Less important |

☐ Related option 1
☐ Related option 2
☐ Related option 3   (need for scrolling is clear without scrolling)

☐ Unrelated option

Less important text | **Important command** |

——— The fold

Secondary text 1
Secondary text 2

☐ Advanced, infrequent, optional

FIGURE 3.17

The most important information is "above the fold", and any reason to scroll is obvious without scrolling. Controls are sized and emphasized based on their purpose and spaced to show their relationships.

- **Layout grids.** An invisible alignment system used to give a page a coordinated, orderly appearance. You can make a layout appear simpler by reducing the number of vertical alignment grids. Reusing layout templates appropriately across your product will give it a consistent appearance.

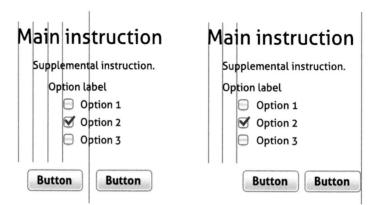

FIGURE 3.18

The layout on the right appears simpler because it uses fewer vertical alignment grid lines.

- **Label alignment.** Shows the relationship between controls and their labels. The most common styles are top-aligned labels, left-aligned labels, right-aligned labels, and left-aligned labels with ragged controls. Placeholders are another option; they are covered in Chapter 2. For large screens, there is no single best alignment approach; each has benefits that depend on how the controls and their labels are used. For smartphones, top-aligned labels work best because users can stay oriented when the screen is zoomed and the vertical format works well with vertical scrolling.

Name
Everett McKay
Street address
410 Memorial Drive
City
Cambridge
State/Province/Region
MA
Postal code
02139

FIGURE 3.19

Top-aligned labels work best when the controls are interactive (such as a form), when users are likely to scan both the labels and the controls vertically, and when ease of localization is important. A downside is that top-aligned labels take a lot of vertical space, so they don't work well with many fields.

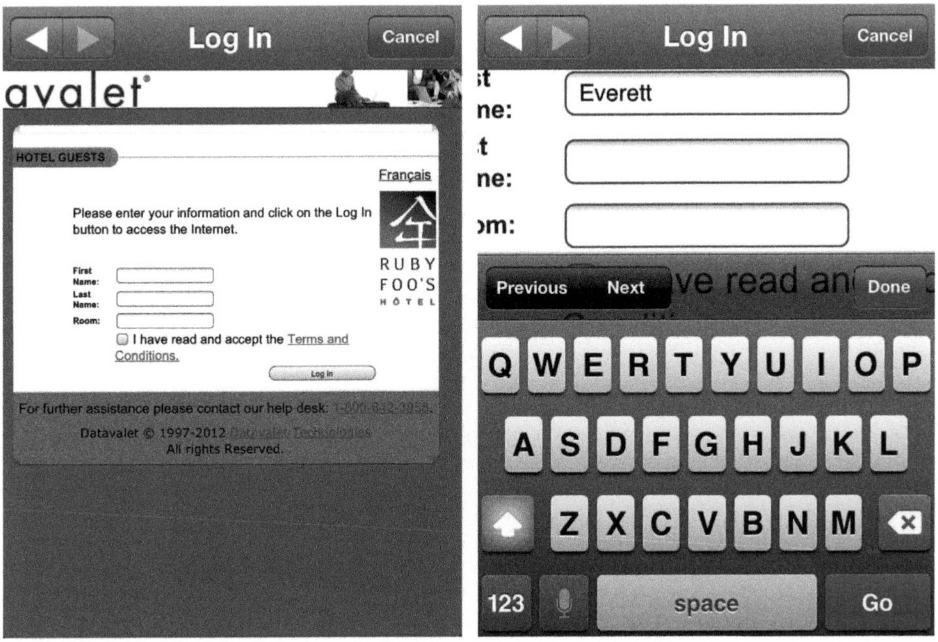

FIGURE 3.20

Because of automatic zooming, top-aligned labels are the best alignment choice for smartphones with small screens. Note how the left-aligned labels aren't visible after zooming.

Communicates
poorly

Name	**Everett McKay**
Street address	**410 Memorial Drive**
City	**Cambridge**
State/Province/Region	**MA**
Postal code	**02139**

FIGURE 3.21

Left-aligned labels work best when users are likely to scan both labels and controls vertically and the labels don't vary much in length. Downsides to this format are that the gaps between the labels and controls can be large if the labels vary in length, the labels and controls look like two individual columns—giving a cluttered appearance, and it takes a lot of horizontal space if there are long labels or controls.

Name	**Everett McKay**
Street address	**410 Memorial Drive**
City	**Cambridge**
State/Province/Region	**MA**
Postal code	**02139**

FIGURE 3.22

Right-aligned labels with left-justified controls work well when users are reading more than they are scanning, such as in a form. In contrast to left-aligned labels, this format's consistent space between the labels and controls makes the pair easier to read and it looks like one column instead of two.

Name	**Everett McKay**
Street address	**410 Memorial Drive**
City	**Cambridge**
State/Province/Region	**MA**
Postal code	**02139**

FIGURE 3.23

Left-aligned labels with ragged controls work best when users are likely to scan vertically to find specific labels but not likely to scan the controls vertically, such as when displaying a set of properties.

- **Grouping.** Use to give related UI elements a clear visual relationship where related items are grouped together; unrelated items are separated. Group boxes can be used to show relationships and lines can be used to show separation, but it is usually better to show these relationships using layout alone to avoid visual clutter.

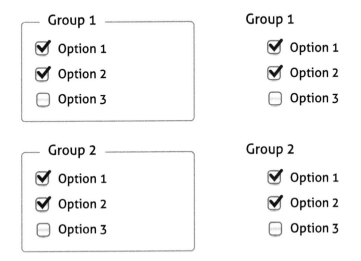

FIGURE 3.24
Show relationships using grouping and separation. Although you can use group boxes and lines to show relationships, using layout alone often works best.

- **Layout efficiency.** Make sure screen space is used efficiently—especially important on mobile devices. Look out for unnecessary scrolling or truncated data, especially when there are large areas of unused space. Users shouldn't have to manually resize anything to make the contents usable.

Poor layout

Select ice cream

☐	Stock No ▲	Name	Notes	Size
☐	6412922	Vermonty Pytho		Pint
☐	8233761	Late Night Snack		Pint
☐	8456821	Bohemian Raspb		Pint
☐	9864125	Festivus	On sale until March 10th	Half Gall

[Continue] [Cancel]

Communicates
poorly

Better layout

Select ice cream

☐	Stock No ▲	Name	Size	Notes
☐	6412922	Vermonty Python	Pint	
☐	8233761	Late Night Snack	Pint	
☐	8456821	Bohemian Raspberry	Pint	
☐	9864125	Festivus	Half Gallon	On sale until March 10th
☐	9893623	Half Baked	Pint	

[Continue] [Cancel]

Communicates
well

FIGURE 3.25

The layout on the top wastes a lot of space

- **Balance.** Content appears evenly distributed across the surface. Imagine placing a fulcrum at the bottom center of a page. If that page looks like it would immediately topple over to one side—usually the left side—your page layout needs more balance.

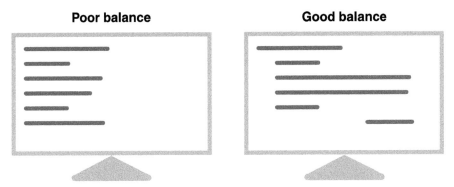

Poor balance   **Good balance**

FIGURE 3.26
The layout on the left appears very left-heavy and looks like it might topple over.

Layout communicates the purpose of the page, how to scan and read the page, and the order in which to use the page elements. Additionally, a well-designed layout appears simple, orderly, easy to scan, efficient, and aesthetically pleasing.

DESIGNING FOR SCANNING

As Steve Krug effectively points out in *Don't Make Me Think!*, users don't read, they scan—so you should design pages specifically for scanning. Don't assume that users will take the time to comprehensively read your pages in a strict left-to-right, top-to-bottom order. Normally they won't.

The goal of scanning is to find things quickly. Users scan a page by looking at those UI elements that attract the most attention and then filter those down to what looks relevant to the task. Here's how you can tell if a page is designed for scanning:

- The most important UI elements attract users' attention at a glance.

- The scanned UI elements make sense on their own and are not misleading.

- Based only on the scanned UI elements, it should be clear (more or less) to target users what to do for the top tasks. It's acceptable if secondary tasks require some reading.

The goal of this section is to take a second look at page layout from the point of view of scanning. (Chapter 5 will present a scanning review process that you can use to determine how well a page is designed for scanning.)

A model for scanning

Here is a simple model for how users scan a page (see Figure 3.27):

- **Users quickly look at the overall visible portion of the page to get an idea what is there.**

- **Users then start to scan at the page's focal point.** The focal point is the element on the page that demands users' attention and they expect to find it toward the upper left or upper center of the page.

- **Users scan the page in roughly a left-to-right, top-to-bottom order.** For large displays, the scan path is usually an arc starting in the upper left and ending in the lower right—per the Gutenberg diagram. Users tend to spend far more time in the upper left than the lower right; this is a consistent pattern in eye-tracking heatmaps. By contrast, for small displays such as smartphones, the scan path is straight down.

- **Along the way, users check any UI elements that attract their attention.** These elements tend to attract attention:

  - Interactive controls and their labels, especially controls that require input and commands. Large interactive controls placed prominently on the scan path get the most attention.

  - Prominent text and icons or anything else that's unexpectedly large, such as graphics.

  - Any controls that the already scanned controls encourage users to look at.

- **Along the way, users skip over any UI elements that repulse their attention, including:**

  - Anything that looks like an advertisement. This phenomenon is known as *banner blindness*, in which users often skip over banners because they assume they are ads. (This is ironic because banners are intended to attract attention.)

  - Large blocks of mostly unformatted text. Users often don't read such text at all because it requires too much effort. (Again, this is ironic because these large blocks of text often address important issues.)

  - Anything that is visually complex or requires a lot of effort to scan.

- **Since the scan path usually ends in the lower right, users expect to find the command to complete the step or task there.** If they don't find anything, their scan will go to the upper right.

- **Users don't optimize, they satisfice.** Another observation from Steve Krug. Once users think they know what to do, they immediately stop scanning and do it. Consequently, if there are better options after the first good one or there are more controls after the commands that complete the step or task, chances are that users won't see them.

- **Users won't scroll the page** unless what they've just scanned gives them a strong reason to do so. Consequently, controls required to understand the page should be visible without scrolling. (But smartphones are different—users expect to have to scroll on their small displays and doing so is very efficient.)

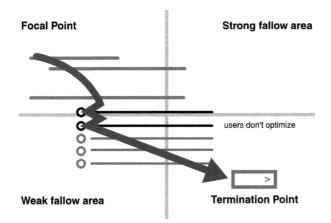

FIGURE 3.27
On large displays, users scan a page by starting at the focal point; scan across the page with a left-to-right, top-to-bottom arc; check UI elements that attract their attention along the way; ignore UI elements that repulse their attention, and end in the lower-right corner.

Designing a layout for scanning

Applying this model, here are steps for designing a layout for scanning:

- **Place UI elements that initiate the task in the upper-left corner or upper-center.** These elements should be visually prominent so that they act as the focal point—where users look at first.

- **Place UI elements that complete the task in the lower-right corner.** These elements should be visually prominent so that they stand out from ordinary commands.

- **If the page scrolls, design the page so that commands to complete the task don't require scrolling.** If that's not possible and the page is long, consider having completion commands at both the right top and right bottom of the scrolling area so that users aren't forced to scroll to complete the task.

- **Place primary UI elements required to perform the task prominently along the scan path** between the starting and ending points.

- **Place secondary UI elements for general tasks in the upper-right corner.** Such commands include sign in, search, and shopping cart.

- **Place secondary UI elements for interacting with the page content in the lower-left corner.** Such commands include performing related tasks. It should be acceptable if users don't see these.

- **Place general information about your product or company or contact information in a footer.** Users ignore the footer during scanning, but they know when it is there and roughly what they should expect to find there.

- **Whenever possible, put crucial text on interactive controls instead of using static text labels.** Users are less likely to scan static text, so they might miss that critical information.

- **Reconsider banners and large blocks of mostly unformatted text.** These formats are often used for the important information, but users are likely to not scan them at all.

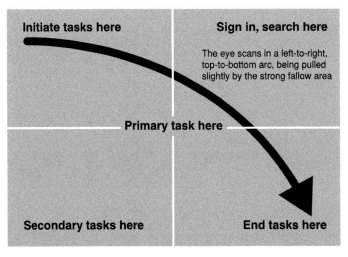

Communicates well

FIGURE 3.28

Here is where common UI elements should go on a typical page based on the scanning model.

The model is slightly different for small screens because users scan straight down and often scroll.

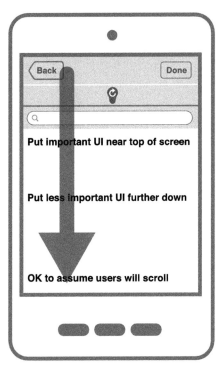

FIGURE 3.29
The layout model for small screens assumes scrolling.

Communicates
well

Quick fixes to scanning problems

Here are some solutions to common scanning problems:

- **Multiple focal points.** A page should have only one focal point; otherwise the eye doesn't know where to look. Make the UI elements that initiate the task the focal point and deemphasize other elements so that they don't compete. You can use location, size, and color to make a focal point.

- **An unnatural flow order.** The flow through the page should mirror the flow through the task. If not, reorder the page elements. It's more important for a page to have a logical flow than to have the most compact layout, so take the space if you need it.

- **Primary elements not attracting enough attention.** If users aren't seeing primary UI elements when they scan a page, you can make them more prominent by:

  - Moving them to a more prominent location on the scan path—perhaps higher on the page.

  - Using a more noticeable control (by size, color, and adding an icon label).

- Giving them a more prominent size. Don't be afraid to use large buttons for the most important commands and larger fonts for the most important text.

- Surrounding with generous space.

- Using more noticeable colors, bold text.

- **Secondary elements attracting too much attention.** If secondary UI elements are drawing more attention than they deserve, you can make them less prominent by:

  - Moving them outside the scan path or lower on the page.

  - Using a less noticeable control (example: a link instead of a push button).

  - Making them smaller.

  - Giving them less space.

  - Using less noticeable colors, normal or deemphasized text.

  - Using progressive disclosure to hide less important information by default.

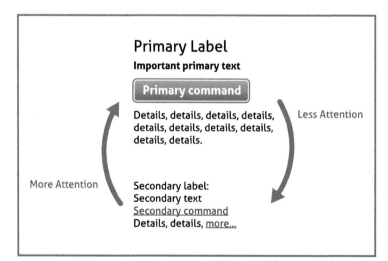

FIGURE 3.30
Some scanning problems can be addressed by attracting the right amount of attention.

Users don't read, they scan—where the goal of scanning is to find things quickly. Scanning is so important that you should design pages specifically for scanning.

TYPOGRAPHY AND TEXT

Well-presented text is beautiful. Calligraphy is the art of stylized writing that has been practiced by all cultures for centuries. Steve Jobs often mentioned that a calligraphy class at Reed College changed his life and that his appreciation of beautiful typography was an important inspiration for the Macintosh.

FIGURE 3.31
Calligraphy is a very human art practiced by all cultures.

 Frankly, the presentation of text in classic UI is so poor that it is embarrassing. We can do better. We tend not to put a lot of thought into the appearance of text, but users interact with text more than any other UI element. Typography and text deserve our attention.
 Modern UI design strives to present text attractively. Here is a summary of what makes modern UI text so good and classic UI text so awful:

- **Better typography.** Modern fonts use subpixel antialiasing to effectively increase screen resolution. Consequently, the text looks solid and smooth instead of thin and jagged.

Subpixel anti-aliasing
Subpixel anti-aliasing

FIGURE 3.32
The text at the top appears smooth, but zooming in reveals how using subpixels achieves that smoothness.

- **Visual hierarchy.** Modern UI text uses a variety of sizes, primarily to draw attention to important text. By contrast, classic UI text tends to be uniformly small and hard to read.

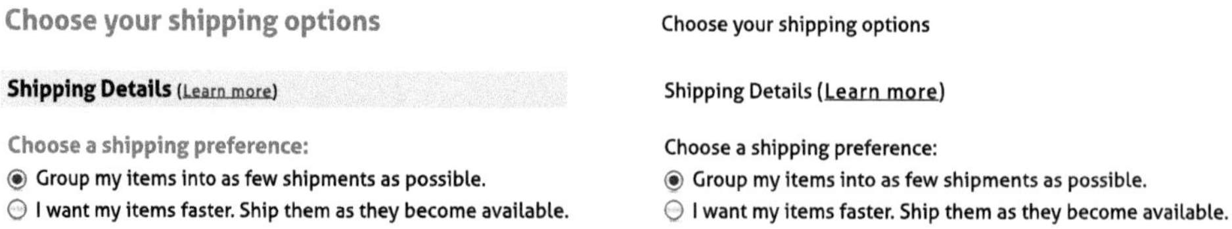

Choose your shipping options

Shipping Details (Learn more)

Choose a shipping preference:
- ◉ Group my items into as few shipments as possible.
- ○ I want my items faster. Ship them as they become available.

Choose your shipping options

Shipping Details (**Learn more**)

Choose a shipping preference:
- ◉ Group my items into as few shipments as possible.
- ○ I want my items faster. Ship them as they become available.

FIGURE 3.33

Using a visual hierarchy makes the text on the left much easier to scan and read.

- **Better, more concise text.** Modern UI text gets right to the point, using progressive disclosure as needed for more detail. By contrast, classic UI text tends to overexplain, often using large blocks of unformatted text.

Better, more concise text

Classic UI text

Modern UI text gets right to the point, using progressive disclosure as needed for more detail. More

By contrast, classic UI text tends to overexplain, often using large blocks of unformatted text. These large blocks of text give details that most users don't really care about. Large blocks of text are hard to read, and uniform text makes them hard to scan as well, so the eye tends to skip right over them. Even the most motivated readers have a hard time reading such text.

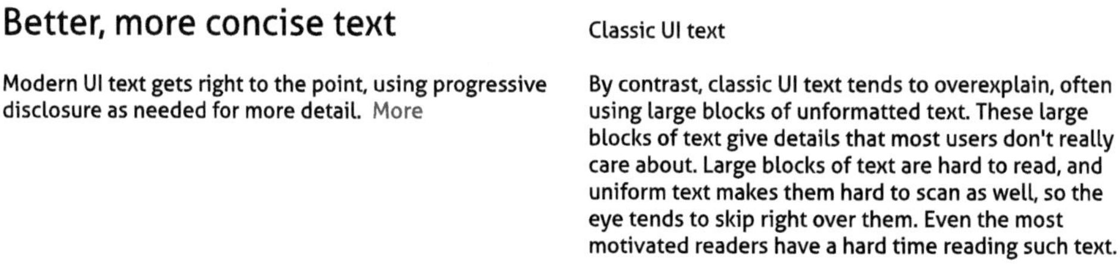

FIGURE 3.34

The concise text on the left gets right to the point, whereas the text on the right overexplains.

Clear, minimal text is beautiful when well presented. Although this is mostly an aesthetic point of view, let's now consider typography from the communication point of view.

Typography and system fonts

Fonts not only have their obvious visual differences in appearance and style, they also have different reading characteristics. Good fonts are *readable*, which means that the font design leads the eye along the horizontal line, making it easy to read large blocks of text (such as documents). Good fonts are *legible*, which means that the individual characters are easy to recognize and differentiate (important for headings and short text such as labels). **Readability and legibility are often tradeoffs** because the most *readable* fonts are usually serif fonts (which have small turns that often finish the strokes of letters), whereas the most *legible* fonts tend to be sans-serif fonts (which lack the serif strokes). Consequently, it is common for books to use sans-serif fonts for headings and serif fonts for the body text. There are so many different fonts for a reason.

Here are the system UI text fonts for common platforms:

- **Web.** Arial, Trebuchet, Verdana (these fonts are "Web safe," meaning that they are supported by all major browsers in all platforms).

- **Windows.** Segoe UI.

- **Mac.** Lucida Grande.

- **iOS.** Helvetica Neue.

- **Android.** Roboto.

Arial Lucida Grande
Trebuchet Helvetica Neue
Verdana Roboto
Segoe UI

FIGURE 3.35

The common system UI text fonts.

Using the appropriate system font for your platform is always a safe choice. UI text needs to be legible (especially on low-resolution displays), so sans-serif fonts are used.

Text attribute guidelines

Here are some guidelines for effective use of UI text:

- **Color.** Large UI text, such as headings and main instructions, can use color for styling and to draw attention. By contrast, normal-sized text shouldn't use color, because color would make it look like a link. By convention, unvisited links (normally blue) are displayed differently than visited links (normally purple), but link colors can be changed through styling. Modern UIs often don't use a different color for visited links, for aesthetic reasons (a poor motivation). Although using a different visited link color often isn't helpful, it can be extremely helpful for tasks that involve exploring lists of items that are otherwise hard to differentiate.

> **UX Design Essentials** Workshop « User Experience Design Training ...
> www.uxdesignedge.com/.../user-experience-design-essentials-worksh...
> A two-day UX design workshop to learn user centered UI design "by doing".
>
> **UX Design Essentials** for Managers « User Experience Design ...
> www.uxdesignedge.com/training/ux-design-essentials-for-managers/
> A two-day course to help managers and executives better understand the **UX design** process to better lead and influence their teams.

FIGURE 3.36

Google uses the visited-link color to make visited items easy to differentiate from the ones you have yet to look at. No question where I've been.

Communicates
well

- **Shade.** Shade (specifically luminosity) is used to distinguish normal text from deemphasized text and disabled text. *Deemphasizing text* means that that it is less important and doesn't need to be scanned, whereas *disabled text* means that it doesn't apply and likely doesn't need to be read at all. Make sure there is a clear visual distinction between the two.

Normal Text	Deemphasized Text	Disabled Text
#000000	#999999	#CCCCCC
100%-80%	80%-70% value of normal	50%-40% value of normal

FIGURE 3.37

This chart shows recommended shades for normal, deemphasized, and disabled text. If your deemphasized text looks like disabled text, users are likely to ignore it.

FIGURE 3.38

Hmmm ... looks like I can't add files or photos.

- **Bold.** Use bold text to emphasize the most important text that users must read or are likely to scan for. Most text isn't the most important (relatively speaking), so most text shouldn't be bold.

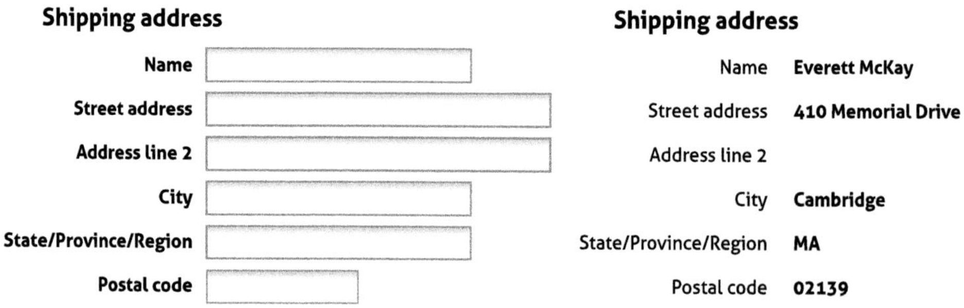

FIGURE 3.39

Consider using bold labels for editable fields because users are likely to scan for specific labels. By contrast, don't use bold labels for reports because users are more likely to scan for specific data, not the labels.

- **Italic.** Use italics as a substitute for quotation marks, primarily when text should be interpreted literally. Use sparingly to emphasize specific words.

- **Bold italic.** Don't use in UI text. There's no need.

- **Underline.** Don't use except for links, because users expect underlined text to be a link. Given that users assume normal-size colored text is a link, there's no need to underline text unless the link is in an unexpected context.

FIGURE 3.40
The blue text clearly indicates a link, so there's no need to underline. Underlining just adds visual clutter.

- **Capitalization.** Different platforms have different capitalization rules, so you should follow them for consistency. If your platform doesn't have capitalization rules, the simplest and best approach is to use everyday capitalization (why be different?). In English, this means using title capitalization (where the first letters of all words are capitalized except articles, conjunctions, and prepositions) for titles and sentence capitalization (where only the first letter of the first word is capitalized) for everything else. Don't use all uppercase or all lowercase. This "everyday" approach is natural, friendly, and flexible.

Background guidelines

Text needs to have good contrast with its background to be legible. (Technically, contrast is defined as a large difference between the luminance of text and its background.) Per the World Wide Web Consortium (W3C) accessibility guidelines, accessible software now must have a 5:1 contrast ratio between text and its background.

Contrast ratios are difficult to calculate (in practice, you should use a contrast calculator), but you can be confident in meeting the accessibility requirement if you follow these guidelines:

- **Normal text.** Most text is black (or near-black) on a white (or near-white) background.

- **Contrasting text.** For visual contrast, some text can be white (or near-white) on a solid dark background.

- **Solid background colors.** Don't put text on harsh gradients or images. Subtle gradients (where you need to look carefully to tell that it's a gradient) are usually acceptable.

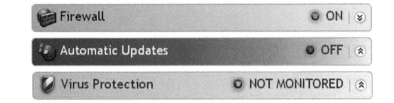

Communicates
poorly

FIGURE 3.41

For accessibility, don't put UI text on harsh gradients. Not a big loss—we won't miss them.

If you want to make sure all users can read your text easily, use dark text on a solid light background.

COLOR

Of all the visual UI elements, the use of color is the most subjective, emotional, and passionate. People have strong opinions about color based on their personal preferences and experiences. And they seem to be surprisingly willing to share their color preferences—managers without design backgrounds especially. Once managers insist that they don't like blue or gray and so the product can't use them, your visual design is in trouble.

FIGURE 3.42

The use of color is subjective, emotional, passionate … even visceral. DILBERT ©2002 Scott Adams. Used by permission of UNIVERSAL UCLICK. All rights reserved.

Beyond aesthetics, the interpretation of color is often culturally dependent. For example, in Western cultures white may symbolize peace and purity, whereas in Eastern cultures white may symbolize death and mourning. Similarly, in Western cultures black may symbolize evil, whereas in Eastern cultures black symbolizes power and strength. Fortunately these connotations don't always carry over to software. It would be very difficult to design a UI without black or white.

FIGURE 3.43

The interpretation of color is culturally dependent. For example, traditional Chinese wedding dresses are red to symbolize love, prosperity, and good luck, whereas red suggests danger in Western cultures. Photo by Kelidimari via Wikimedia Commons.

Another challenge is that color affects your product's accessibility. Users with blindness or low vision may not be able to see the colors well, if at all. Approximately 8 percent of adult males (yes, 8 percent!) have some form of color confusion (often incorrectly referred to as "color blindness"), of which red-green color confusion (deuteranopia) is the most common.

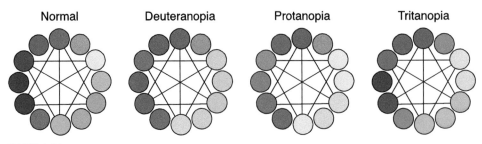

FIGURE 3.44

The primary colors as seen with normal color vision, with deuteranopia (6% of the male population), with protanopia (1% of the male population), and with tritanopia (1% of the male population).

Never use color as the only method of communication. Instead, make sure that color is used to reinforce other design elements such as text, icons, graphics, and physical size and location.

FIGURE 3.45

The color red demands attention, but the button's icon and text label clearly communicate its purpose independently of color. Also, its size and separate physical location reinforce the button's significance.

There is a lot of subjectivity in regard to color, but there is a fair amount of objectivity that you can take advantage of. Let's start with the basics. Here are the standard colors used to communicate status:

Color	Examples	Meaning
Red		Error, stop/stopped, critical, required, requires immediate attention
Yellow		Warning, proceed with caution

Color	Examples	Meaning
Green		Normal, proceed, life is good

Using status color appropriately allows you to communicate meaning at a glance.

The interpretation of these status colors is globally consistent. This is due to the United Nations *Convention on Road Signs and Signals*, which defines the worldwide convention for traffic lights. Even though red means "good luck" in Chinese culture, a red traffic light in Beijing still means stop.

FIGURE 3.46
Stop! ... and good luck!

What if you want to use red, yellow, or green without suggesting status? Users associate the status to hues that have high saturation and midlevel luminosity, so you can avoid these meanings by choosing colors that have low saturation or high or low luminosity.

FIGURE 3.47
The left folder looks yellow, not like a warning. By contrast, the saturated folder in the middle looks like a warning.

Here are the typical human perceptions of some colors, independent of status or cultural interpretation:

Color	Examples	Human Perception
Gray	**Ordinary button**	Neutral, doesn't demand attention.
Blue	Item **Neutral highlight** Item	Neutral, traditional, conservative, cool, doesn't demand attention.
Green	**Call to action**	Relaxing, organic, fresh, cool, doesn't demand attention.
Yellow	Item **Attention getting highlight** Item	Harsh, organic, (luke)warm, demands attention. Best color for highlighting.
Orange	**Call to action**	Aggressive, fun, energetic, warm, demands attention.
Red	**⚠ Error!**	Aggressive, emotional, energetic, warm, demands attention.
Purple	**Call to action**	Aggressive, cheerful, cool, demands attention.

These perceptions suggest that color can be used strategically to help users scan a page:

- **Focal point.** For the focal point, use the strongest color on the page to demand the user's attention. To have a single focal point, avoid using that color elsewhere on the page. Shades of orange, red, or purple are often used for this purpose.

- **Next step.** For the control to advance to the next step, use a color with medium strength to stand out from the other controls without demanding attention. Shades of green or blue are often used for this purpose.

- **Differentiation.** To make certain controls stand out, use a neutral color. Shades of blue or gray are often used for this purpose.

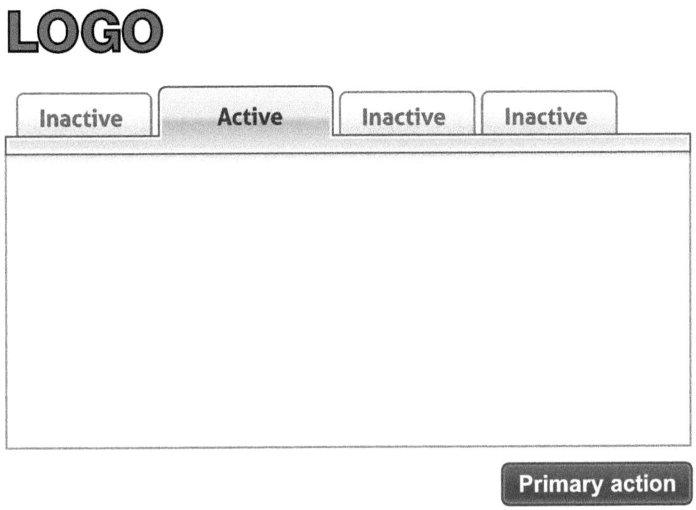

FIGURE 3.48
Here the strongest color is used for the focal point. Medium colors are used to draw attention to the next step, and neutral colors are used for differentiation.

Even though there is flexibility with these colors, you should keep these perceptions in mind when you're choosing colors. For example, the *Register Now* buttons shown in Figure 3.49 are identical except for their color. How does each make you feel? Which one do you think communicates its message best?

FIGURE 3.49

The color of these *Register Now* buttons has a strong connotation. The gray button feels too neutral—as if to suggest that you *can't* register now. The blue button also feels neutral but without the discouraging connotation of the gray. The red button certainly demands attention, but the error status association makes you feel like you shouldn't click it. Oranges feels similar to the red in that it demands attention but without the feeling of error status. Finally, green feels the most encouraging—yes, you can click this button to proceed safely.

Here are some recommendations for designing with color:

- **Start your design process using monochrome wireframes.** Ironically, the best way to design for color is to start by designing without color and then add color later. Doing so places focus in the right place (which, early in the process, *isn't* color) and ensures that that information isn't being communicated using color alone for accessibility.

- **Keep your use of color simple.** Limit the use of color to design themes, key visual elements, visual communication, and branding. Anything outside these goals should probably be a neutral color.

- **When you're choosing colors, consider what each UI element communicates and choose a color consistent with that communication.** Make sure the resulting color has the right meanings, is consistent with your product-branding guidelines, and is aesthetically pleasing and appropriate for your product. When in doubt, use a shade of gray or blue.

- **Use a graphic designer if you want to use complex color** such as color schemes, gradients, or unusual colors. It's all too obvious when a nondesigner creates a complex color scheme. Don't do it!

In choosing colors, consider what the UI element communicates and choose a color that helps communicate that meaning at a glance. For accessibility, never use color as the only method of communication.

AFFORDANCES

***Affordances* are the visual properties of a UI element that indicate how to perform an interaction.** Standard controls all have affordances. For example, push buttons have frames that visually suggest they can be pushed (that is, clicked or touched).

iOS
Save Draft
Cancel
Android
Save
Cancel
Mac
Cancel
Save
Windows
OK
Cancel

FIGURE 3.50

Push buttons have frames that visually suggest they can be pushed.

To contrast with labels, affordances indicate how to interact with a control mechanically, whereas labels communicate the results of an interaction functionally.

Tap to enter title
From
Sat 03/16/2013
1:00 AM
To
Sat 03/16/2013
2:00 AM
Time zone
(GMT-4:00) Eastern Daylight Time
All day

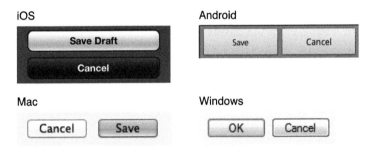

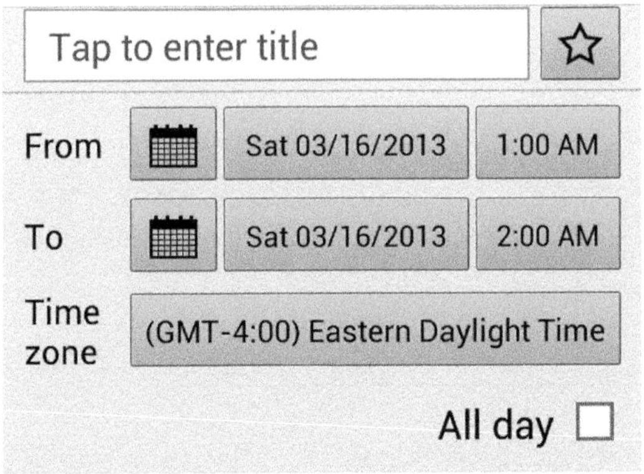

FIGURE 3.51

The button, text box, checkbox affordances indicate the interaction, whereas the labels indicate their meaning.

The consistent use of affordances is essential to having an intuitive UI. To help you achieve consistency, here are the common affordances with their effects, usage details, and examples, starting with plain text as a baseline:

Plain text	Ordinary UI text, such as a label or an instruction.	**UI Is Communication**
Button frame	Indicates that the element is clickable.	[UI Is Communication]
Link	Indicates that the element is clickable. Shown with normal-sized colored text. Maybe underlined, but an underline isn't necessary if the text is obviously a link from its context. Hovering changes cursor to a hand to confirm that the text is a link.	UI Is Communication
Edit box	Indicates that the text is editable. The box appearance might be subtle until the user clicks on it. Clicking displays a caret to indicate where the interaction will take place.	UI Is Communication |
Arrow	Indicates that a pop-up menu will be displayed where the arrow points.	UI Is Communication ▼
Arrows	Indicates that a list is scrollable in the direction of the arrow. Always used in pairs.	UI Is Communication / Intuitive / Affordance
Chevron	Indicates that any remaining items will be shown (or hidden) where the chevron points. For iOS, a right-pointing chevron indicates selection will advance to another screen. For Android, a left-pointing chevron indicates moving up in the navigation hierarchy.	UI Is Communication >

Colored background	Indicates that the item has been selected.	 UI Is Communication Intuitive Affordance
Check	Indicates that the item had been selected.	✔ UI Is Communication
Check box	Indicates that the item is independently selectable.	☑ UI Is Communication
Option circle	Indicates that the item is a mutually exclusive selection.	◉ UI Is Communication
Open/Close	Indicates that the item is a container that can be expanded or collapsed.	⊞ UI Is Communication ⊟ UI Is Communication
Handles	Indicates that the object can be moved or resized.	UI Is Communication
Separator	Adding a line shows separation. For example, adding a line to a menu button makes it a split button.	UI Is Communication ▾
Bold text	Indicates that the UI element is important but doesn't change its interaction.	**UI Is Communication**
Gray text	Indicates that the UI element is disabled.	UI Is Communication
Flashing	Rapid flashing indicates that the user must respond immediately. Slow flashing (pulsing) attracts attention but doesn't demand it.	UI Is Communication
X	Indicates that a window or pane can be closed.	UI Is Communication ⊗

Some of these affordances have multiple meanings, but their meaning is usually clear from the context.

A downside to affordances is that they can add a significant amount of visual clutter, especially when they aren't really needed. Consider removing affordances when the interaction is already clear or the affordance is redundant. Chapter 1, "*Strategically Unintuitive UI*," explored the cost of affordances.

FIGURE 3.52
The Windows taskbar icons could have arrow affordances to indicate pop-up menus, but these would add visual clutter without sufficient benefit.

FIGURE 3.53
The arrow indicates that clicking the button advances to the next step, but so does the label. Better off without the arrow here.

How do you get the intuitive benefits of using affordances without the visual clutter downside? Here's a good solution:

- Always display nonobvious primary affordances so that users can easily discover them.

- Display secondary affordances dynamically when users interact with the object.

This approach strikes the right balance by displaying the most important affordances but avoiding the clutter of the secondary affordances only until they are relevant. For more information, refer to "*Dynamic Secondary Commands and Affordances*" in Chapter 2.

> Affordances are visual properties of a UI element that indicate how to perform an interaction, and the consistent use of affordances is essential to having an intuitive UI. But there is a downside to affordances, so make sure they are worth any visual clutter they add.

ICONS AND GLYPHS

An *icon* is a small picture—often rendered using 3-D, full color, and shading—that's used to label a command, option, or object. A *glyph* is a flat (2-D without shading), monochrome symbol or shape used for the same purpose. **Modern UIs tend to use fewer icons than classic UIs and tend to use glyphs instead of icons.**

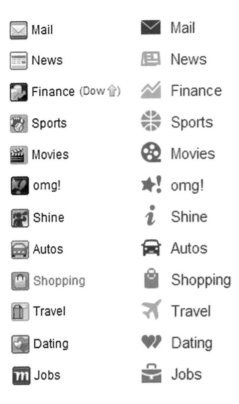

FIGURE 3.54
Icons (on left) and glyphs (on right). Note how the glyphs tend to be easier to understand at a glance.

Icons and glyphs vs. labels

> A picture is worth a thousand words ... unless it's an icon!

If it's an icon or glyph, it is worth up to three words—at best! The oft-cited cliché is misleading because icons are a poor way to communicate. (Important exceptions: when the target audience can't read, as with young children, or when the target audience's language is unknown, as in an airport.) With the exception of well-known standard icons, people understand text labels much better than icons. As Jef Raskin noted in *The Human Interface*, "Instead of icons explaining, we have found that icons often require explanation."

Don't believe that icons are a poor way to communicate meaning? Take the "icon challenge" by removing all labels and tooltips and see if you can correctly determine what the controls do based on their icons alone. For example, try to figure out the meaning of the commands on the Insert tab in Microsoft Word.

FIGURE 3.55

The "icon challenge" for Microsoft Word: Try to figure out what these icons mean.

When I tried this challenge, I scored only 10 out of 24 for this ribbon tab. Keep in mind that Word is a familiar program and Microsoft Office uses excellent iconography, so I would expect the typical score to be even lower, especially if there are many custom icons.

I recommended using this approach to evaluate your product's icons. Don't expect the results to be encouraging.

Recognition versus comprehension

If icons are so poor at communicating, why bother with them? First, I should reiterate that well-known standard icons communicate their one to three words quite effectively. It is the not-well-known, nonstandard icons—the ones that require time and thought to figure out—that are the ones in question.

Icons are all about efficient visual recognition, so nonstandard icons help users recognize and distinguish commands visually. Although users understand text labels quickly, they recognize and distinguish icons faster still. For example, users might remember that the command they are looking for has a blue globe on it and locate it immediately, even though they might not understand exactly what the globe means. When there are many commands, using a labeled icon works well because the icon enables quick visual recognition and the text label enables quick comprehension.

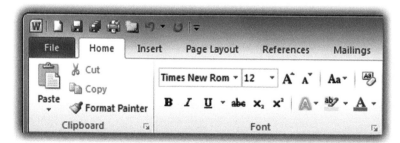

FIGURE 3.56

Quick: Find the New Comment command Based on the icon alone, can you determine what the Format Painter command does? Try this exercise enough, and you'll see that labels are best for comprehension, icons are best for recognition, and labeled icons are best for both.

To help users distinguish between your icons, make sure the icons are visually distinct in terms of design, shape, and color. If all the icons in a specific context have a common theme (for example, a database), remove the common theme to focus on the differentiation.

FIGURE 3.57
The icons on the left have distinct shapes and colors, whereas the icons on the right have similar shapes, colors, and designs and are more likely to be confused.

If your target user's comprehension of your icons is low, it's likely that you need to reconsider your labeling strategy more than the icon design itself. Efficient recognition is valuable—just keep in mind that it's not a substitute for comprehension.

Intuitive icon designs

The user's ability to understand an icon is primarily determined by the icon type. The follow icon types are easy to understand:

- Standard symbols

- Preview of results

- Simple nouns

- Simple nouns doing simple verbs

- Simple nouns showing simple adjectives

- Well-known logos

- All of the above with a single standard overlay (error, warning, disabled, etc.)

Standard and simple works well. This list reveals an interesting challenge to icon design: Icons are symbols, and symbols are nouns. Yet icons are often used to represent commands, and commands are verbs. Consequently, many icons boil down to a noun representing or doing the verb.

The following icon types are moderately difficult to understand:

- **Metaphors.** When an object with similar behaviors or properties is used as a substitute.

- **Metonyms.** When a completely different but related object is used as a substitute.

- **Synecdoche.** When a part represents the whole.

Metonyms and synecdoche are related to metaphors, but I listed them explicitly to show that metaphors aren't the only game in town. Using a fork on a map to represent a restaurant is a synecdoche, not a metaphor. Again, simplicity and familiarity are the key to success here. For example, a star is a successful metonym for "favorite" because people often rate things they like using stars.

Communicates
well

FIGURE 3.58

Icons using metaphors, metonyms, and synecdoche.

The following icon types are difficult to understand:

- Unfamiliar nouns

- Complex, detailed icons

- Abstract concepts

- Obscure logos

- Puns

To work through an example, what is a good icon for fidelity? Fidelity is an abstract concept, so it's very difficult (if not impossible) to create an understandable icon to represent it. Dogs are known for having fidelity to their masters, but a dog icon is far more likely to be interpreted literally.

In addition to type, context plays an important role in helping users easily deduce meaning. For example, a zebra icon (an unfamiliar noun, icon-wise) is meaningless out of context, but in the context of monkey, turtle, bird, and snake icons, a zebra most likely represents savanna animals.

FIGURE 3.59

In the context of a database program, users can figure out that this funnel icon is a metaphor for filtering. But the meaning of this icon is unclear in any other context. Martinis, anyone?

Everett's Laws of Icon Design

I have a couple laws for icon design:

The longer it takes to come up with an idea for an icon, the less comprehensible the icon is going to be.

and

If an icon requires a tooltip to understand, it's not comprehensible. At best, such icons help in recognition.

If you are wracking your brain trying to come up with an idea for a good icon, most likely it's because there isn't one. Once you've made this realization (and if you really must have an icon), better to focus on the recognition consolation prize.

What to do if your icons aren't good

If you are dissatisfied with your icons, consider the following, in priority order:

- **Reconsider the need.** Icons are overused and are often not necessary. Text labels are just as recognizable when there are only a few items, and icons help recognition when there are many. But when they aren't really needed, icons just add visual clutter. You can design a good UI without them.

- **Reconsider consistency.** Using icons in some places doesn't mean that you have to use them everywhere. In Figure 3.60, note how Yahoo only uses icons for their most well-known sites.

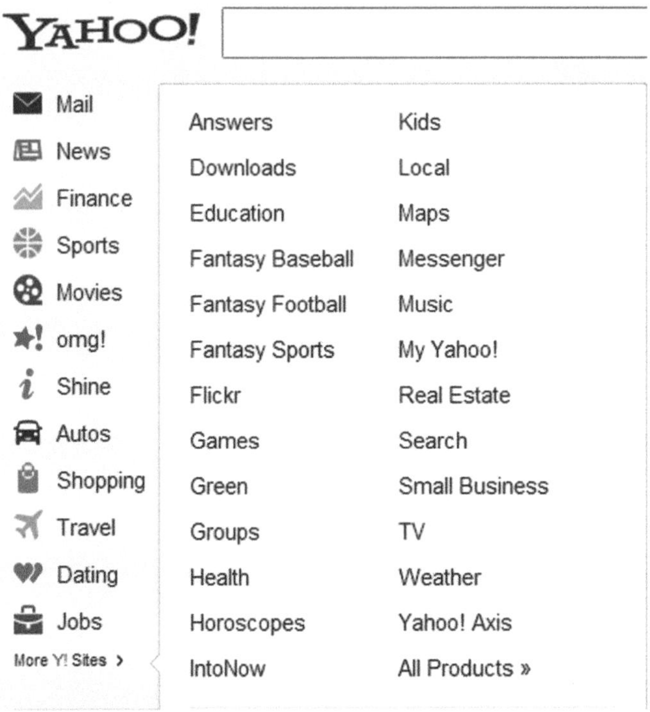

FIGURE 3.60
You don't need an icon for every command.

- **Hire an icon design specialist.** Icon design is a specialized talent, so you'll need to either buy suitable preexisting icons or hire a specialist to design custom professional, comprehensible icons. Keep in mind that creating custom icons is very time intensive, so don't expect to get off cheap. (And whatever you do, don't attempt to design them yourself.)

Standard icons and glyphs

Here's a list of standard icons (glyphs, actually) with their meanings (from a variety of sources):

Symbol	Meaning
◀ ▶ ▲ ▼	Directional actions, back/forward, next/previous, up/down
➕	Add
📎	Attachment
◀	Back
📖	Bookmarks
📷	Camera
⊗	Close
🖊	Compose
✂ 📄 📋	Cut, copy, paste
⊖ ⌫	Delete
📄	Document
★ ♥	Favorite, rating
✉	Email
⊗	Error
📁	Folder

Symbol	Meaning
	Full size/normal size
	Grabber
	Help
	Home
	Information
	Like, dislike
	Location service
	Lock, security
	Menu
	More
	Move, organize
	Near me now
	Phone
	Plus/minus, more/less, zoom in/out
	Power
	Print

Symbol	Meaning
	Refresh, reload
	Reply
	Save
	Search
	Settings, options
	Share
	Speech input
	Stop
B *I* <u>U</u> a̶b̶c̶	Text bold, italic, underline, strikethrough
	Text left, center, right, indent, unindent
	Trash, delete
	Undo/redo
	Video/audio transport controls
	Warning
	Audio volume indicator
	Battery-strength indicator

Symbol	Meaning
☼ ☀	Brightness indicator
◑	Contrast
▄▁▁▁▁ ▄▅▆▁▁ ▄▅▆▇█	Phone signal strength indicator
📶 📶 📶	Wi-Fi signal strength indicator

To reinforce the meaning of these standard icons, choose them based on their meanings, not their appearance. If you need a different meaning, use another icon. So, scissors means Cut, not office supplies; a magnifying glass means Find, not Zoom.

Word is saving Chapter 3 Visual Design.docx: ▭▭▭▭ ⊗

FIGURE 3.61

You can cancel a document save in Microsoft Word ... by clicking an error icon. Oops!

Communicates
poorly

You can use these standard icons unlabeled and be confident that users will understand them. For all other icons, you should use either a labeled icon (a static label or tooltip) or a text label without an icon. Still, there may be situations where you must use an unlabeled nonstandard icon—perhaps because the UI framework you are using requires it or you just don't have the screen space for a label.

For unlabeled, nonstandard icons, assume that users won't understand them and will experiment to figure them out, which, of course, you want to avoid. But if necessary, make sure those experiments are immediately self-explanatory and easy to undo if undesired.

> Choose (and design) icons based on what they communicate. Standard icons work best and don't require labeling. All other icons should be labeled; otherwise users may have to experiment to figure them out.

Icon overlays

Overlays are used to modify the meaning of an icon. Here's a list of some standard overlays (from a variety of sources):

Overlay	Meaning
	Delete
	Error (there's a problem)
	New, add
	New items or notifications
	Unavailable, disabled
	Warning (needs attention)

The only trick to icon overlays is to use only one at a time. If more than one applies, use the overlay that is the most important or urgent.

FIGURE 3.62

A single overlay is easy to understand, but more than one is confusing. What does this icon hieroglyphic mean?

ANIMATIONS AND TRANSITIONS

Using animations and transitions appropriately can make your product easier to understand, feel smoother and more natural, and have a modern, engaging, high-quality feel. *Animations* give the appearance of motion or change over time. You can use animations to give feedback, show relationships, draw attention to important change, or explain tasks visually. *Transitions* are animations that keep users oriented during a state change and that make those changes feel smooth and natural instead of jarring.

Effective animations and transitions communicate what is happening visually. Animations and transitions don't have to demand the user's attention to be successful. In fact, the opposite is often true: Transitions are often used to *not* draw attention, but instead to make state changes smooth and natural. The ideal transition is so natural that users don't even notice it's there—and would only notice its absence.

Communicates well

FIGURE 3.63

The ideal transition is so smooth that users don't even notice it is there.

By contrast, the classic "flaming logo" types of animations communicate nothing and serve only to draw unnecessary attention to themselves. Remove any such animations.

Communicates
poorly

FIGURE 3.64
Pointless animations aren't cool. Trust me!

Effective nonverbal communication

Animations and transitions are all about effective visual communication, and consistent meaning is crucial to their effectiveness. The best way to achieve consistency is to define an animation vocabulary for all *meaningful* animations and transitions. By contrast, making arbitrary one-off, spur-of-the-moment animation choices because they look "kind of cool" undermines effective visual communication. Such animations offer little more than eye candy.

Meaningful animations should be assigned a single meaning, and that meaning should be applied consistently throughout the product. An animation is *meaningful* when it communicates a specific meaning. For example, a right-to-left page transition might be used to communicate that page content is being replaced by the next item in a sequence. Using that transition for other meanings would be confusing or surprising.

Communicates
well

FIGURE 3.65
A right-to-left transition shows that the page content is being replaced by the next item.

By contrast, a cross-fade transition (where the old content is faded out and the new content is faded in) has no particular meaning and can be used for many purposes without confusion.

FIGURE 3.66
Cross-fade transitions don't have a specific meaning and can be used for many purposes without confusion.

Page transitions used by presentation software such as PowerPoint usually have no meaning and are intended to draw the user's attention to the slide transition instead of making the transition feel natural. Consequently, these transitions are a poor design model for your UI.

An example transition vocabulary

To give you an example of an effective animation vocabulary, here are the common transitions used by iOS, along with their consistent meanings:

Name/Meaning	Transition
Sign in	Cut page in half horizontally, slide top up and bottom down to return
Zoom in	Emerge from center of screen
Zoom out	Collapse to center of screen
Slide in	Choreographed slide in from right
Slide out	Choreographed slide in from left
Next item	Slide in from right
Previous item	Slide in from left
Show options or keyboard	Slide up from bottom
Remove options or keyboard	Slide down to bottom
Show dialog	Slide up from bottom, dim background
Flip left/right	Reveal options (on back side)
Curl up/down	Reveal options (underneath)
Cross fade	Change view
Enter passcode	Slide numeric keypad up and passcode input from left
Shrink	Display in higher-level context
Restore	Restore to original context
Expand/contract	Show more/less information
Edit mode	Shift in editing affordances from both left and right sides of screen

And here are the common iOS animations:

Name/Meaning	Animation
Searchlight	Draw attention to "Slide to unlock"
Rubber band bounce	Indicate at top or bottom of document

Name/Meaning	Animation
Genie	Move item to object
Move	Show move to new location
Determinate progress	Progress bar
Indeterminate progress	Spinner
Stretch	The refresh control stretches as users drag down
Wiggling icons	Rearrange the Home screen icons mode

Consider defining a similarly consistent animation and transition vocabulary for your app.

Designing an appropriate personality

When you're communicating, it's not just what you say but how you say it. For animations and transitions, the "what you say" is the meaning of the effect and the "how you say it" is its personality. We will explore personality in detail in Chapter 4, but for now make sure that the personality you choose for your animations is consistent and appropriate for your product.

An animation's personality can be relaxed, energetic, or even happy. For example, suppose you are using an animation to show that an object needs attention. A relaxed personality might show this feedback with a slow animation that has an economy of movement.

FIGURE 3.67

An Attention animation for a product with a relaxed personality.

An energetic personality might show the feedback with a faster animation that has much more movement and a jarring ending. A happy animation might bounce with delight.

FIGURE 3.68
An Attention animation for a product with an energetic personality.

FIGURE 3.69
An Attention animation for a product with a happy personality.

When in doubt, animations and transitions that are natural, subdued, and efficient yet relaxed are a safe bet.

Animation and transition guidelines

Here are some general animation and transition guidelines:

- **Don't use animations and transitions just because you can.** The gratuitous use of animations can easily make your product distracting and annoying.

- **For accessibility, never use animations as the only method to communicate important information.** Make sure that low-vision users can find that important information some other way.

- **Choose transitions that don't harm users' productivity.** Such transitions happen quickly (200 milliseconds or less, 100 milliseconds or less if frequent) and don't interfere with interaction. No matter how good your transitions, nobody is going to want to wait for them.

- **Choose transitions that feel responsive.** If a transition looks slow, it will feel slow—regardless of what the clock says. A good approach is a "shotgun/pillow," where the animation starts quickly to feel fast but ends with a soft landing to feel smooth.

- **Choose animations and transitions that aren't tiresome after repeated viewings.** Design for the long run. The ideal animation or transition is as engaging the 1,000th time as it was the first. Gratuitous animations that draw unnecessary attention to themselves are the most vulnerable here—they feel tiresome quickly.

> Use animations and transitions to communicate what is happening visually. To ensure effective communication, define an animation and transition vocabulary and apply it consistently across your product.

DEMANDING ATTENTION

Well designed UIs are often described as *invisible* in the sense that once users are in a state of *flow*, they aren't even aware of the UI. Normally this is what you want. Users don't read, they scan, and they are immersed in their work and aren't too concerned with the details of using your product. Great visual designs recognize this fact and are designed for efficient user decision making while scanning. That way, users will do the right thing even if they aren't paying full attention to the UI.

In some situations you want to do the opposite: break the user's concentration, demand their full attention, and address a pressing issue thoughtfully. In such situations, if users were to maintain their flow, there's a good chance that they would make a mistake with significant consequences—perhaps without even realizing it.

Here are some situations worthy of breaking users' flow and demanding their full attention:

- **Potential for physical harm.** Example: disabling a carbon monoxide detector.

- **Potential harm to device (hardware or software) or access to it.** Example: installing software from an untrusted source.

- **Critical change in status.** Examples: low battery, low storage, long-term loss of connectivity.

- **Potential for significant loss of data or user effort.** Example: erasing or formatting a storage device.

- **Disclosure personal or sensitive information.** Example: disclosing user's physical location.

Attention-getting techniques

Your first choice should be to avoid the need to demand attention, but here are some techniques to demand the user's attention (in order of least obtrusive first):

- **Put critical text on control labels.** Although users scan most UI text, they usually read control labels before they click on them. If there is critical information users must know before giving a command, put it on the label.

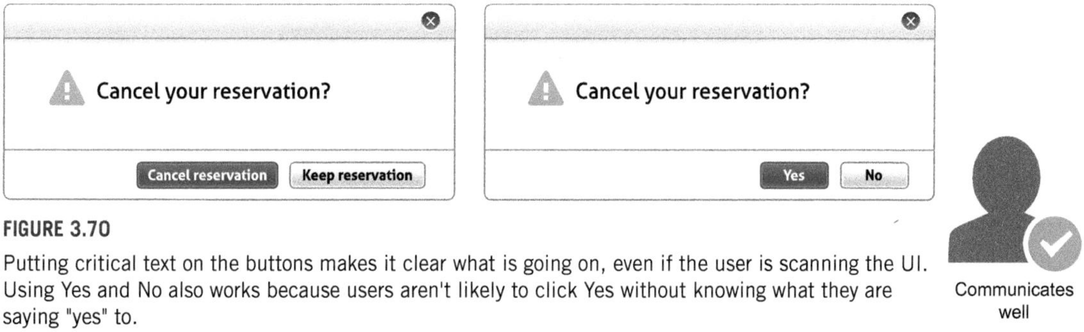

FIGURE 3.70

Putting critical text on the buttons makes it clear what is going on, even if the user is scanning the UI. Using Yes and No also works because users aren't likely to click Yes without knowing what they are saying "yes" to.

Communicates well

- **Use an attention-getting presentation.** Critical or urgent UIs should look critical or urgent instead of normal, so make these controls stand out using layout, control size, color, and highlighting.

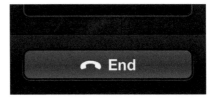

Communicates
well

FIGURE 3.71

By making the End call button large, red, and physically separate, the iPhone ensures that this button gets users' attention, even when they're distracted. Users are unlikely to tap this button by accident.

FIGURE 3.72

The iPhone uses update overlays to show when there is a new email, message, or app update. The red overlay gets the user's attention without demanding it.

- **Use warning icons.** Nothing communicates *warning* more concisely than a warning icon, which suggests that users should pay special attention to the task at hand. But displaying many warning icons runs the risk of causing users to ignore them all.

- **Animations.** Obvious animations draw attention without demanding it (unlike flashing, which demands attention). Larger, faster animations draw more attention than smaller, slower ones.

- **Notifications.** A UI (supported by many platforms) that shows timely, important events unrelated to the current activity and that are useful and relevant, but not critical—*without* breaking users' flow. The top question designers have about notifications: "How can I make sure users see my notification?" The answer: "You can't—the fact that users can ignore them is their entire point!"

- **Modal dialog boxes.** Modal dialog boxes interrupt users and force them to respond before they can continue. This makes modal dialogs a good choice for information users must see (and a poor choice for everything else).

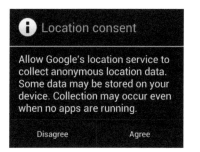

FIGURE 3.73
Modal dialog boxes are a good choice for information users must see, but they're not so good for other stuff.

- **Flashing.** Flashing demands attention, especially when it's rapid. A slow pulsing makes an object noticeable without demanding immediate attention. Rapid flashing is best reserved for only the most urgent problems (which should rarely occur).

FIGURE 3.74
If you end a call by pressing the Sleep button instead of the End button, the iPhone will flash the End button to confirm your intention.

- **Beeping and alarms.** Beeping and alarms definitely demand people's attention, especially when they're loud. They make it hard to do anything else. These are best reserved for only the most urgent, critical problems—like preventing a disaster.

Although flashing and beeping are the most obtrusive and annoying, they aren't always effective in getting people to act. People are very motivated to get the annoyance to stop, but they won't necessarily make an effort to address any underlying problems.

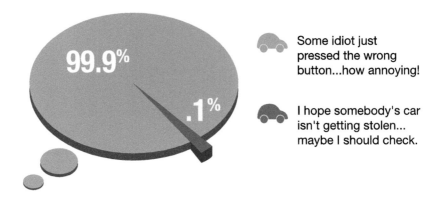

FIGURE 3.75

When was the last time you looked for vandals when a car alarm went off? Your only goal is to get the noise to stop.

Abuse and habituation

All the previous techniques can be abused if overused or if the attention they draw is undeserved. For example, just about anything you can do with a computer has the potential for going badly, but using warning icons for every potential problem accomplishes nothing but makes your product feel hazard-prone.

Communicates poorly

FIGURE 3.76

Overwarning accomplishes nothing except making your product feel hazard prone ... and designed by a lawyer.

> **Worse, if users perceive any these attention-getting techniques as normal, they just start to filter them out.** Your effort to demand attention just becomes a routine extra step.

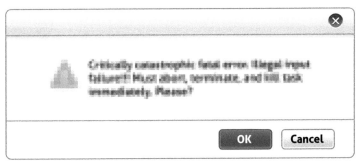

FIGURE 3.77
Have you seen this dialog box lately?

Recommendations

Here are some ways to get attention when needed, without overdoing it:

- **Think about what you would do in person.** Would you interrupt someone immersed in their work to report this issue? If so, how would you do it? Make sure the issue is worthy of the interruption.

FIGURE 3.78
Do you really need to ask? Not worthy of the interruption.

- **Use the least obtrusive attention-getting technique that does the job.** This means using different techniques instead of a single favorite one. Often, doing nothing special is that least obtrusive technique.

- **Make sure that the need to demand attention is rare.** If a feature constantly needs the user's immediate attention, redesign the feature.

- **Use progressive escalation.** If an issue gets progressively worse, start unobtrusively but become more obtrusive as the situation warrants.

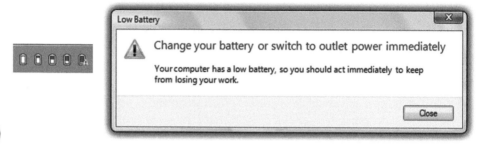

Communicates well

FIGURE 3.79

The Windows low-battery indicator becomes progressively obtrusive as power gets low.

If an interruption would be inappropriate in person, it is equally inappropriate for your product.

SUMMARY

If you remember only 12 things:

1. **UI form follows communication.** At the wireframe level, every visual design element should be justified by what it communicates. If a UI element doesn't communicate anything, it should be removed. If it communicates poorly, it should be redesigned. Through the lens of communication, many visual design decisions that initially appear subjective, emotional, arbitrary, and aesthetic are actually objective, rational, coordinated, and principled.

2. **People are emotional and react emotionally to a product's visual appearance.** Your product should look the part—it should look like it fulfills its purpose well. But if instead your product's visual appearance is of questionable quality, users will naturally assume that the rest of the product has the same level of quality. Don't assume that users will see the beauty that lies beneath; they won't.

3. **If you want a beautiful product, hire a professional graphic designer** … even if you are on a tight budget. It's money well spent.

4. **A page's layout communicates the purpose of the page, how to scan and read the page, and the order in which to use the page elements.** Additionally, a well-designed layout appears simple, orderly, easy to scan, efficient, and aesthetically pleasing.

5. **In designing a page's presentation, think about how you would present the content in person.** Unless you would present the content as a continuous monologue that covers everything without interruption, choose a presentation model that lets users drive the conversation.

6. **Generally, users don't read, they scan—where the goal of scanning is to find things quickly.** Scanning is so important that you should design pages specifically for scanning. On large displays, users scan a page by starting at the focal point (usually in the upper-left corner), scanning across the page with a left-to-right, top-to-bottom arc, checking UI elements that attract users' attention along the way, ignoring UI elements that repulse their attention, and ending in the lower-right corner.

7. **Well-presented text is beautiful, with attractive, easy-to-read typography, a clear visual hierarchy, and concise text.** It's always a safe choice to use the appropriate system font for your platform. Use color, shade, attributes, and capitalization to help users understand the text. If you want to make sure all users can read your text easily, use dark text on a solid light background.

8. **When choosing color, consider what the UI element communicates and choose a color that communicates the meaning at a glance.** The interpretation of color is culturally dependent, but the meaning of red, yellow, and green as status indicators is globally consistent. Also, color has a human perception (warm versus cool, neutral versus aggressive) that is independent of cultural interpretation. For accessibility, never use color as the only method of communication.

9. **Not everything needs an affordance.** Affordances are the visual properties of a UI element that indicate how to perform an interaction, and the consistent use of affordances is essential to having an intuitive UI. But affordances potentially add visual clutter, so make sure they are worth it. Do this by always displaying unobvious primary affordances and displaying secondary affordances dynamically.

10. **Choose (and design) icons based on what they communicate.** Standard icons communicate their meaning well, but nonstandard icons are primarily for visual recognition. For good visual recognition, make sure your icons are visually distinct in terms of design, shape, and color. Standard icons don't require labeling, but all other icons should be labeled to avoid the need for experimentation to figure them out.

11. **Effective animations and transitions communicate what is happening visually.** Use animations to give feedback, show relationships, draw attention to important change, or explain tasks visually. Use transitions to keep users oriented during a state change, and make those changes feel smooth and natural instead of jarring. To ensure effective communication, define an animation and transition vocabulary and apply it consistently across your product.

12. **Sometimes you need to break the user's flow and demand their full attention.** If you do, use the least obtrusive attention-getting technique that does the job. To avoid habituation, make sure that the need to demand users' attention is rare.

All the good examples in this chapter have something in common: They use visual design to communicate effectively. Even though aesthetics are important, effective communication should drive most visual design decisions.

EXERCISES

To improve your visual design skills, try the following exercises. *Assume that anything is possible. Don't let concerns about development costs or current technology limitations inhibit your thinking.*

1. **Design is the product.** Make a list of all the high-quality products that you enjoy using that have a poor visual appearance. How long is that list? What does that tell you?

2. **Visual communication.** Find or create a wireframe design for a UI. Pass through the wireframe and evaluate each element based on what it communicates. Remove any elements that don't communicate anything. Redesign any elements that don't communicate well. Better?

3. **Using conversation patterns.** Find a UI that contains a significant amount of information. Think about how you would present this information to the target user in person. Choose a presentation pattern that mirrors that conversation and redesign the page to use it. Better?

4. **Designing for scanning.** Take a printout of a UI, apply the scanning rules to determine what users will see, and highlight those elements. Now read the page in a left-to-right, top-to-bottom order, reading only the highlighted elements. Is it still clear what to do? Does your own scanning behavior match the scanning rules? For example, do any banners attract or repulse your attention?

5. **Using good text presentation.** Find some pages that don't present text well. Identify the specific problems with the text, including fonts, colors, backgrounds, and attributes. Now redesign the page to address these problems. Better?

6. **Using color for communication.** Find some pages that make poor use of color. Make black-and-white photocopies, and restore the color only when needed to communicate status or draw needed attention. Better?

7. **Using affordances effectively.** Review several products for their use of affordances. Can you find any affordances that are used incorrectly based on their interaction and effect? Are there any that result in unnecessary visual clutter? Can you reduce the clutter by displaying secondary affordances dynamically?

8. **Using icons for communication.** Find a product that makes heavy use of icons. Evaluate its icons based on what they communicate (removing any text labels or tooltips). Do all the icons communicate equally well? Can you improve the icons that communicate poorly? Should text labels be used? What would happen to the design if these icons were removed or replaced with text labels?

9. **Using transitions.** Find a product that uses transitions extensively and document its transition vocabulary. Are the transitions meaningful? Are they used consistently? How could they be improved?

10. **Demanding attention.** Find a product that uses several different attention-getting techniques. Is the user's attention really required? Are the techniques used appropriately? Could less obtrusive techniques be used instead?

Communicating to People

4

"If we want users to like our software, we should design it to behave like a likeable person."

—*ALAN COOPER*

"Designing an interface to be usable is like a chef creating edible food."

—*AARON WALTER*

If our user interfaces were designed to communicate with robots—robots whose only requirement is mechanical usability—we would be largely done at this point. But our target users aren't robots. Our UIs are designed to communicate with humans—emotional humans who have incomplete knowledge, who constantly make small mistakes, who want to feel productive and don't like wasting time, who want to be treated with respect, and who want to enjoy what they are doing and don't want to be bored. These emotional humans want our UIs to be worth the trouble to learn and use and to feel confident when they're using them.

Traditionally UI design focuses on completing tasks mechanically, where the UI boils down to performing individual transactions through features. The UI presents some set of inputs, users perform some actions, then the UI responds with some output. The user's goals are presumed to be achieved on the first try, after which the user immediately moves on to the next task. Lather, rinse, repeat until done.

If enough users can perform the tasks in a reasonable amount of time, the UI is declared *usable.* **But at the human level, being merely usable is a rather low bar.** As Aaron Walter describes, it's like eating food that is merely edible. If you have ever screamed in frustration while doing a simple task with a "usable" product (a common occurrence for me), you know exactly how low that bar is.

Great UI design transcends mechanical usability by recognizing that there is an emotional, impatient, error-prone human at the other end of the interaction, so well-designed interfaces strive to make a personal connection. We need higher expectations than

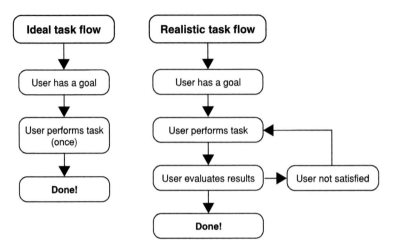

FIGURE 4.1

Users rarely perform complex tasks perfectly on the first try, yet complex tasks are usually designed with that ideal task flow.

mechanical usability. Aaron illustrated this well by remapping *Maslow's hierarchy of needs* to a hierarchy of user-experience needs. To this idea I have taken the liberty of adding a bit more detail in Figure 4.2. As Aaron points out, the pleasurable top of the pyramid is often missing, and users generally take useful and usable for granted—as they should.

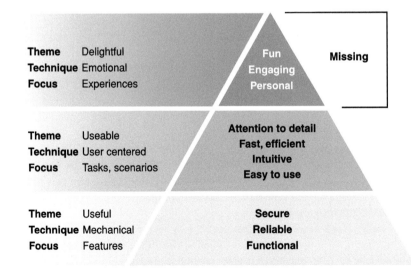

FIGURE 4.2

Maslow's hierarchy of needs remapped to user-experience needs; gives a new meaning to "missing the point."

The goal of this chapter is to explore the human side of human/computer interaction. Most of the topics presented here have a clear communication angle, but for some the relationship to communication is less obvious. But in all cases the topics go beyond mechanical usability and address how tasks are communicated on a human level.

THE IMPORTANCE OF MAKING AN EMOTIONAL CONNECTION

Great modern user experiences go beyond usability—they are so engaging that people *want* to use them and develop an emotional attachment to them. Consider two competing products. Suppose both products fulfill their purpose equally well *mechanically*, but the first product is unattractive, has no recognizable personality and feels technical and unengaging, whereas the second product presents itself in a way that is beautiful, engaging, and delightful. Which product would you prefer to use? That's not a hard decision—in most circumstances, the beautiful, engaging product wins.

Just because users can perform tasks mechanically doesn't mean they will. And it doesn't mean that they will like it. If your product solves real problems, has a simple, intuitive interaction and an appealing, easy-to-read visual design, yet people aren't using it, chances are your product is failing to communicate at a human level.

When Steve Jobs introduced the first Macintosh in 1984, half the story was a self-contained, high-tech, low-cost graphical user interface (GUI)-based computer. The other half was that the Mac had a personality. Its personality is what made the most impact and is the part that has endured long after the original technology became obsolete.

FIGURE 4.3
Hello, I am Macintosh. It sure is great to get out of that bag!

We must have the same standards for software interaction as we do for social interaction. If an interaction wouldn't be acceptable between people, we shouldn't expect users to accept it with software. For all the talk about user-centered design, the truly human side of design is often ignored. Thinking about UI design as human communication forces that consideration.

HAVING A PERSONALITY

Personality **refers to the characteristics of a product that connect emotionally with users.** All software has a personality—whether intentional or not—so it is better to have a personality that is carefully designed than one that is accidental.

What we see　　　　　　　　　**What users see**

FIGURE 4.4

What we see in our software isn't what our users see. We see the technical challenges required to get the project done. Users don't see any of that, but they do see its personality—which we don't see at all.

Personality is not a minor detail. Think about a recent experience, whether real world or with technology, that you really enjoyed. Why was that? Now think about a recent experience that you strongly disliked. Why was that? Consider the difference between the two.

Although it is possible that this difference was your mechanical ability to get tasks done, it is more likely that the difference was your emotional reaction to your experience. As users, we react emotionally to:

- Wasting time

- Rudeness and inconsiderate behavior

- Arrogance

- Stupidity

- Lack of attention to detail

We react badly to such experiences in real life, but we tend to lower our expectations when we're dealing with technology. We shouldn't. With technology, we are often thrilled if it just works the way we expect.

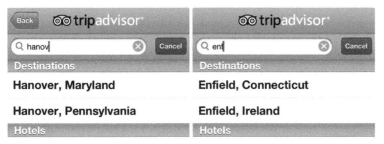

FIGURE 4.5
These would be good guesses if I did this search anywhere other than Hanover and Enfield, New Hampshire. We shouldn't lower our expectations when we're dealing with technology.

Designed for robots

We rationalize rude, arrogant, unintelligent behavior from technology because we know that technology isn't human. But we recognize that technology is crafted by humans, so we often transfer our feelings about an experience to the organization that designed the technology. If the experience is poor, we think "Those idiots! What were they thinking when they designed this?" If the technology's tone is cold and impersonal, we think that the organization that created it is also cold and impersonal. Whether good or bad, a user experience says a lot about the organization that designed it. The best user experiences feel like they were designed by intelligent, thoughtful, caring, respectful people.

FIGURE 4.6
In *2001: A Space Odyssey*, the HAL 9000 computer was more human than the depersonalized crew.

Anthropomorphism **gives human characteristics or behaviors to objects that are not human. To have a personality, it isn't necessary and often isn't appropriate to present software as a person.** In fact, doing so is off-putting in some contexts and cultures. There are many modern products that have a human personality.

Goshdarnit!

Something has gone wrong with our servers. It's probably Matt's fault.

We've just been notified of the problem.

Hopefully this should be fixed ASAP, so kindly reload in a minute and things should be back to normal.

Communicates well

FIGURE 4.7

A casual, friendly personality works great for casual applications …

But this approach is risky in more formal environments where there are significant consequences, such as physical well-being, destruction, or personal loss.

Communicates poorly

FIGURE 4.8

… but not for products that have significant consequences.

All software has a personality—whether intentional or not—so it is better to have a personality that is carefully designed than one that is accidental.

PERSONALITY ATTRIBUTES

Since personality refers to the characteristics of a product that connect emotionally with users, it's not surprising that software personality characteristics mirror those of human personality. Here are some common personality attributes:

- Human (versus robotic, mechanical, technical, unemotional)
- Friendly (versus impersonal, aloof, hostile)
- Professional (versus casual, overly familiar)
- Respectful and polite (versus rude, disrespectful)
- Humble (versus arrogant, condescending)
- Sincere, genuine, honest (versus patronizing, fake)
- Encouraging (versus discouraging, negative, harsh)
- Relaxing (versus stressful, hazard prone)
- Flexible, adaptive (versus stiff, unforgiving, bureaucratic)
- Fun (versus boring, dull, pedantic)
- Humorous (versus dry, factual)
- Concise (versus chatty, verbose, curt)

   A simple way to design a software personality is to define a short list of desirable attributes and make sure that your design decisions are consistent with them. Those personality attributes should be appropriate for your product and its target users. For example, a Web-based photo sharing app targeting young users might be friendly, casual, fun, and humorous. By contrast, an emergency room triage app should be professional, respectful, concise, and sincere.

   A great way to communicate a product or feature personality is through its name. Although there is nothing wrong with choosing a name that reflects its technical functionality, modern software names often reflect personality and attitude.

FIGURE 4.9
Apple's OS X Time Machine feature name and icon suggests its purpose without getting technical. By contrast, Microsoft Windows' Shadow Copy feature has the personality of … a property page.

HAVING A GOOD TONE

Tone **is the attitude a UI conveys to users.** Tone is an important personality attribute and is conveyed through the use of language, text presentation, and icons. Here are some tones that you might see in software:

- **Friendly tone.** Feels like users are having a casual conversation with a friend.

- **Professional tone.** Feels like users are having a business conversation with a colleague at work.

- **Encouraging tone.** Feels encouraging, positive, and goal focused, inspiring users' confidence.

- **Robotic tone.** Feels like users are having an impersonal, mechanical conversation with a robot.

- **Corporate tone.** Feels like users are being told what to do by a powerful corporation.

- **Salesman tone.** Feels like users are being sold something, perhaps contrary to their best interests.

- **Law enforcement tone.** Feels like users are being interrogated with a barrage of intrusive questions and being forced to explain their questionable actions.

- **Lawyerly tone.** Feels like users are being asked to perform some legally significant act and acknowledging that they will bear all the responsibility if anything goes wrong.

- **Negative tone.** Feels like the software is obsessed with user mistakes and doing everything perfectly.

- **Arrogant, condescending tone.** Feels like the product is belittling non-expert users and makes them feel foolish for their mistakes—as though it's the user's fault that the UI is confusing and hard to use.

- **Boastful tone.** Feels like the software is bragging about its accomplishments—as though it wants praise from users for actually working correctly.

- **Flippant tone.** Feels like users aren't being taken seriously or being taken for granted.

Of these, **a combination of professional, friendly, and encouraging tone is a good choice because it is always appropriate.** The other tones are undesirable and even antisocial.

FIGURE 4.10
Some products have a negative, arrogant, condescending tone. You're welcome!

Do designers actually use these undesirable tones? All the time—usually unintentionally. You just have to look for them.

Review Order and Prepare for Checkout

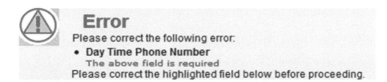

FIGURE 4.11
This error message has a law enforcement tone. The big red "Error" heading, the cultish-looking error icon, and the extreme overexplanation of a minor problem convey its tone. Saying "please" twice doesn't improve the tone but rather gives it a "good cop/bad cop" feel.

Designed for robots

To get the right tone, be careful with the words you use (and their connotations), the way you phrase sentences, and the way you present problems. If the text and tone reflect what you would actually say to the target user in person, it is probably the right tone. As the Google Android Design Guidelines recommend, "Pretend you're speaking to someone who's smart and competent, but doesn't know technical jargon and may not speak English very well." Great advice!

If a tone would be inappropriate in person, it is equally inappropriate for your product.

Speaking the user's language

Speaking the user's language is important not only because it is the language that your target users understand but because it is the best way to communicate on a human level. Here are some steps you can take to speak the user's language:

- **Define a *minimal* vocabulary list.** Make a list of terms that your target users routinely use in performing your app's tasks, eliminate any redundancy, and use that vocabulary consistently.

- **Remove *unnecessary* jargon.** Jargon exists for a reason—it is a specialized language for precise communication for a particular profession or field. Using jargon is fine as long as your target users routinely use it, but if they don't, use plain-language alternatives instead.

- **Avoid unnecessary abbreviations and acronyms.** A well-designed layout usually gives enough space to make most abbreviations and acronyms unnecessary, so spell these words out if you can.

- **Avoid unnecessary negative phrasing.** Use positive phrasing if it is more concise, natural, and encouraging. Negative phrasing has a discouraging tone and can be harder to understand.

- **Use clean data.** If your database is displayed in your UI, you need to make sure it is clear, natural, and easy to understand. Why say "1KNG 1BDRM EVO STE NSMK" when you can say "Evolution Suite with 1 King Bed (nonsmoking)"? Yes, you have the screen space to spell this out. Also, note how using abbreviations and all capital letters gives the data a very unfriendly, technical feel.

- **Refer to users as you would in person.** Address users as *you* and their objects with *your.* Use the active voice for user actions.

- **Use complete sentences.** Use sentence fragments only if you would in person. Use explicit verbs unless they go without saying (such as "view" and "go").

- **Be polite but not too polite.** Design your product to be polite, but be careful not to go too far. For example, say "Please" when users are inconvenienced or when its absence would be rude. The overuse of "please" sounds patronizing.

> If language would be inappropriate in person, it is equally inappropriate in your product.

MOTIVATING USERS BY PROVIDING OBVIOUS VALUE

Your product helps users perform some task, solve some problem, or achieve some goal. If your users *must* use your product, then of course they will. But if they *should* use your product, there is a strong possibility that they won't—unless your product delivers obvious value.

Providing clear value motivates people to use your product. Solving a problem isn't good enough. Users measure value by comparing a product's benefits relative to their cost—the cost of owning the product plus the time and effort required to use it. It's a classic design mistake to assume that all you need to do is solve a problem to have a successful design.

Your product should maximize value by maximizing its benefits while minimizing its costs. And your product should be designed to make its value obvious; don't assume that users are going to invest time and effort to figure it out on their own. If you have a great product that people aren't using, chances are the design isn't clearly communicating its value.

To address to benefit side of value, don't just allow users to perform tasks; encourage them to achieve their goals better than they could with the alternatives. For example, a mobile photo-sharing app must be designed to share photos quickly and easily while on the go, especially compared to the alternatives. If there's another solution that's quicker and easier to use, that's what users will use instead.

To address the cost side, design your product to eliminate any unnecessary effort (and the perception of effort) required to see the value—especially for first-time users. Does using your product require an account? Do users have to sign in to do anything? Do they have to perform some initial configuration to perform a task? Do they have to do a lot of typing or answer a lot of questions? Do they have to plan how they will use your product in advance? All this work requires a great deal of motivation. To deliver value, do everything you can to make such steps unnecessary.

Why My Company Lost to Mint

A number of people have asked and speculated about why the company I co-founded, Wesabe, shut down earlier this summer. I thought I'd add my own opinion.

Mint (our competitor) focused on making the user do almost no work at all, by automatically editing and categorizing their data, reducing the number of fields in their signup form, and **giving them immediate gratification** as soon as they possibly could. We completely sucked at all of that.

I was focused on trying to make the usability of editing data as easy and functional as it could be; Mint was focused on making it so you never had to do that at all. Their approach completely kicked our approach's ass. **It was far easier to have a good experience on Mint, and that good experience came far more quickly.**

Everything I've mentioned … are great, rational reasons to pursue what we pursued. **But none of them matter if the product is harder to use, since most people simply won't care enough** or get enough benefit from long-term features if a shorter-term alternative is available.

Focus on what really matters: making users happy with your product as quickly as you can, and helping them as much as you can after that. If you do those better than anyone else out there you'll win.

By Marc Hedlund

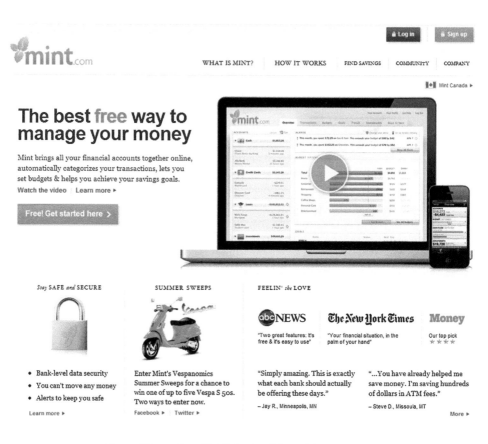

FIGURE 4.12

The Mint homepage is completely focused on communicating its value. It doesn't assume that users are going to take the time and effort to figure out Mint's value on their own.

> Great products clearly communicate their value.

MINIMIZING EFFORT

Well-designed UIs reduce the effort required to perform tasks, as well as the perception of effort. Robots don't care how much effort is required to perform a task, but people certainly do.

Assuming that users want to get a task done as quickly as possible (which, with the exception of games, you should always assume), of the two plans that follow, which approach do you think users would rather take?

Plan A:

1. Perform the task immediately (perhaps as a guest with default settings).

2. Optionally refine the results or save the work for later.

Plan B:

1. Register to create an account.

2. Sign in.

3. Configure a whole bunch of settings and account information.

4. Answer a whole bunch of questions about the task.

5. Specify how to display the results.

6. Tweak the UI to make it usable.

7. Perform the task.

Plan B is likely easier to program, but users would rather get right down to business with Plan A. Plan B has an inconsiderate personality that says the user's time doesn't matter. Instead, put results users want ahead of knobs, dials, and questions whenever you can.

Here are some techniques to reduce the effort (and perception of the effort) required to perform a task:

- **Remove any hurdles that get in the way of users satisfying their goals.** Don't require users to have an account or sign in to perform basic tasks.

FIGURE 4.13

Please don't make me do a CAPTCHA on my smartphone just to read a post. In my opinion, *CAPTCHA* stands for "Crappy Automated Public Turing test to Completely piss off HumAn users." Robots don't mind them but people do.

Designed for robots

- **Don't require users to set options before performing a task.** Better to have good defaults and delay any changes until users know what they want.

- **Start with the top task.** If there is a top task that users almost always do, just start there instead of making them choose it. For mobile apps, consider eliminating homepages and surface the most important info instead.

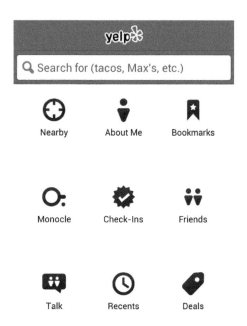

FIGURE 4.14

The Yelp app has a home screen, even though the top task ("help me find good places to go near me now") is by far the most likely action. The home screen is just an unnecessary step.

- **Don't require users to tweak the UI to make it usable.** Display objects with the right size and format so that they don't have to scroll, resize, sort, or the like to do the task.

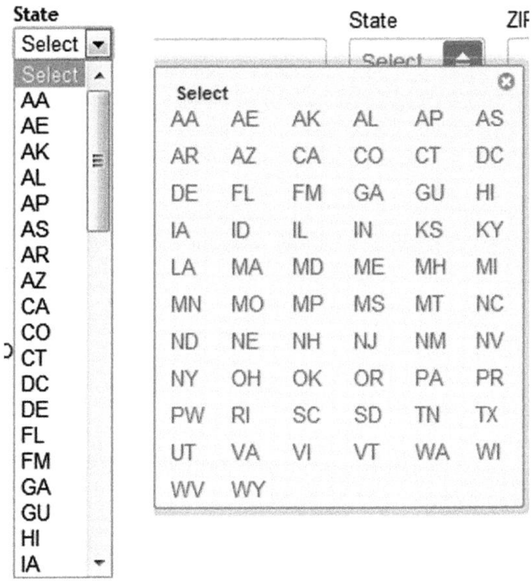

FIGURE 4.15
Users shouldn't have to scroll to select a state.

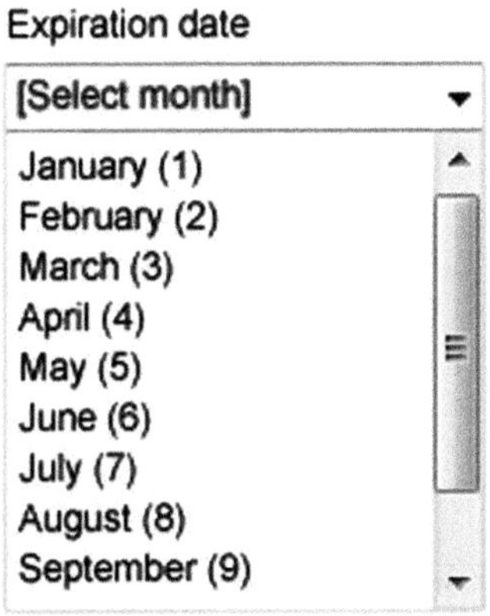

FIGURE 4.16
This list is short enough to eliminate the scrollbar by making it slightly longer.

- **Don't require users to save work.** If users might want to save their work, either save the work automatically or offer the option at the end instead of requiring the effort at the beginning.

- **Respect the user's privacy.** Don't ask for personal, sensitive, or complex information until users are about to make a commitment. Otherwise, let them explore freely.

Here is a simple test to determine if you are minimizing effort: Take any task that users are likely to repeat and perform it twice in a row. Ideally, the second try should have been a streamlined version of the first. If by contrast you had to repeat everything, redesign the task to eliminate unnecessary steps and input.

HAVING FORGIVENESS

Robots might perform tasks perfectly, but people make small interaction mistakes all the time. Users tend to blame themselves, ignore any design problems, and redo the interaction until they get it right. But what if the user's intent is clear and unambiguous? What if there is a simple design alternative that prevents the problem or makes it easy to fix? Must we force users to redo the work even when we know what they want?

Your product can be forgiving by:

- **Preventing the mistake.** Use constrained controls to restrict input to valid values. Use appropriately sized controls to prevent mistargets.

- **Doing the right thing anyway.** Recognize when the user's intent is clear and unambiguous and just do the right thing by default. Don't punish the user for not knowing the "correct" way.

- **Making problems easy to correct.** Provide users the ability to fix small interaction mistakes with minimal effort. Users shouldn't have to redo a task or reenter input.

Whenever you see users frequently make mistakes with your product, ask yourself whether the problem could be prevented or easily fixed with a better design.

With this is mind, I would like to propose *Everett's Law of Forgiving UI*:

For every UI that requires users to constantly correct small mistakes, there exists an alternative design that prevents the mistake, makes it easy to recover from the mistake, or does the right thing anyway.

Beyond supporting the obvious Undo/Redo commands, let's review some common minor interaction mistakes and what we can do about them.

Mistargeting

Users often miss their intended targets by a few pixels. You can prevent mistargeting by using controls of appropriate size. Different platforms have different sizing guidelines.

For example, Windows recommends a minimum control size of 16 × 16 pixels with a minimum of 7 pixels between controls, whereas Macintosh has standard regular, small, and mini control sizes with regular-sized controls recommended for most UI. Touch-based UI has larger minimum sizes that are based on the size of the typical finger. Research shows that touch targets of 9mm square or larger greatly improve touch accuracy, but translating this minimum physical size into points or pixels requires knowing the resolution of the display used.

Since arguably all modern UIs should be designed for touch, you should consider designing desktop UI for touch as well. iOS recommends using a 44 × 44 point layout grid for comfortable touch support, whereas Android recommends 48 × 48 points. Figure 4.17 shows a sizing approach that should work well for most platforms.

FIGURE 4.17
Minimum control sizes for accurate interaction.

You can also prevent mistargeting by providing a margin for error. One approach is to make click targets larger than they appear on screen.

Don't design like a programmer

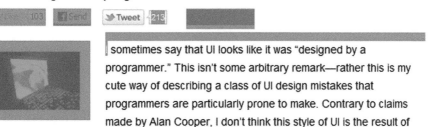

sometimes say that UI looks like it was "designed by a programmer." This isn't some arbitrary remark—rather this is my cute way of describing a class of UI design mistakes that programmers are particularly prone to make. Contrary to claims made by Alan Cooper, I don't think this style of UI is the result of

FIGURE 4.18
Selecting text in most browsers is a very mechanical and unforgiving process. One pixel too short and you have a partial selection. One pixel too many and you select the entire document.

Another approach is to put noninteractive space between objects that respond to similar direct manipulations.

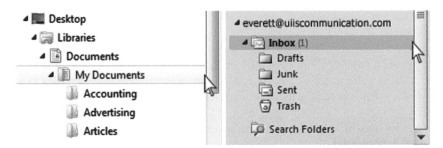

FIGURE 4.19
Windows Explorer and Microsoft Outlook have no margin for error between the folders and their scrollbars. If users are off by one pixel, they end up moving a folder instead of scrolling—usually without even realizing it.

You can reduce the consequences of mistargeting by keeping disruptive controls physically separate from other controls. A control is *disruptive* when accidentally clicking it results in lost work or having to start a task over.

FIGURE 4.20
The disruptive control (the End button) is physically separate from the keypad.

Finally, if you are designing custom controls, always provide a way to abandon a mistaken interaction before completion—usually by holding and releasing the control.

FIGURE 4.21

Standard controls always provide a way to abandon mistaken interactions before completion. Make sure your custom controls do, too. For example, moving the mouse off a control before releasing the mouse button abandons the click.

Performing (slightly) wrong interactions

Users often perform slightly wrong interactions. The following common interactions are often confused:

Single-click Select or invoke the object being clicked.

Double-click Select the object being clicked, then perform its default action.

Right-click Show an object's context menu.

Shift+click Extend a selection or display a link in another window.

There are similar problems with touch-based UI. For example, touch-based UIs often confuse flick gestures for scrolling with press gestures for selection.

Often these distinctions are important, and if users make a mistake, they must correct it. But what about situations in which the user's intention is clear and the distinction isn't important? For example, suppose an object isn't selectable (making double-click technically unnecessary), but the user double-clicks anyway? Should that double-click be interpreted as one single click or two—where the second is likely to undo the effect of the first? Should we do the right thing or must we teach those users a lesson? I vote for doing the right thing and performing one single click.

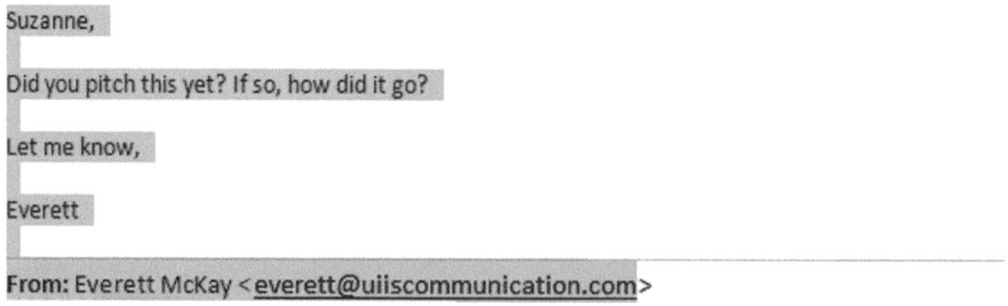

Suzanne,

Did you pitch this yet? If so, how did it go?

Let me know,

Everett

From: Everett McKay <everett@uiiscommunication.com>

FIGURE 4.22

In a browser, Shift+clicking a link means display the link target in another window. It could mean the same thing in Outlook, but since the Shift is technically unnecessary (because the link must be displayed in another window), Shift+clicking a link in Outlook "extends the selection" by selecting the entire document to the click point. This is never the user's intention.

Providing wrong data, typos

Users often enter wrong data, especially in unconstrained text boxes. Users might type the wrong word or make a typo. Does your product make users start completely over?

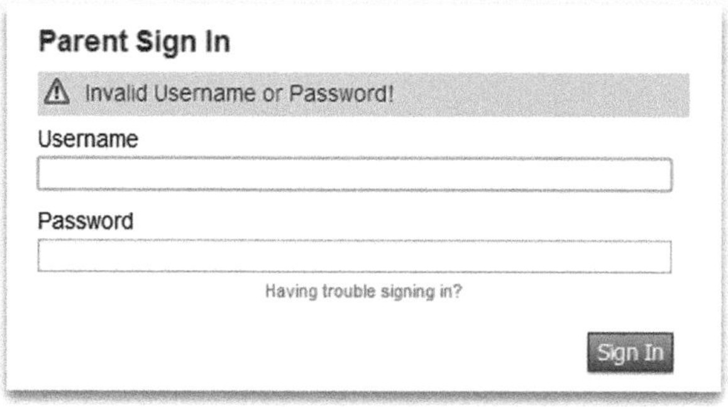

Parent Sign In

⚠ Invalid Username or Password!

Username

Password

Having trouble signing in?

Sign In

Designed for robots

FIGURE 4.23

I typed in the wrong password. For that, I get the pleasure of retyping my username, too.

Does your product return an error message or the most likely intended matches? For sites like Google and Amazon, returning an error message is leaving money on the table, so they boldly provide the closest matches without asking. After all, you can't sell things customers can't find.

FIGURE 4.24

Google automatically corrects simple typos. Returning an error message would frustrate users and leave money on the table.

FIGURE 4.25

Expedia points out that the arrival and departure cities aren't the same in case that wasn't the user's intention. This UI is designed for scanning and to avoid surprises.

Communicates well

Working in the "wrong" order

Many products are designed for users to perform steps in a strict sequence, even if that sequence isn't necessary or obvious. If users work out of sequence, the previous input might get reset. Should we provide flexibility or must we teach those users a lesson? I vote for providing flexibility and letting users work the way they prefer.

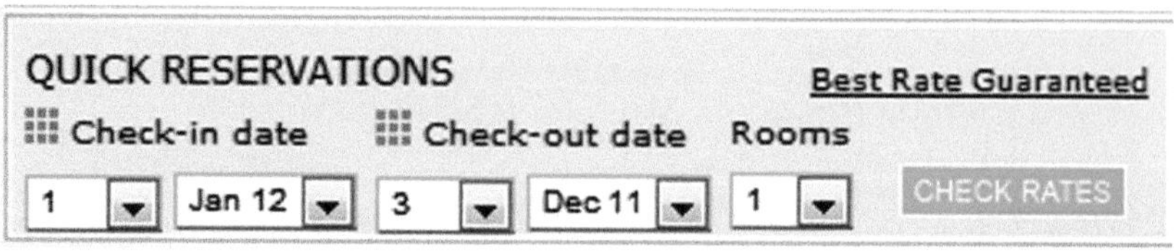

FIGURE 4.26

When making a reservation with this UI, the obvious steps are to provide a check-in day, then a check-in month. Wrong! Changing the month resets the day to 1, forcing users to reselect the day. Quick indeed!

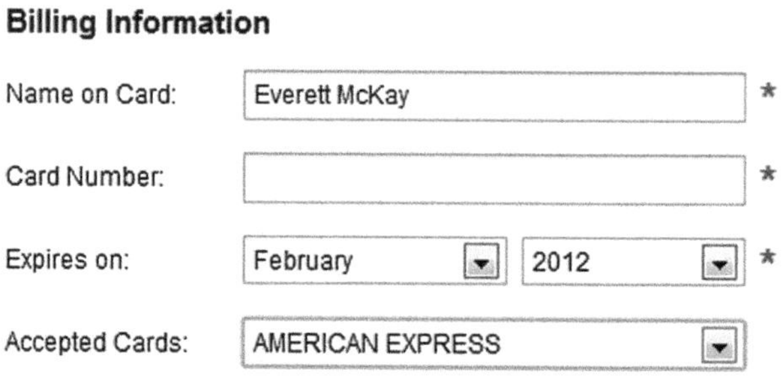

FIGURE 4.27

When making a reservation, I provided my credit card number, then selected the credit card type, as suggested by the control order. But selecting the credit card type (which is unnecessary based on the number) clears the number. How rude!

Not reading text carefully

As Steve Krug points out in *Don't Make Me Think!,* users don't read, they scan—yet UI text is often written to require careful, complete reading to avoid confusion. Here are some techniques to avoid user confusion with your UI if text isn't read carefully:

- **Make distinctions distinct.** If it is different, make it look different using both labeling and visual distinctions.

FIGURE 4.28

Users aren't likely to confuse ordering with pre-ordering on Amazon. Not only are the labels different, but their look is different as well.

- **Use self-explanatory, yet simple, concise labels.** Say enough to be self-explanatory, but remember that the longer the label, the more effort required to read and understand it.

 ✖ From a Setup Wizard screen　　　　✔ From a Setup Wizard screen

FIGURE 4.29

The better label is self-explanatory yet concise. (From Google's Android guidelines.)

- **Use explicit verbs.** A few verbs such as "view" and "go" go without saying, but most don't. Put the explicit verb near the beginning of the label.

- **Avoid nuanced phrasing.** Users shouldn't have to give it deep thought to understand the meaning of the label.

- **Avoid redundancy in related options.** For sets of related options, don't repeat the similarities. Put the most important information and any differences toward the beginning of the label.

- **Avoid negative phrasing, especially double negatives.** Users who are scanning are likely to miss those negatives and therefore completely misunderstand the label.

If you find that users are constantly misinterpreting your UI text, rewrite it! Adding a word or two for clarity can make a big difference.

FIGURE 4.30

Got it! Wait … what?

Accidentally choosing catastrophic actions

Catastrophic actions **are actions with significant, often irreversible results that are cata-strophic when unintended.** Catastrophic actions should be difficult to trigger, but all too often they are presented as an ordinary command like any other. Combine this misleading presentation with users' tendency to not read carefully and you have a hazard-prone experi-ence. In his book, *About Face*, Alan Cooper describes this as not hiding ejector-seat levers.

FIGURE 4.31
Apparently that wasn't the light switch.

One simple way to avoid catastrophic actions is to assume that users want to save their work and they should have to take some action *not* to do so. Classic UI takes the opposite approach, requiring users to save their work explicitly.

Another simple approach is to make catastrophic actions hard to do, either by asking for a confirmation or by making these actions hard to do accidentally.

FIGURE 4.32
The iPhone Calculator app hides the draconian All Clean (AC) button, revealing it when users tap Clear (C). This prevents accidents and saves a button in the process. Clever!

Make it easy to correct or undo the last interaction. Never make users reenter previously entered text. Never make users start completely over because of a small mistake. Most important, make catastrophic mistakes really hard to commit. Users should never lose anything by accident that isn't easily replaceable.

> Great design recognizes that users make small mistakes all the time.

BUILDING TRUSTWORTHINESS

Trust **is a relationship that is earned by consistently demonstrating competent, open, honest behavior so that people are willing to rely on or take risks with something or someone.** In a risk-free world, trust wouldn't matter much.

In the real world, trust is required because risks are everywhere. Users are constantly being asked to reveal their names, email addresses, physical addresses, personal information, financial information—even their current physical location. Financial and medical apps usually involve sensitive or private information. Search engine queries reveal a tremendous amount of personal information that could be abused in the wrong hands.

Beyond protecting sensitive information, trustworthiness requires basic competence. Purchasing products online requires users to trust that companies will ship the right product to the right location at the right time for the right price in the right physical condition. Even something as basic as an alarm clock app has no value if users can't depend on it to sound an alarm audibly at the appropriate time. Risks that require trust can be as small as wasting time or being disappointed.

As designers, we usually take users' trust for granted. We assume that users will trust that our product will do the job competently and satisfy their goals. We assume that users will provide personal information whenever we ask for it. But if we haven't earned their trust, why should they? If users aren't willing to depend on your product, chances are it is failing to earn their trust.

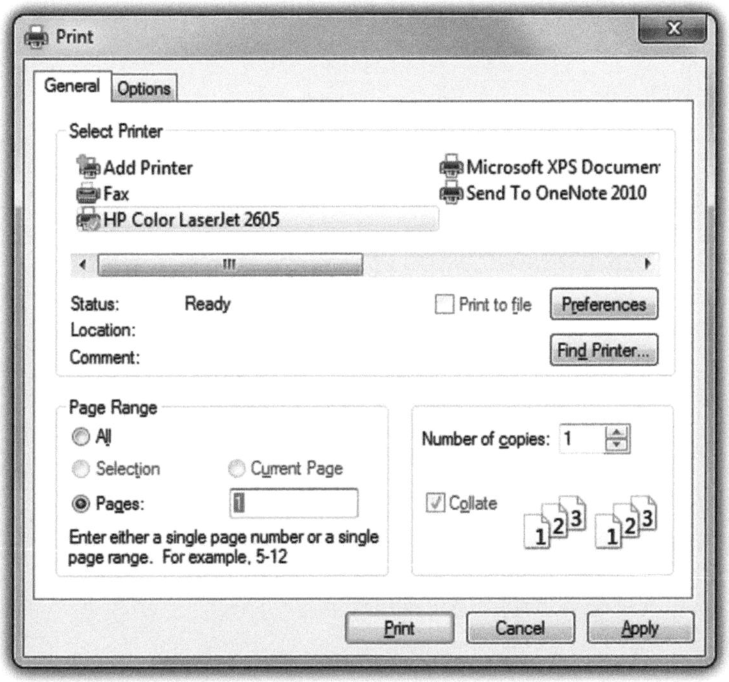

FIGURE 4.33

I don't use the Print Current Page option in Microsoft Windows, even though I frequently want to print only the current page. Why? Because I don't trust that Windows' assumption of the current page is the same as mine. This dialog box takes my trust for granted.

FIGURE 4.34

By contrast, I frequently use the Print Current Page option in Microsoft Office and Adobe Reader. Why? Because they earn my trust by showing me the current page. Making the effort to earn my trust makes all the difference.

Your product can earn the user's trust by:

- **Demonstrating competence.** Yes, your product can do the task, but is that obvious to users? In working with valuable assets (such as documents and photos), are they never lost, corrupted, or misplaced? When users view information, is it clearly accurate, credible, and timely? Explicitly setting accurate expectations and providing timely feedback are essential here.

Your Request Cannot Be Completed

What can you do?
Simply wait a moment or two then resubmit your booking request.

 **Start search over**

 Cancel and go to the home page.

FIGURE 4.35

Their mistake, but I pay the price. And when they say "start search over," they mean *completely* over.

- **... for the small things, too.** Developers tend to worry about the primary functionality but not too much about the details. But if simple tasks aren't done competently, why should users assume that the more challenging functionality will be done right?

FIGURE 4.36

I set an appointment to start at 1:00 P.M. and end at 2:00 P.M. Microsoft Outlook somehow concluded that my appointment ran for 25 hours. If my personal assistant did this, he or she would be looking for a new job.

- **Avoiding surprises.** If users are unpleasantly surprised by the results, your product isn't trustworthy, even if it does the job correctly in the technical sense. Common offenders are commitment points that aren't obvious, promising but not delivering special offers, and unreasonably high fees and shipping charges that are either hidden or revealed very late in the task.

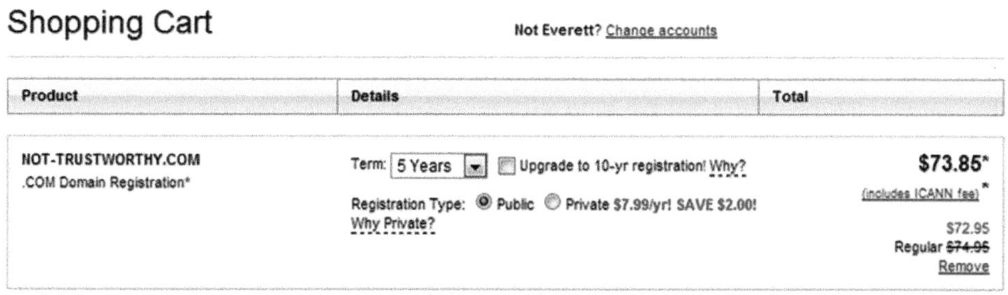

FIGURE 4.37

Go Daddy is offering a fantastic sale on one-year domain registrations on its homepage. You don't get that sale price by default but instead get a longer registration at the normal price. To get the sale price, you have to manually change the registration length back to one year, but that isn't made obvious here. Surprise!

- **Providing specific information.** Vague information or feedback doesn't build trust because users can't distinguish real problems from false alarms or routine mistakes. Does my account have insufficient funds? If so, tell me so that I don't try the task again. Is there a security risk? Tell me specifically what the risk is so that I can make an informed decision. Is there really a problem? Tell me what is specifically wrong so that I can fix or prevent it.

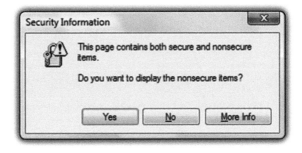

FIGURE 4.38

Do I need to display the nonsecure items? What is the specific security risk here? How can I possibly answer the question without knowing? But I am feeling lucky ...

- **Providing timely information.** Present information required to build the user's trust as soon as you can. Users who lack confidence might not see it later.

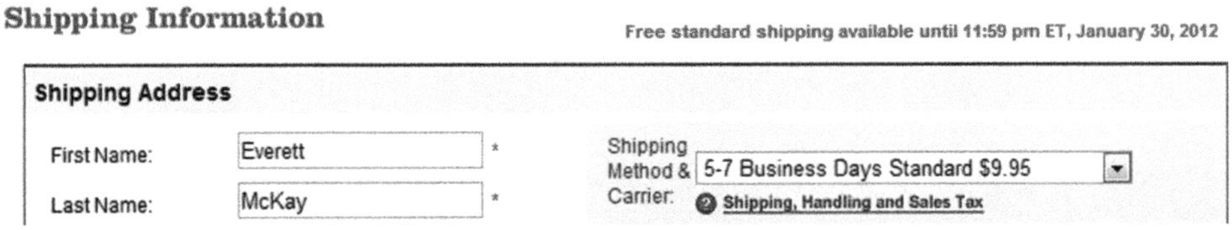

FIGURE 4.39

This site promises free standard shipping, so why can't I find that option here? Turns out that I will see it on the last step, but I might not get there.

- **Taking responsibility.** If your product performs tasks that involve risk, it shouldn't evade responsibility by asking a bunch of questions users can't answer.

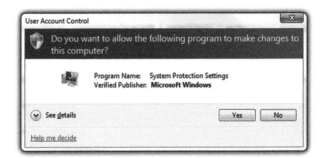

FIGURE 4.40
Umm ... where's the "I haven't a clue" button?

- **Putting the user's goals ahead of yours.** Are you offering options for your business goals and not the user's? If so, make their effect clear and disable them by default (that is, users must opt in rather than opt out). You won't earn trust by tricking users into accepting options they don't want.

FIGURE 4.41
These privacy options should be disabled by default.

- **Not requiring unnecessary sensitive information.** If sensitive information isn't clearly required to perform a task, make it optional. To improve conversion rates, consider explicitly labeling such info as optional to build users' confidence. If the need for information isn't obvious, explain why it's required.

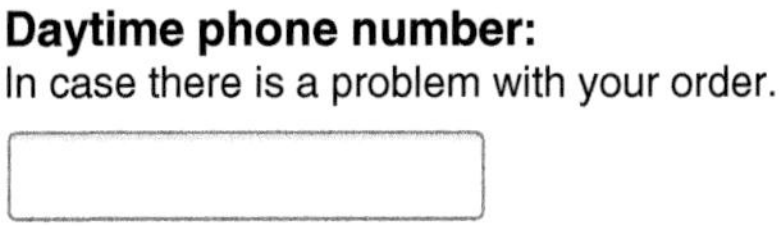

Daytime phone number:
In case there is a problem with your order.

FIGURE 4.42
This form explains the benefit of providing optional personal information.

- **Making it feel right emotionally.** Success should look like success. Failure should look like failure. Never the twain shall meet.

Designed for robots

FIGURE 4.43

This success sure feels like failure. This is the feedback you get if even a single file can't be backed up.

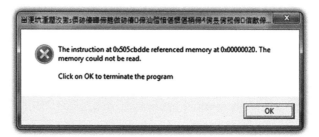

FIGURE 4.44

Hmmm ... I'm lacking confidence right now. Have I been hacked?

Earn the user's trust and do everything you can to keep it—even if it conflicts with your business goals. Once that trust is broken, it is very hard to earn back.

Go out of your way to earn the user's trust. Don't take it for granted.

BEING SMART WITHOUT LOOKING STUPID

Modern user interfaces are aware of what users are doing now, along with users' preferences and past behavior. Robots don't mind if they are interacting with something that lacks intelligence—they are used to that—but people certainly do. Consequently, modern UIs are better able to focus on what users are likely to want by presenting the right contextual commands, options, and defaults. Past performance really is the best indicator of future performance, so modern UI has a memory and takes advantage of it.

　Your product can appear intelligent by performing an appropriate combination of these qualities:

- **Paying attention to user input.** Keep track of previous user input and reuse it automatically as appropriate. The user should never have to reenter previous (nonsensitive) input to complete a task, even if the user changes options, goes back to a previous step, restarts the task, or the task times out. Don't reset anything unless you must.

FIGURE 4.45
My favorite hotel just offered me a special rate for my birthday. I entered my arrival and departure dates, plus the number of adults and children. Not liking the deal, I clicked Specials and tried another offer, again having to enter my arrival and departure dates, plus the number of adults and children. Not liking that deal either, I decided to make a regular reservation. Guess what they are asking me again.

- **Paying attention to user preferences.** The user's preferred way of working is always right, so your product should adapt to user preferences—not the other way around. Presenting tasks the way the code works and not being flexible is easier to implement, but that doesn't make it right.

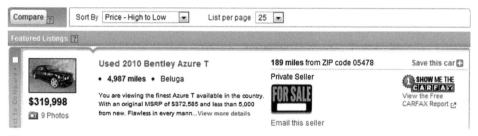

FIGURE 4.46

Nearly every time I save a PowerPoint deck to a .pdf file, I publish Handouts with six slides per page and frame the slides. You would never know that from the Options, which appear to prefer publishing Slides. PowerPoint likes having its way better than accommodating mine.

- **Understanding the target users and their goals.** Your product's behavior should make sense for its target users and their goals. Being unaware doesn't look very smart.

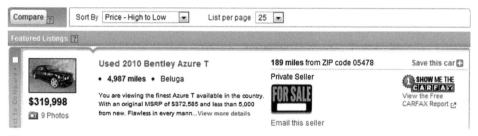

FIGURE 4.47

People buying cars usually want the lowest-priced car that meets their needs. So why does AutoTrader show search results starting with the highest price first by default? As if ...

- **Knowing what makes sense in the current context.** Taking full advantage of the current context is a great way to simplify a UI because you can eliminate actions and options that don't make sense. If an option is impossible now, why even offer it?

Designed for robots

FIGURE 4.48
I'm planning a trip for four months from now and the return date must be after the departure date. So why is the default return date today?

FIGURE 4.49
The iPhone keypad is optimized for the type of data being requested—in this case, Website addresses. Nice!

There are more advanced techniques to appear intelligent, such as applying heuristics and using data mining. **But keep in mind that you risk looking stupid if you try too hard to look intelligent—especially if you do so in a very visible way.**

FIGURE 4.50
Office Clippy tried way too hard to look intelligent—and failed, in a very visible way. No, I'm not writing a letter. Please don't ask again! OK/Cancel ©2005 Tom Chi and Kevin Cheng. Used by permission.

Set a high bar when trying to appear intelligent, and don't draw attention to your product's intelligence. The more attention you draw, the more embarrassing the mistakes. As Abraham Lincoln once said, "It is better to remain silent and be thought a fool than to speak and remove all doubt." Good advice.

> If a behavior would be stupid for a person to do, it is equally stupid for your product to do.

NOT BEING ANNOYING

Robots have no emotions, so they can't be annoyed. People, on the other hand, are easily annoyed. The techniques we already mentioned for being smart are a great start.
Here are some annoyances your UI should avoid:

- **Constantly demanding attention.** Products that constantly demand attention are annoying. They demand your attention by being in your face, drawing attention to themselves (flashing being the worst way), and constantly requiring maintenance and handholding. Any UIs that users routinely dismiss without performing any action should be reconsidered.

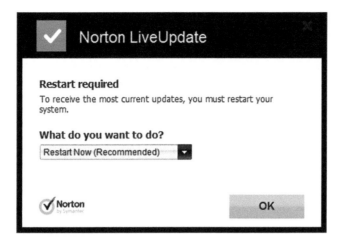

FIGURE 4.51
I have better things to do than restart my computer, and the constant reminders aren't helping.

- **Interrupting.** Products that interrupt users to ask unimportant questions or point out minor problems are annoying. Don't interrupt users and break their flow unless it is truly warranted. Don't ask users to confirm an action unless you can give a strong reason not to proceed.

FIGURE 4.52
Unnecessary confirmations are annoying ...

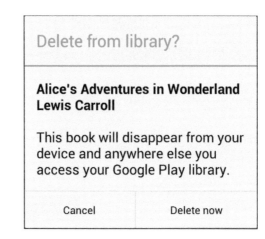

Communicates
well

FIGURE 4.53

... but necessary confirmations are acceptable.

- **Repeating.** Interrupting users once without good reason is annoying; repeating the same or similar interruptions is infuriating. Interrupt once—at most—unless the situation changes dramatically.

FIGURE 4.54

I didn't forget the reminder from an hour ago; no need to remind me again. And honestly, the message isn't that critical.

- **Not paying attention to user input, preferences, or context.** I mentioned these in the last section. Very annoying!

Many tasks are designed as though they were individual transactions that users perform perfectly on the first try. In reality, achieving users' goals might require research-based refinement involving many related transactions. For example, comparison shopping might involve finding and comparing several related products with minor variations. Requiring users to repeat all or most of the steps each time can be really frustrating.

> If a behavior would be annoying for a person to do, it is equally annoying for your product to do.

USING COURAGEOUS DESIGN

Suppose you have a question, and there's a 99 percent chance you know the answer but a 1 percent chance you don't. Do you ask anyway? Apparently many designers don't like those odds. For example, here I've told Expedia that I want to travel to Ontario, California. I think my request is pretty clear. (Note that CA is the U.S. Postal Service's abbreviation for California and that I performed this search in the United States.) So, is this question really necessary?

Please help us with a little more information

1 We found more than one airport that matched 'ontario, ca'. Please select an airport from the list below.

Going to:

○ Toronto, ON, Canada (YTO-All Airports)
○ Ottawa, ON, Canada (YOW-All Airports)
○ Fort Frances, ON, Canada (YAG-Fort Frances Municipal)
○ Hamilton, ON, Canada (YHM-John C. Munro Hamilton Intl.)
○ Kenora, ON, Canada (YQK-Kenora Airport)
○ Kingston, ON, Canada (YGK-Norman Rogers)
○ Kitchener, ON, Canada (YKF-Region of Waterloo Intl.)
○ London, ON, Canada (YXU-London Intl.)
○ North Bay, ON, Canada (YYB-Jack Garland)
○ Ontario, CA (ONT-Ontario Intl.)
See all results for 'ontario, ca'

FIGURE 4.55

Yes, there is such a thing as a stupid question. Fort Frances sounds like fun, though.

Designed for robots

If you were to tell someone in the United States that you wanted to travel to "Ontario, CA," and they asked if you really meant Fort Frances, Ontario, Canada, what would you think? Would you be impressed by their meticulousness?

Well-designed UIs have the courage to take *intelligent* risks to do the right thing without asking. When users' input is clear and unambiguous, you can't always be certain, but you can usually be right. The only reason to ask anyway is to avoid responsibility.

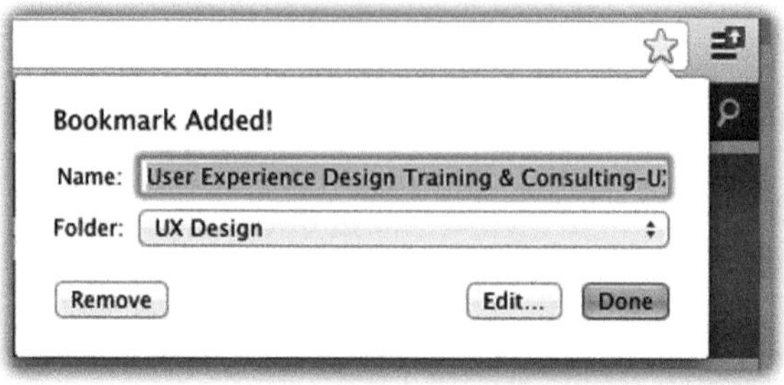

FIGURE 4.56

Google Chrome makes the courageous bet that I want to save this favorite in the same folder as the last one. If it wins the bet, I set the favorite in one click. If it loses, I set it in four—still fewer clicks than with other browsers. A winning bet either way.

> If a question would be stupid for a person to ask, it is equally stupid for your product to ask.

WHY BE DULL? MAKE IT FUN!

Any task has the potential to be engaging. Robots might not care if tasks are drudgery (in fact, robots tend to be really good at such tasks), but people want to be engaged by what they do and definitely don't want to be bored.

If you were to make a list of the most boring tasks you could think of, chances are many of them would involve using forms. Yet Wufoo, a Web service that enables you to create, manage, and use forms, is one of the most delightful apps I use regularly.

FIGURE 4.57

Why be dull? Even form building can be engaging. Note that this is a solid error message because it explains a specific problem and provides a solution. But unlike typical error messages, it isn't scolding and it doesn't draw attention to the user's mistake.

Communicates
well

Wufoo's fun personality and attitude are very much by design, as its lead designer Kevin Hale describes:

> The inspiration for our color palette did come from our competitors. It was really depressing to see so much software designed to remind people they're making databases in a windowless office and so we immediately knew we wanted to go in the opposite direction. My goal was to design Wufoo to feel like something Fisher-Price would make. We were determined to make sure Wufoo was fun.

Special experiences

Special experiences are opportunities for special user engagement, product differentiation, and branding. Although you might assume that special experiences are situations in which a product fulfills its purpose particularly well, in practice they are usually the opposite. That is, specific experiences tend to be those necessary evils required to use a product and that don't necessarily relate to fulfilling its primary purpose.

Here are common opportunities for special experiences:

- Startup, shutdown

- Signing in or out

- Adjusting or transitioning

- Waiting

- Problems, service unavailable

- Customer service

In these situations, users aren't yet fully productive or engaged with getting their work done. Rather, they are distracted by getting your product to work properly, making this an excellent time to engage users with special experiences that have a human touch. Why be dull?

FIGURE 4.58

This page communicate in a playful way that Twitter is over capacity.

Communicates
well

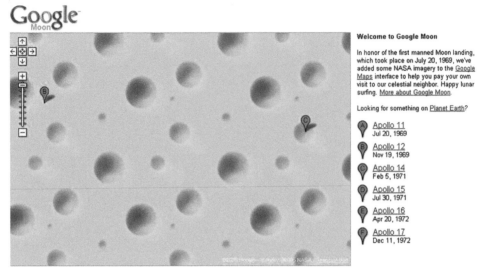

Communicates
well

FIGURE 4.59

If you zoom too far into Google Moon, you discover that it really is made of Swiss cheese. They could have used a routine error message (to avoid confusing astronauts), but why be dull?

Why be dull? Make using your product enjoyable and engaging!

SUMMARY

If you remember only 10 things:

1. **Users are humans, not robots. Humans are emotional.** They want to enjoy what they are doing. They make small mistakes all the time. They are focused on their work and are easily distracted. Your product should communicate to users at a human level, so it's not just what you say but how you say it. Good software interaction should have the same standards as good social interaction.

2. **Mechanically enabling tasks is only the first step in great design, not the last.** Great UI design transcends mechanical usability by recognizing that there is an emotional, error-prone human at the other end of the interaction. We need higher expectations than mechanical usability.

3. **Give your product a likeable personality to make an emotional connection with users.** All software has a personality, so it is better to have a personality that is carefully designed than one that is accidental. You can design a personality by defining a short list of desirable attributes, being consistent in using them, and choosing a name to match.

4. **Motivate people to use your product by providing obvious value.** Maximize its benefits and reduce its costs compared to the alternatives. Don't assume that your product's value is obvious just because it solves some problem. Remove any hurdles that get in the way of users finding your product's value. Don't assume that users will invest a lot of time and effort to find it.

5. **People make mistakes all the time, so design your product to prevent mistakes, do the right thing anyway, or make mistakes easy to correct.** Never make users reenter text or start completely over. Make catastrophic mistakes really hard to do. If you find a common interaction mistake, look for simple design alternatives that prevent the problem or make it easy to fix.

6. **Earn the user's trust** by consistently demonstrating competence, avoiding surprises, providing specific information, taking responsibility, and putting the user's goals ahead of your business goals. Once that trust is broken, it is very hard to earn back.

7. **Make your product intelligent** by understanding the target users and their goals, paying attention to user input and preferences, and taking advantage of the current context. But have a high bar for intelligence, and don't draw attention to your product's intelligence.

8. **Avoid your product being annoying** by making it appear intelligent, and not demanding attention, interrupting users, or repeating itself.

9. **Show design courage** by doing the right thing without asking based on the information you have rather than playing it safe and asking every possible question.

10. **Be engaging and fun!** Any task has the potential to be engaging, so engage users whenever appropriate. Special experiences are excellent opportunities to engage users because they are usually points of low productivity when users aren't getting their work done. Why be dull?

All the good examples in this chapter have something in common: They feel like natural, friendly conversations between people. By contrast, the bad examples often feel like mindless, mechanical interactions between robots. If your user interface feels professional yet friendly and reflects what you would actually say in person to the target user, the design is probably good.

EXERCISES

To improve your ability to design UIs that communicate on a human level, try the following exercises. *Assume that anything is possible. Don't let concerns about development costs or current technology limitations inhibit your thinking.*

1. **People are motivated by value.** Can you think of a product that solved a real problem and that appeared well designed, yet you didn't end up using it as expected? Can you explain why?

2. **People are emotional.** Can you think of a time when you yelled or screamed at a product while using it? What specifically made you scream and yell?

3. **Software is crafted by humans.** Can you think of a time when you had a low opinion of a company or its employees because of the way its products are designed? What was the specific design problem? What did you think about the product's designers?

4. **Having a good personality.** Find a product that has a good personality. Characterize its personality in human terms and find the specific design elements that reinforce that personality. Would you feel differently about the product if it didn't have that personality?

5. **Avoiding a poor personality.** Find a product that has a poor personality. Characterize its personality in human terms and find the specific design elements that reinforce that personality. Redesign three aspects of the product to improve its personality.

6. **Having a good tone.** Write an error message for a situation in which the user removes a storage device while it is being formatted. How is the tone? Does it match what you would say in person? Does it make sense from the user's point of view?

7. **Preventing small mistakes.** Find a product that you often use on a daily basis. While performing several typical tasks, monitor *every* mistake that you make, no matter now small (have a friend record your mistakes if necessary). When you're done, analyze your mistakes for the type and cause. Was the UI confusing? Was your intention clear and unambiguous? Are there alternative designs that could have prevented the mistakes?

8. **Having intelligence.** Find a product that lacks intelligence. Review the list of UI elements that improve intelligence and use them to redesign a product. Can you think of ways in which trying to appear intelligent might appear unintelligent?

9. **Building trust and confidence.** Can you think of a time when you didn't complete a task because you didn't trust the product or lacked confidence that it would do what you wanted? What did you do instead? Can you think of design alternatives that would fix the problem?

10. **Avoiding being rude.** Find a product that has rude error messages. Redesign the error messages to address the problem without the rudeness.

A Communication-Driven Design Process

5

Getting the right design and the design right.

—BILL BUXTON

The Marshmallow Challenge is design exercise that encourages teams to experience simple but profound lessons in collaboration, innovation, and creativity. The task is simple: In 18 minutes, teams must build the tallest freestanding structure out of 20 sticks of spaghetti, one yard of tape, one yard of string, and one marshmallow. The marshmallow needs to be on top.

FIGURE 5.1
The Marshmallow Challenge.

There are surprising trends in team performance. Teams consisting of MBA graduates tend to perform poorly. They are trained to analyze the problem, identify the best solution, assign roles and responsibilities, develop a plan, execute the plan ... then realize it's wrong and run out of time.

But teams of kindergarteners tend to perform surprisingly well. They dispense with politics and planning and get right down to business by trying out ideas. They quickly learn what works through trial and error and find creative solutions to improve their designs.

There are several important takeaways here:

- Effective collaboration, innovation, flexibility, and creativity are keys to success.

- Quick trial and error leads to rapid innovation.

- Careful planning doesn't work well if you don't know what you are doing and don't have a lot of time.

But before we draw any more conclusions, let's take a step back and think about the nature of the Marshmallow Challenge for the typical participant:

- Time is extremely short; speed is critical.

- The resulting product is unlike any product team participants have used before, making their past experience irrelevant.

- The challenge is unlike any design problem team participants have done before, potentially making careful planning counterproductive.

- The challenge is modest; the teams are small, focused, and in the same physical location; there is no need to coordinate or integrate with anything or anybody outside the team.

- The resulting product doesn't have to be useful to anyone. There are no target users, no important user goals or scenarios, no design principles or guidelines to follow, no customer training or support to worry about, and no customer expectations. Nobody has to like it or want to use it. A successful design just has to be tall and freestanding.

- Failure has no significant financial or career penalty. You won't lose customers or market opportunities, nor will you harm your company or product's reputation or brand. Nobody's bonus is on the line. Crazy is good—as long as it is tall and freestanding.

- All the competition has to follow exactly the same rules. No exceptions.

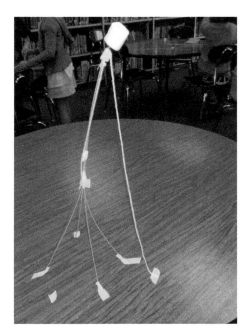

FIGURE 5.2
What was the user scenario again?

Although some user interface design problems are similar to the Marshmallow
Challenge, most are not. It would be a mistake to conclude that careful planning and
design are generally counterproductive. My top takeaways from the Marshmallow Challenge
are that there is no single best design process and that you must recognize and adapt to
the situation at hand.

A COMMUNICATION-DRIVEN DESIGN PROCESS

Imagine having a UI design perspective where you could consistently leverage past
experience. Design is iterative and the first efforts are never right, but what if you could
make them close to right—or at least closer than you usually do?

UI design is very similar to golf in this respect. In golf, every hole and every lie is
different, every hole requires iteration, and getting a hole-in-one is never a realistic
expectation. To play well, you need to keep the ball on the fairway consistently and on
the green instead of whacking it into the weeds. Although you can learn from your
mistakes, there are other ways to learn that are less haphazard, less risky, and less time
consuming.

FIGURE 5.3
Golf is also an iterative process, but hitting the ball into the weeds isn't considered a beneficial learning experience.

I believe that effective human communication is that design perspective. A user interface is essentially a conversation between users and a product to perform tasks that achieve users' goals—except that it uses the language of UI instead of natural language. If we focus the UI design process on effective communication, we can leverage our understanding of the target users, their goals, their tasks, and the way the UI needs to communicate to users on a human level.

At the highest level, a communication-driven design process looks like this:

1. Determine a solid product concept that provides clear value.

2. Understand the target users, their goals, tasks, and problems.

3. Determine the top scenarios that achieve those goals, and let them drive most design decisions.

4. Design task flows and pages that communicate effectively, for both interaction and visual design.

5. Get the other details right.

6. Evaluate, test with real users, and iterate until you have achieved your design objectives.

This communication-driven approach allows you to leverage everyday interpersonal communication skills that you have been practicing all your life. If you can explain how to perform a task in person in a way that's clear and concise, this process will help you map that explanation into the language of UI—both in terms of interaction and visual design—in a way that feels simple, natural, easy to understand, and humane. The outcome of this approach is naturally user and user-goal centered.

Although there is no single best design process, a communication-driven approach works well for most situations and removes much of the mystery and subjectivity.

Yes, collaboration, innovation, flexibility, and creativity are very important, but you no longer have to resort to trial and error to drive the process. Let's save trial and error for those innovative situations in which we really do need it. Routine tasks like having users fill in a form to buy a product online don't require innovation—they require basic competence.

The goal of this chapter is to present a communication-driven design process. Covering the entire UX design process in complete detail is a subject worthy of its own book (Kim Goodwin wrote that book—it's called *Designing for the Digital Age*), so I will only outline the process but will focus on the details that are communication related. In the next chapter, we will apply this process to some real design problems.

Another important goal for this chapter is to discourage what I call "sketching a pile of features." Too often teams design UI by creating a list of features, then sketching to explore different ways the features could be presented *physically*. Aimlessly "sketching a pile of features" by focusing on controls and their physical placement leaves to chance important objectives such as having value, achieving user goals, and, of course, effective communication. We can do better by focusing on these goals deliberately.

> There is no single best design process, but a communication-driven approach works well for most situations and it allows you to leverage everyday interpersonal communication skills. We need a better process than "sketching a pile of features."

DON'T DESIGN LIKE A PROGRAMMER

I sometimes say that a user interface looks like it was designed by a programmer, which is my way of describing UI design mistakes that programmers are particularly prone to make. These designs happen because programmers find them easier to develop, don't notice their usability problems, and often aren't aware that there are better solutions.

The root cause of designing like a programmer is to believe that a well-designed UI mechanically enables a task. Programmers tend to let the features and technology drive their UI design decisions.

A "designing like a programmer" process looks like this:

1. Identify a problem to solve.

2. Design a technology and set of features that solve the problem.

3. Directly expose in the UI whatever the features need from users.

4. Lay out the UI based on where things fit, not where they belong. Use as few pages and as little whitespace as possible. (I call this *UI Tetris* in Chapter 3.)

5. Have the marketing department declare the UI to be "intuitive and easy to use," regardless of its actual usability.

6. Done! (What could possibly go wrong?)

Even though this approach enables users to perform the task mechanically, it doesn't mean that the results are usable.

Mechanically enabling a task isn't the last step, it's just the first! To see the potential problems, suppose the technology needs the following information (presented as a C++ data structure):

```
struct UserOptions {
         bool        Option1;
         bool        Option2;
         String      Option3;
         String      Option4;
         ...
};
```

It's natural to assume that a good UI might look something like Figure 5.4.

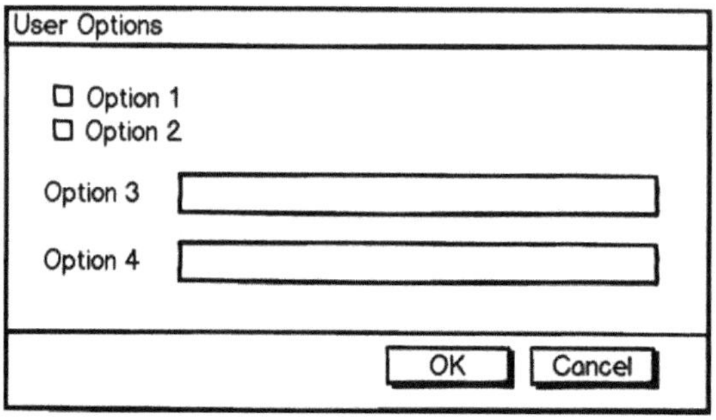

FIGURE 5.4
A well-designed UI is obvious, right?

But consider these potential problems:

- What if the technical descriptions in the data structure aren't meaningful? (Example: Duplex printing vs. printing on both sides of paper.)

- What if users don't know the right value? (Example: How would a user know to set a volume to 47?)

- What if users know roughly what they want but not the exact value? (Example: User wants to fly to a city but doesn't know the nearest airport or airport code.)

- What if users provide the right value but in the wrong format? (Example: Program requires a phone number or date in a specific format.)

- What if users don't want to give the information because it is personal or unrelated to the task? (Example: UI requires a credit card number for a task that shouldn't require one.)

- What if the date format isn't appropriate for the task? (Example: User is performing a task that requires an age, but the program asks for a birth date.)

- What if providing the data is unnecessarily difficult? (Example: User has to select from a long, unsorted list or has to provide the same information repeatedly.)

- What if providing the data is more trouble than it's worth? (Example: Program requires a lot of input for a simple task.)

- What if providing the value is error prone? (Example: The control isn't constrained to valid input [such as a text box] or gives vague, unspecific errors for minor, easily correctable problems.)

Displaying the raw data structure enables users to perform the task mechanically, but it doesn't mean that they will understand it or want to use it or that it satisfies their goals.

FIGURE 5.5
This design meets all the specified requirements and it has all the required features. What could possibly go wrong?

A well-designed user interface must go beyond mechanically enabling a task; enabling a task is the first step, not the last. You need to do some work to map what the technology wants into a UI that users can understand and can use easily and that meets their goals. Designing a UI based on what the technology needs completely misses this important design step.

WHAT EXACTLY IS DESIGN?

A good place to start is by asking: What exactly is design? There are many definitions, but here is the one I use:

> Design is making creative decisions on behalf of target users to create a product that satisfies their goals.

I like this definition because it explains the essential ingredients of a good design process:

- **Design is to create a product.** Of course, a product is the output of the design process.

- **Design is driven by decision making.** Design, and therefore the design process, is ultimately about making decisions. But to make decisions, we must have options to choose from.

- **Design is on behalf of target users.** We are making those decisions on behalf of our target users, not ourselves. Therefore, what we personally like or dislike doesn't really matter.

- **Design is creative.** We can choose any practical solution we can think of, so this is where creativity comes into play. Usually nobody is forcing a solution on us.

- **Design is to satisfy users' goals.** Satisfying users' goals is ultimately the point of the design process. Otherwise, why bother?

A BASIC DESIGN PROCESS

The design process is ultimately a decision-making process. Fortunately, there's already a well-known process for making good decisions, known as the *rational decision-making process.* We routinely use it to make important, potentially risky decisions. Here are the steps:

1. Define the problem.

2. Identify decision criteria (goals, requirements, resources, priorities) as a basis to choose.

3. Determine the possible options (that you can choose from).

4. Make a choice (by applying decision criteria to the options).

5. Evaluate the choice (make sure it's the right choice).

6. Iterate as needed until satisfied goals are achieved.

A good design process should have these essential elements.

The UI design process is generally broken into planning, design, and refinement phases. **Here is a basic design process that mirrors the rational decision-making process, with the traditional design steps filled in:**

Planning phase
1. Define the product concept and vision.
2. Determine target users, their goals, tasks, and problems.
3. Determine how to prioritize by determining schedules, resources, budgets, and project themes.

Design phase
1. Brainstorm and sketch to generate many ideas.
2. Identify best ideas by applying criteria from planning phase.
3. Propose alternative designs, perhaps using prototypes.
4. Make a choice.

Refinement phase
1. Review and evaluate quickly using "expert" evaluation.
2. Perform usability testing.
3. Iterate as needed until you're satisfied that design objectives are achieved.

Design, like golf, is an iterative process. Designs are seldom right the first time; there is always room for improvement. Holes-in-one are rare in both domains. Consequently, finding and correcting problems during the refinement phase is a sign of success, not failure. Iteration is the price we must pay to do our best work; *not* finding problems is failure here.

Although this process works well in general, remember that there is no single best design process and that you must recognize and adapt to unusual situations. So, if you need to design the tallest freestanding structure in only 18 minutes, you might want to try something different.

THE CLASSIC DESIGN PROCESS MISTAKES

To fully appreciate a good design process, we need to understand what an ineffective process looks like. Doing so will help you understand why intelligent, capable, well-motivated teams with the best of intentions so often fail to create good designs. Bad design happens for a reason. I already mentioned what an ineffective design process looks like for programmers: merely enabling a task mechanically by directly exposing what the technology needs.

For more experienced designers, an ineffective process often looks like this:

1. Do lots of user research.

2. Do lots of brainstorming, sketching, explorations, stuff with walls and sticky notes.

3. Poof! Magic happens! ... or not.

4. Do many high-fidelity prototype variations in Photoshop.

5. Get buy-in from management, customers, and other stakeholders.

6. Oops! Ran out of time, so ship what you've got.

… or something like that.

This approach can work well—especially when your product needs innovative ideas— but it's very labor and time intensive and there is too much left to chance. As with the Marshmallow Challenge, if you brainstorm quickly enough you are likely to stumble on a good design idea or two.

But why leave your design to chance when you can make it more deliberate and principled? And what if that magic doesn't happen? Many fundamental product design blunders can be traced back to some process mistake. If you review the previous design process outline, you will see that there is opportunity to make disastrous mistakes at every step.

Here are the most significant mistakes that everyone tends to make, which I call the *classic process mistakes*:

- Trying to do too much (instead of setting clear goals and priorities)

- Designing for yourself or for everyone (instead of having clear target users)

- Focusing on technology and features (instead of target users and their goals)

- Falling in love with one—usually the first—design solution (instead of considering design alternatives)

- Worrying about feasibility during brainstorming (which dampens the creative process by discouraging the free flow of ideas)

- Prototyping at the wrong level (usually too high-fidelity too early, which takes too long, has too much commitment, and discourages feedback)

- Not scheduling time for iteration and refinement (instead assuming that you'll get it right the first time)

- Not fixing the small bugs, releasing before ready (instead assuming that your customers won't care about such details)

Pay attention to what your team is doing and look out for these classic process mistakes. My experience suggests that your team is making many of them and not doing its best work as a result.

THE PLANNING PHASE

For the planning phase, I will focus on to whom you are communicating (personas), what they want to accomplish (scenarios), why they are going to use your product (value propositions), and staying focused (project themes).

1. Define the product concept and vision.
2. Determine target users, their goals, tasks, and problems.
3. Determine how to prioritize by determining schedules, resources, budgets, and project themes.

Together, the scenarios, personas, and value propositions form a decision-making framework to help you make the right decisions for the right reason. Use this decision-making framework to drive the design process.

Let's start with value propositions.

Use value propositions to deliver obvious value

A *value proposition* **briefly states the reason your target users will want to buy and use your product or feature, so in defining your concept and vision there's no better place to start.** It's a classic process mistake to assume that having technology to solve a problem is sufficient. You can use value propositions to make sure that your product or feature delivers value.

Why bother? Because value motivates people! People ultimately decide to use a product or feature based on its value; value is often the first thing users think about. If you ask someone if they are going to buy or use a product or feature, the answer they give will be their value proposition. When people say things like "No, I won't use it—it's too much trouble," they are really saying that they don't see value.

Value is best measured by comparing a product's benefits to its costs. Surprisingly, most value propositions I see completely ignore costs, as though the products were free and users' time and effort have no value. Most people think of cost first.

Users have choices, so a good value proposition states a product's or feature's value in both absolute and relative terms compared to the alternatives. Doing nothing is always an alternative and sometimes a formidable one, so make sure your product concept is much better than doing nothing! If your design's acceptance or usage isn't meeting expectations, chances are it's not delivering value compared to the alternatives. Why do customers need your product or feature? Why are your customers going to care? You must know the answer to these questions.

If your product or feature lacks value, nothing else in the design process matters, because your customers simply aren't going to care. Putting all this together, a good value proposition identifies:

- The target users and their motivation for using a product or feature

- The alternatives

- The benefits of the product or feature (compared to the alternatives)

- The costs of the product or feature (compared to the alternatives)

- Why target users will prefer the product or feature over its alternatives

One more thing: A good value proposition sounds like something target users will actually say. If a value proposition sounds like it was written by an executive or a public relations firm, it's not real and isn't going to be useful.

By *costs*, I'm not referring to just economic costs—so, even free software has a cost! To use a free service on the Web or a free mobile app, users must take the time and effort to:

- Find the product

- Try, learn, and evaluate the product

- Build confidence and change expectations

- Change routines and habits

- Change any legacy, such as saved work

Make sure your team knows your product's value proposition and actively uses it when making design decisions. If you have a marketing team, they will own the product's value proposition. (But they probably won't have feature-level value propositions.) Many marketing teams have a habit of keeping the value proposition to themselves, but clearly this technique has no value unless it is used to drive design decisions.

For an example, here is a value proposition for a handheld package tracking device:

A BladtBlaster value proposition
Compared to our existing solution, the BladtBlaster 2000 provides:
- Ability to access package-tracking information during delivery (using wireless)
- Touch-based interaction (instead of requiring a pen or keyboard)
- Different IT systems consolidated into a single mobile device
- Reduced training costs, especially for frequently performed tasks
- Improved battery life so that it doesn't require recharging during delivery

---

FIGURE 5.6
A value proposition for a handheld package-tracking device.

You are using value propositions correctly when:

- Everybody on your team knows and uses the value proposition to make design decisions that improve the product or feature.

- The design maximizes the product's or feature's benefit relative to the alternatives.

- The design minimizes the product's or feature's cost to users.

- The design makes its value obvious so that users understand it right away.

The last point is especially important: Don't expect users to spend a lot of time trying to figure out your product's or feature's value. They won't—so make it obvious!

Define a value proposition—the reason your target users will want to use your product or feature—and ensure that the design delivers it by maximizing its benefits, minimizing its costs, and making its value obvious.

Use scenarios to understand what users want to do

User-centered design requires us to understand what users are going to do with our product from their point of view. If you have ever wondered why a design looks good to you and your team but not to users, scenarios are the best place to start.

A *scenario* **describes a specific target user trying to achieve a specific goal or perform a specific task in a specific context.** Concisely:

Secnario = user + task + context

All three elements are important. Since some products might support hundreds or even thousands of scenarios, it helps to identify the top scenarios. The *top scenarios* are the ones users care about the most—the tasks they are most likely to perform and what delights them when it's done especially well.

To fully appreciate scenario-based design, it helps to compare it to feature- and task-based design. In feature-based design, the design process is focused on adding features to the product—on the assumption that features are what users want and that more features are better. The problem is that users don't do features, they do tasks—so it's very easy to add features that have little practical value. Having a long list of features might initially appear impressive, but having many complex, poorly coordinated features doesn't necessarily help users get their work done. Unfortunately, feature-based design is the way many teams work.

FIGURE 5.7

Makes sense ... "ease of use" is just another feature, right? DILBERT ©2001 Scott Adams. Used by permission of UNIVERSAL UCLICK. All rights reserved.

Task-based design recognizes this problem, so it focuses on enabling tasks—where *tasks* **are a unit of activity with your program.** Given this focus, task-based design tends to produce designs that are much more useful than feature-based design.

Task-based design sounds pretty good, so what's the problem? The problem is that great user experiences are designed for their target users, and task-based design often doesn't consider target users, their goals, or their context at all. Do users really want to do those tasks? Can they really use them? Do they like them? Add the tendency for people to design for themselves, and task-based design often leads to designs that their developers love but customers don't. Great user-centered design requires designing for clear targets. That's what scenario-based design is all about!

You can't use scenarios to determine the right solution if the solution is already baked into the scenario. Good scenarios focus on the users' goals, their problems, and their context, without providing any solutions. The purpose of scenarios is to help you make the right decisions quickly and confidently, so if your scenarios don't achieve that goal, rewrite them!

Unfortunately, scenarios have a spotty track record in practice. I have seen many scenarios that aren't very useful. Consider this scenario:

> ### A BladtBaster scenario
> Joe works at a Fortune 500 company. On occasion, he needs to access Snarfbladt info for his customers. He discovered that the BladtBlaster 2000 allows him to access Snarfbladts from the BladtBlaster Website. Joe is thrilled!

FIGURE 5.8
A first attempt at a scenario for a handheld package-tracking device.

What's wrong with this scenario? In short, everything. Although it provides a task (Joe needs to access Snarfbladts), we have no clear idea who the user is, what he is doing, where he is doing it, or why. By saying "Joe is thrilled," this scenario is basically saying that customers will be thrilled if we ship a feature. That is feature-based design! Clearly, this scenario has little value, but scenarios like this are surprisingly typical. Such scenarios tend to live in specs, unused.

Here is a better scenario:

> ### An improved BladtBaster scenario
> Joe works in the shipping department of a large company, where he is responsible for the pickup and delivery of about 200 packages a day across 10 buildings. To maintain his aggressive schedule, he is always on the move, either with a cart or carrying a few packages underarm.
>
> Between deliveries, Joe occasionally needs to access Snarfbladt info for his customers. The BladtBlaster 2000 allows him to access the Snarfbladt info instantly. Best of all, he can do it while walking, using a single hand with only five thumb strokes or less.

FIGURE 5.9
A better scenario for a handheld package-tracking device.

Note that the task in the two scenarios is exactly the same, but we now know who Joe is, what he is doing, where, and why. We can now make good design decisions on Joe's behalf.

Context is a crucial part of a scenario, but it's something we tend to overlook. The context might be where the users are physically (are they at their desk or somewhere else?), where they are in a task flow or other context (what's the big picture?), or perhaps where they are mentally (are they under stress or in a hurry?)

In fact, understanding the users' context is so important that it is often the difference between a good design and a great design. Here are some levels of design greatness:

- **Acceptable design.** Enables tasks *mechanically*.

- **Good design.** Performs tasks *smoothly* for target users.

- **Better design.** *Achieves goals* well for target users.

- **Great design.** Achieves goals well for target users in their *context*.

Great design requires clear targets, and scenarios provide those targets! You can't design well by having random people doing random things for random reasons in random contexts.

> Use scenarios to understand your product from the customers' point of view. Great design requires clear targets, and scenarios provide those targets.

Use personas to understand your users

Great design requires clear target users. It's a classic process mistake to design for yourself (assuming your target users are just like you) or to design for everyone (because designing for everyone is equivalent to designing for no one). You can't hit a target if you don't have one, so you can use personas to set clear target users for your design process.

A *persona* is a fake person constructed using real user research data to represent a class of real target users. Personas are the actors in our scenarios. In a nutshell, you create personas by determining the entire space of possible users, picking the classes of users that you care about most, defining personas to represent those classes, and using these personas to drive design decisions. The key concept is that if your design delights a persona, it will delight everyone in that space of users.

Choosing personas from the space of users

FIGURE 5.10
Personas identify the classes of users you care about the most.

Without personas, everyone on your team forms their own independent picture of the target users. And somehow, those target users are always remarkably similar to the people on the team. Furthermore, that undefined target user may change from feature to feature or even from discussion to discussion. Ultimately, without a clear definition, target users are basically whatever the person who is speaking wants them to be at the time—not a very solid foundation for user-centered design. This problem is known as the *elastic user*.

FIGURE 5.11

If your personas look like your team members, you are probably doing it wrong. DILBERT ©2012 Scott Adams. Used by permission of UNIVERSAL UCLICK. All rights reserved.

Personas provide clear, well-defined targets. A typical persona includes a name, a general description, a list of specific attributes, and perhaps even a picture. To have value, everyone on your team needs to know these personas and their specific attributes and use them to make design decisions.

Unfortunately, personas have a spotty track record in practice. Many teams have tried and abandoned them because they can consume a substantial amount of time and may accomplish very little. User researchers would start the process by spending a significant amount of time gathering data about target users, defining personas to represent them, and crafting long, detailed persona documents. These documents would be filled with irrelevant life-story details like the persona's kids, coffee, cars, cats, and so on. The fact is, people don't read long documents, and those details weren't all that useful in make design decisions anyway. Such personas are created and talked about but not really used in making design decisions.

Often design teams would use those personas by learning the persona names, their high-level descriptions, and … well, that's about it. In practice, "using personas" often boiled down to replacing an elastic user with an equally elastic persona with a very specific first name. Not really a big step forward in user-centered design.

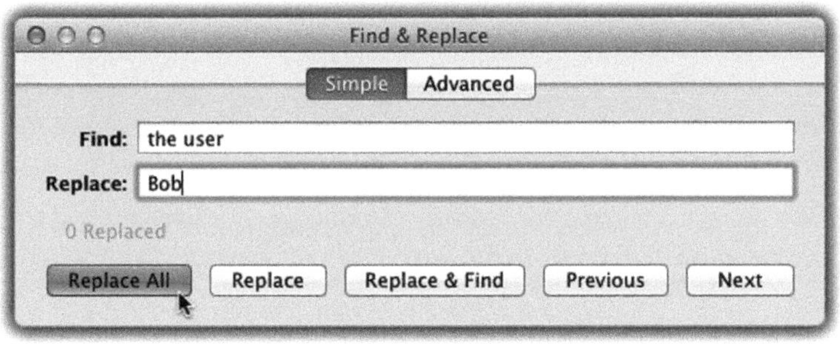

FIGURE 5.12
If this is what your persona strategy boils down to, don't bother.

That said, I am a strong believer in personas. The solution to these common persona problems is simple: Instead of creating long documents with many irrelevant details, create short user models with relevant details focused on the task at hand. Include the details that are relevant to making good design decisions, and exclude everything else. Don't bother to make the persona feel like a real person. If the persona reads like an online dating profile, you're doing it wrong.

Here are some useful characteristics that should be in most personas:

- **Their general computer knowledge.** Are your target users experts, intermediates, or novices? What relevant computer concepts can you safely assume that they know?

- **Their domain knowledge.** Are your target users domain experts, intermediates, or novices? What specifically do they know about the tasks and the data involved? This affects the domain concepts that you can safely assume. Note that a computer expert can be a domain novice and vice versa.

- **Their goals, tasks.** What exactly are your users going to do with your product, and why?

- **Their frequency of using the product and doing tasks.** A heavy UI might be appropriate for rarely performed tasks, but a lightweight UI is much better for frequently performed tasks.

- **Their vocabulary.** So that your UI speaks the user's language, determine what terms your users know and use regularly.

- **Their motivation.** How motivated are the target users to get the task done? Highly motivated users will do whatever it takes, whereas unmotivated users will abandon tasks that require too much effort.

- **Their context.** In what physical conditions do your users work? Is the environment relaxed and casual, or high stress and fasted paced? What is the scale? Do they work with a few things? Hundreds? Thousands? Hundreds of thousands?

- **Their age, physical abilities, access preferences.** Studies have shown that about 37 percent of the workforce has some physical impairment. If that number seems high, think about impairments such as poor eyesight, color confusion (often called *color blindness*), or carpel tunnel syndrome. Consider the fine motor skills required to hit small targets. These are all quite common issues that affect design.

For example, here is a persona for "Joe the shipping guy," who is the target user for our handheld package-tracking device:

BladtBlaster persona: Joe the Shipping Guy
Joe works in the shipping department of a large company, where he is responsible for the pickup and delivery of about 200 packages a day across 10 buildings. Here are his personal details regarding BladtBlaster usage:
- Joe has basic computer literacy.
- He is likely right-handed, but he may be left-handed.
- He has received 20 minutes of BladtBlaster training.
- His top six tasks are 95 percent of his BladtBlaster usage.
- He is familiar with Snarfbladt info but doesn't have it memorized.
- He looks up only one Snarfbladt at a time.
- He uses a cart if delivering many packages; otherwise he carries them.
- He prefers to use the BladtBlaster with a single hand using his thumb.
- He works mostly indoors but has to travel outdoors between buildings, so he may wear gloves during cold weather.
- He is always in a hurry—and appreciates things that save time.

FIGURE 5.13
A persona for the target user for a handheld package-tracking device.

That's it. That's all we need! Given this simple model, we have what we need to design for Joe. We don't need Joe's life story and every detail about his daily routine. Although the scenario in the previous section provided a lot of useful information, the persona fills in many important details about Joe that were missing.

Every decision you make should be consistent with the relevant persona. Any discrepancies reveal design problems. You are making design decisions on behalf of your target users, so having personas like these help you understand exactly who you are designing for. To be practical, everyone on your team needs to know the personas from memory so that they can aim for the same target. If someone makes an assertion about Joe that's not in the model, you can easily flag it and either validate it or reject it. Having a one-page handout for each persona on every team member's desk is a great way to get started.

In creating personas, keep in mind that the entire purpose is to help you make better design decisions. Anything that gets in the way of the goal should be reconsidered. If the persona has irrelevant, too vague, or overly specific details that don't potentially impact decisions—remove them. If you have too many personas, eliminate the less important ones. Specific details are useful when they provide goals and context for the class of users, but they're harmful if they narrow the class down to a few individuals.

Details that probably shouldn't be in a persona definition:
- Age
- Marital status
- Income level
- Personal details about kids, coffee, cars, cats, colors, hobbies, etc.
- Overly specific details that describe specific individuals instead of classes of users
- Loves piña coladas and walks in the rain

FIGURE 5.14
Details that probably shouldn't be in a persona. If a persona reads like an online dating profile, you're doing it wrong.

Consider age. People often put ages in their personas, but I recommend against doing so unless age is relevant to the target class of users. Clearly, if a product is targeted at children, teenagers, or the elderly, age is relevant. But does age matter for business software? Is a business app or feature only targeted at certain age groups? Probably not. Sometimes ages are used to imply work details, such as level of experience, willingness to make changes in work style, interest in technology, or preferences for email versus texting. If so, I recommend skipping the age and putting those assumptions in directly.

For more information on creating and using personas, I recommend *The Essential Persona Lifecycle: Your Guide to Building and Using Personas,* by Tamara Adlin and John Pruitt.

> Define personas to have a clear set of target users. Instead of long documents with irrelevant details, create short user models with relevant details that are focused on the task at hand. Every decision you make should be consistent with the relevant persona. Any discrepancies reveal design problems!

Staying focused with project themes

When they're working on a release of a product, your team can't do everything that it would like to do—and it certainly can't do everything well. Staying focused is a key to success, and trying to do too much is a classic process mistake. Prefer to "do less better" than to attempt to do everything poorly.

There are many ways to stay focused. Traditionally, project schedules, staffing, and budgets are used to keep project scopes in check. This is a practical technique because it limits the project scope to what the team can actually produce with the resources it has.

A shortcoming of this resource-based approach is that it is focused purely on delivering a project mechanically. The resource-based approach doesn't give any guidance on the product design unless a proposed UI is a budget buster. The resulting user experience needs to be considered as well.

A more user-centered way to stay focused is to create *project themes***, which identify a small number of high-level user experience goals for a project.** Everything your team works on should tie into the project's themes in some way. For example, here are project themes for a typical project:

BladtBlaster project themes
- **Mobile scenarios.** Redesign features to take full advantage of the wireless capability and location awareness.
- **Touch.** Redesign the pages to use larger, touchable targets, use simple interactions, and reduce the need for typing.
- **Larger screen.** Take advantage of the larger screen size to make tasks more self-explanatory and reduce the need for training.
- **Performance.** Design pages to be displayed and mostly interactive within 300 milliseconds.

FIGURE 5.15
Possible project themes for a handheld package-tracking device. Better to focus on doing a few things well.

An important benefit to using project themes is that they help customers appreciate what you are doing in a new release. Customers might not appreciate a release with hundreds of new features and thousands of bug fixes, but they can easily appreciate a product release with five new capabilities they really care about.

FIGURE 5.16
Can you identify the project themes for the new iPad? (Hint: There are three.) Having clear project themes makes it easier for customers to appreciate what Apple did.

Although perfection isn't required for a great UX, staying focused is. Use project themes to stay focused. Your themes should be obvious in the product design.

THE DESIGN PHASE

1. Brainstorm and sketch to generate many ideas.
2. Identify best ideas by applying criteria from the planning phase.
3. Propose alternative designs, perhaps using prototypes.
4. Make a choice.

For our discussion of the design phase, I want to focus on how effective communication should drive brainstorming, task design, and the decision-making process.

Traditionally, the design phase starts by understanding the goals of the project determined in the planning phase, brainstorming ideas on how to achieve those goals, then sketching and prototyping the *physical presentation of the UI* (such as page layouts) to explore, refine, confirm, or reject those ideas. In turn, the evaluation of these sketches is largely visual.

However, if UI is essentially a conversation between users and a product to perform tasks, there is a crucial missing step here: The traditional process skips understanding the natural in-person conversation. So, going directly from brainstorming to sketching the physical presentation skips the most important step!

How can you determine the best way to present the conversation physically when you don't even know what it is yet? Not designing the personal conversation is a huge missed opportunity because the quality of the communication is an excellent predictor of the quality of a design. Instead, focusing on physical presentation encourages the very technology- and feature-focused design approach that we want to avoid.

> The traditional UI design process skips understanding the natural in-person conversation and immediately focuses on the physical presentation instead. Better to figure out what you want to communicate before worrying about how to present it physically.

Imagine a conversation with the target user

For a communication-driven design process, imagine a conversation between you and the target user who is performing the task you are now designing. If that person were to ask you, "How do I perform this task?" think about what you would say: the steps you would give, their order, the language you would use, the questions you would ask, and the details you would provide. Think about the various questions and details that you *wouldn't* mention until they were relevant, because you already know the answer, or because they were too early or too late in the conversation or otherwise inappropriate. Also, think about the questions and details that you wouldn't bother mentioning at all because they just aren't important enough. Finally, think about this conversation from the user's point of view. Would the user be able to answer your questions or perform the steps? Will the user want to?

For example, suppose you own a small store and a first-time customer just walked in the door. Would you immediately make that customer create an account, sign in, and recommend that he follow you on Twitter? Would you make him prove that he is really human? Agree to terms of use? Would you offer him a tour and instructions on how to interact with your merchandise? Would you constantly remind him that you are there to help and to feel free to ask questions? Would you make him start completely over if there is a problem? Probably not! You would let the customer explore first and let him ask questions when he is ready. Your UI should do the same. A polite UI doesn't behave like it is on a commission.

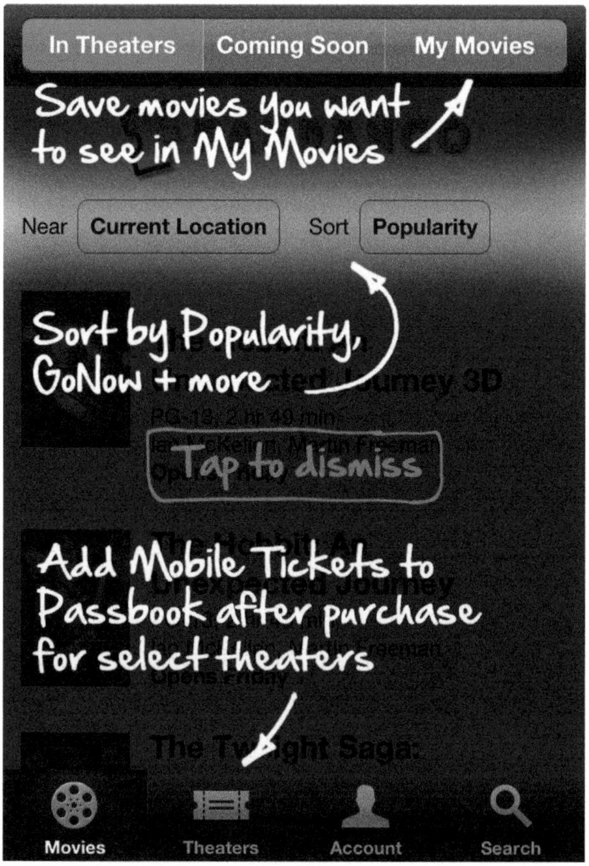

FIGURE 5.17

Thanks for the tour, but I'm just not ready yet. Let me explore first and I'll ask for help when I need it.

Continuing with our handheld package-tracking device, imagine a friend asks you, "How do I look up a Snarfbladt?" Here is what you might say as a response:

A conversation to find a Snarfbladt—follow these steps:
1. Go to the home screen (if you aren't there already).
2. Give the Lookup Snarfbladt command.
3. Provide information about the Snarfbladt you are looking for (preferably enough to identify it uniquely, but whatever is most convenient), then give the Search command.
4. Review the list of matching Snarfbladts (displayed in order of relevance) and select the one you are looking for. (Skip this step if there is only one match.)
5. Review the displayed Snarfbladt info.
6. When done, return to the home screen.

FIGURE 5.18
Start a design by writing down the steps that you would explain to the user in person.

I call these high-level task outlines *conversations*. **They are a high-level guide for the task flow and page design.** These task step descriptions can be used for main instructions to help make the task flow more intuitive. If you aren't familiar with these main instructions, you might want to review the "Inductive UI" section in Chapter 1 before continuing.

Focusing on effective communication suggests that if there is a discrepancy between what you would say in person and what is in the proposed UI, most likely the personal conversation is right and the proposed design is wrong. Why? Because what you would say in person is the most natural, concise, intuitive way to explain the task. What we put in UI is often technical, unnatural, and unintuitive. Such technical UIs tend to reflect how the code works, not how users think about the task.

A mechanical description of how to find a Snarfbladt—follow these steps:
1. Provide credentials.
2. Lookup Snarfbladt.
3. Enter query.
4. Choose match.
5. Display record.

FIGURE 5.19
If we don't think about the personal conversation, the task becomes mechanical and resembles the way the code works instead. In this case, the steps are roughly the same, but all the human nuances are missing.

Use these conversations, plus the scenarios, personas, and value proposition from the planning phase, to help you make design decisions. Once you have determined the right communication, most other significant decisions naturally follow. It's much easier to get the communication right, then figure out the right presentation and details, than to start with a presentation and details, then try to figure out a way to communicate that conforms to them. Sketching a pile of features is the hard way.

Join Twitter today.

Full name

Everett McKay   ✓ Name looks great.

Email address

everett@uiiscommunication.com

Confirm email address

everett@uiiscommunication.com   ✓ Email addresses match!

Create a password

| 6 characters or more! Be tricky.

FIGURE 5.20

A good UI is like a conversation between friends. Let's use those conversations to drive the design process.

Communicates well

I'm assuming that you have the basic skills required to communicate to your target users effectively in person—which isn't always a safe assumption. If you have trouble here, please review Chapter 1, "Communication Design Principles," before continuing.

Finally, if you can't explain how to perform the task to someone in person, you aren't ready to design yet. Before designing, be sure to do enough research and analysis so that you can explain the task.

Imagine a conversation between you and a friend or colleague who is the target user and is performing the task you are now designing. That conversation, plus the scenarios, personas, and value propositions from the planning phase, should drive the design process.

Communication brainstorming to generate ideas

Brainstorming is an interactive group process for generating many ideas rapidly in order to discover creative and unobvious solutions to a challenging problem. The key to success is to encourage the free flow of ideas—without inhibition. It's a classic process mistake to explore only one design idea, so brainstorming helps teams to look at many.

Here are some rules for effective brainstorming:

- **Have a facilitator.** The facilitator keeps things moving, prods people with questions, enforces rules, challenges assumptions, and prevents dwelling on one idea.

- **Have clear goals.** The brainstorming session should have clear goals, and the facilitator should keep the session focused on them.

- **Focus on quantity, not quality.** Finding the creative and unobvious requires looking at many ideas, whereas looking at ideas in depth doesn't achieve that goal. Simply put, dwelling on the details is a waste of time during brainstorming.

- **Record, don't debate.** The facilitator should write ideas down quickly and move on. The facilitator should not let anyone say "no," critique, judge, or debate the ideas.

- **Don't worry about feasibility.** The facilitator should discourage concerns about feasibility. It's a classic process mistake to worry about feasibility too early in the process. The wild and impractical can encourage ideas that are innovative and practical, so don't inhibit them.

- **No ego.** Nobody owns the ideas, so the facilitator should discourage team members from referring to "my idea" versus "your idea." Owning ideas makes them personal and encourages advocacy and bias.

- **Build on ideas.** However, the facilitator should encourage people to build on, extend, and combine other ideas. That's what brainstorming is all about.

From the communication angle, at least part of a brainstorming session should be directed toward effective, natural communication. When appropriate, the facilitator might direct the team to discuss "What are we really asking the user here?" or "How would you explain that in person?" If the responses sound unnatural or mechanical, the facilitator should keep prodding for new communication ideas by asking, "Would anyone say it differently?"

FIGURE 5.21

What a typical brainstorming session looks like. Note that the facilitator is writing the ideas down quickly.

Use brainstorming to rapidly discover creative, unobvious ideas. The facilitator should direct part of the brainstorming sessions toward effective, natural communication. When appropriate, the facilitator might ask, "What are we really asking the user here?" or "How would you explain that in person?"

Sketching to explore ideas quickly

Sketching **is a quick way to conceive, suggest, and explore design ideas with your team, usually on paper or whiteboards.** Sketching is used to explore design directions in the first place, whereas prototyping is used to communicate, improve, and test established ideas. And to be clear, you don't want to be prototyping yet; prototypes are too heavy and time consuming for quick exploration. Sketches are easy and quick to make, timely, and inexpensive without commitment. As Bill Buxton said in *Sketching User Experiences*, a rough sketch screams, "This is an idea! I'm not done!"

An important benefit to sketches is that they are ambiguous and may be interpreted in a variety of ways. As Buxton emphasizes, this is a good thing. Many times I have seen (mis)interpretations of sketches that were much better than the originally intended idea.

Your current sketching skills should serve you well here, but be aware of what you are proposing, suggesting, and exploring. Are you exploring different ways to communicate with users, or different visual presentations? As I suggested previously, your sketching efforts will be more productive if you initially focus on exploring ways to communicate. Postpone sketching the physical presentation until you have a strong understanding of what you need to present.

FIGURE 5.22

When sketching, are you thinking, "How can I best explain this task?" or are you thinking, "Where can I fit this widget?"

For more information on sketching and its value to the UI design process, check out Bill Buxton's *Sketching User Experiences*.

Use sketching during the idea generation phase to quickly express and explore ideas with your team.

Exploring many design alternatives is much better than one

Design is ultimately about making good decisions. Can you make a good decision by exploring only one option? Suppose that one option is really good—but how do you know it's really that good if you don't compare it to the alternatives?

You can't make a decision *confidently* if you don't know the alternatives. It's a classic process mistake to fall in love with one design. Consequently, experienced designers force themselves to explore alternatives. However, I have observed that inexperienced designers have a very hard time doing this. Once they come up with a solution, they find it very difficult to see other alternatives, because that one solution seems so obvious and natural to them. This is a classic mistake for a reason.

I would like to encourage you to come up with radically different design alternatives (minor layout variations don't count) during this early part of the design phase. **But if you are absolutely convinced that you couldn't possibly have a better design, here are some possible variations that you should consider:**

- Try a simpler, more streamlined variation.

- Try an automatic variation.

- Try a more standard variation (using standard interactions and patterns).

- Try a radically innovative variation.

- Try a deluxe "five-star" version.

- Try a version optimized for a different goal or platform (such as a mobile device).

Even if you stick with your original design idea, these variations will make the idea stronger and give you more confidence. But my bet is that at least one of these variations (probably the simpler, automatic, or standard one) will be much better.

Design is ultimately about making good decisions. You must explore more than one option to choose the best design idea confidently.

Innovation sometimes considered harmful

Designers often want to create *innovative designs*—novel approaches that have a form or function that hasn't been done before. Although that certainly sounds good, using an innovative design might be counterproductive if it isn't necessary for the task at hand.

In my experience, many of the "innovative" designs are unnecessary, poorly done, and not readily understood—created primarily because their designers didn't recognize more standard, familiar solutions. Don't get me wrong; I love great, innovative designs as much as the next guy. But it's better to use standard, familiar approaches based on established design patterns for your environment than to come up with radically different approaches without a clear justification. The best innovations have the right motivation. Start with the standard and familiar first, then innovate if the familiar fails to do the job well.

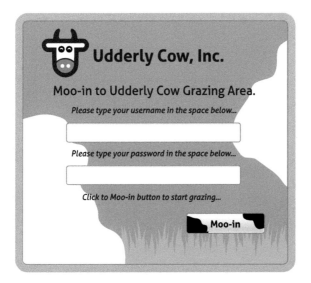

FIGURE 5.23
But we wanted to have an innovative sign-in page ...

Innovation is great—but only when standard, familiar designs fail to do the job well.

Identify the best design ideas

Working with many ideas early in the design phase helps you understand the possibilities before making a commitment with confidence.

To help make that commitment, you need to narrow the ideas down in order to focus on the most promising. Bill Buxton illustrates this process quite well with a diagram from *Sketching User Experiences* (see Figure 5.24). The idea is that you start the design process with a single starting point—the product concept—then expand your thinking to many options through brainstorming. Now you have to start to reduce those options to a single focal point—the product you actually intend to build.

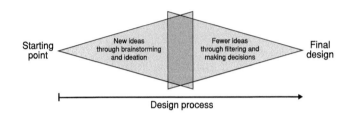

FIGURE 5.24

Brainstorming expands our thinking by looking for new opportunities, but now we need to narrow our focus by making decisions. (Based on a concept by Paul Laseau.)

How do you do this? The decision-making framework we established during the planning phase, plus the effective communication analysis at the start of the design phase, will show the way. There are many other possible considerations, but they are often secondary.

Here are some criteria to consider, roughly in order:

- **Scenarios.** Which design alternatives best support the top scenarios?

- **Personas.** Which design alternatives best match the target user characteristics?

- **Effective communication.** Which design alternatives communicate the task best?

- **Value proposition.** Which design alternatives deliver the most benefit or have the least cost?

- **Design principles.** Which design alternatives best uphold our design principles (such as the intuitive design attributes from Chapter 1)?

- **Resources, themes.** Which design alternatives are realistic with our available resources? Which best support our project themes?

At this point in the process, you'll probably want to settle on about three design directions before starting to prototype. You want to build your confidence, but you don't want to waste time.

> Apply the decision-making framework from the planning phase to narrow down to three design directions at most before you start to prototype.

Prototyping to communicate and improve established ideas

A *prototype* **is an interface mockup that demonstrates how a program or feature is going to look or behave.** Effective prototypes have clear goals; you shouldn't prototype for the sake of prototyping.

Common goals for prototyping are to:

- Communicate and visualize design ideas.

- Evaluate, compare, get feedback, and improve design ideas.

- Usability-test specific designs.

And most important, the ultimate goal of effective prototyping is to achieve your goals more efficiently than with production code. It's all about efficiency because the prototype is always a means but rarely an end.

Prototypes can have different levels of visual and functional fidelity:

- **Low fidelity.** A sketch or wireframe, with no attempt to look real. Not all functionality needs to be included. May show task flows.

- **Medium fidelity.** A modest attempt to look real, but obviously not. May show task flows and minimal functionality.

- **High fidelity.** Looks like a real program. May be interactive or demonstrate some functionality.

Generally, the lowest-fidelity prototype that achieves your goals is best. Choosing the right level of fidelity is an important decision—it's a classic process mistake to prototype at the wrong level. Lower-fidelity prototypes:

- Enable quick design, faster iteration, and creativity.

- Have the least investment and commitment.

- Focus on the high-level issues instead of details.

- Are perceived as unfinished and easily changeable, so they don't discourage feedback.

The last benefit is especially important: If your goal is to improve the design, the last thing you want is the presentation of your prototype to discourage feedback. I find that people react emotionally to beautiful things and that beauty hides flaws. Consequently, beautifully rendered prototypes often receive less critical feedback than rough ones—which isn't what you want here.

Designers often add fidelity to their prototypes as they progress through the design phrase. Low-fidelity prototypes are useful for determining task flows, rough page layouts, and basic interaction, whereas high-fidelity prototypes are great for getting pixel-level visual details like fonts, colors, and exact layout, plus high-level visual goals such as visual appearance and appeal, scannability, and personality.

> Use prototypes to confirm, communicate, improve, and test established ideas
> efficiently. Have a clear goal for your prototype and choose the lowest-level prototype
> that achieves your goals.

Getting the details right

Once you have the interaction and visual design established, it's time to think about the details. Here are some important details that you should not overlook:

- **Performance.** Great performance is the ultimate feature because it benefits all users in all scenarios. Design tasks to be responsive, give great feedback, and avoid unnecessary waiting.

- **Efficiency.** Make sure frequent tasks can be performed efficiently, especially by advanced users. Design shortcuts and gestures for minimal user effort.

- **Defaults and recommendations.** Good defaults and recommendations make tasks more efficient and give users confidence in their selections.

- **Animations and transitions.** Animations and transitions give your UI a modern, realistic feel. The best transitions don't demand attention but rather make state changes more natural and less noticeable.

- **Forgiveness.** Users make small mistakes all the time, so strive to handle such mistakes gracefully. Avoid giving big punishments for small mistakes.

- **Error handing.** Good error handling must be designed in instead of being an afterthought. Good error messages are specific, actionable, and helpful.

THE REFINEMENT PHASE

1. Review and evaluate quickly using "expert" evaluation.
2. Perform usability testing.
3. Iterate as needed until you're satisfied that design objectives are achieved.

Designs are never right the first time. UI design is an iterative process, so you need to review and evaluate your design decisions throughout. Effective evaluations are crucial for your team to do its best work. I find the techniques that nondesigners tend to use aren't very effective. The feedback tends to be arbitrary, visual, and emotional, and the reception tends to be defensive. We can do better.

There are many evaluation techniques, but they boil down into two categories:

- **User-based evaluation.** A UI is evaluated using actual target users. Usability lab studies are the most commonly employed user-based evaluation.

- **"Expert"-based evaluation.** A UI is evaluated using "experts" who represent target users. Simply put, the "experts" aren't actual target users. An expert evaluation might involve your team applying an evaluation method or a set of design principles to a design.

Between these two options, user-based evaluation clearly has the advantage of testing with actual users. For example, a *usability lab study* evaluates a design by having actual target users perform realistic tasks to determine if they can complete them successfully. Will your target users understand your UI? You will never know until you test with real users.

Usability lab studies are the ultimate measure of usability and user behavior (prede-ployment), and they always trump expert-based evaluation, speculation, and personal opinion. As a result, usability lab studies are considered the gold standard for design evaluation. For more information, I recommend *Usability Engineering,* by Jakob Nielsen, and *Rocket Surgery Made Easy,* by Steve Krug.

Expert evaluations have the less obvious advantage of being quick, inexpensive, and focused. There is no single best technique; use the technique that best achieves your evaluation goals.

There are too many evaluation techniques to cover them all, so I will focus on those that evaluate how well a design communicates. These evaluation techniques tend to be quick, easy to do, and very effective.

That said, there are several "expert"-based evaluation techniques that I won't cover that you effectively already know. Everything you do during the planning phase can be used to evaluate a design by looking for discrepancies. For example, you can evaluate a product's value proposition by evaluating how well a design maximizes its benefits while minimizing its costs. Design principle reviews are also very effective. For example, you apply the attributes of intuitive UI from Chapter 1 to help you determine whether a design is intuitive.

> Usability lab studies evaluate a design by having actual target users perform realistic tasks to determine whether they can complete them successfully. These studies always trump expert-based evaluation and are considered the gold standard for design evaluation.

(Ineffective) Team-based design reviews

Team-based design reviews, where the designer presents a UI to the team during a meeting, is quite common, so let's start there. As I suggested earlier, these reviews usually aren't very effective.

Here is the format for a typical team-based design review:

1. The designer explains the project and its goals, plus the goals of the design review.

2. The designer walks through the UI page by page.

3. Team members make random comments about the design, usually based on personal preferences.

4. To address the feedback, the designer defends the various design decisions.

5. Someone starts to propose new design ideas during the meeting.

6. A debate breaks out over some random topic completely unrelated to the goal of the design review.

7. A developer points out that the design is going to be really hard to implement within current technology and schedule.

8. The team lead points out that he or she doesn't like the colors, fonts, and icons, and quibbles over minor text details.

9. Someone mentions that his or her mom would never use the proposed design.

This is the worst case, but this worst case happens quite often. Nothing good comes from this.

In the best case, the designer manages to make it all the way through and the team says "Looks good!" for each page. But this is still an ineffective design review. Why? Because the "Looks good!" assessment likely based on the design's visual appearance—the mockup itself literally looks good to the reviewers. This is a visual, largely emotional response, not a real assessment of the quality of the design.

> Team-based design reviews are often ineffective. Saying "looks good!"—though encouraging—isn't effective feedback.

A better approach: Scenario-based reviews

Instead of this undisciplined approach, consider setting some design review rules. Here are some rules that I recommend: staying on topic; no defending, designing, or debating; give specific, actionable feedback; your mom isn't the target user, and so on. I present these design review rules in more detail in Chapter 6, "UI Design Examples."

But effective design reviews strive to evaluate the design from the user's point of view instead of random, emotional, visual feedback. How can we do that? With scenarios!

Here is the format for a scenario-based design review:

1. The designer explains the project and its goals plus the goals and rules of the design review.

2. The designer presents the top scenarios for the review.

3. The team walks through each scenario step by step.

4. Team members give specific, actionable feedback in terms of the scenario and its target users instead of personal opinion.

5. The designer records the feedback quickly and moves on. No defending, designing, debating, or going off topic.

6. The team lead points out that he doesn't like the colors, fonts, and icons and they all quibbles over minor text details—because he can't resist. *But because this is off topic, he does it after the meeting, through email!*

Much better!

Use scenario-based design reviews and set some design review rules to keep the meetings productive. Doing so evaluates designs from the target users' point of view and discourages random feedback.

Communication reviews

A *communication review* evaluates how well a design communicates by comparing it to what you would say in person, as I described earlier in the section "Imagine a Conversation with the Target User." If the UI feels like a natural, friendly conversation, it is probably a good design. By contrast, if you wouldn't say something in person, why say it in a UI? There's little point in doing a usability lab study with designs that don't communicate well.

You could perform a communication review as a separate step, but I usually do it while I'm performing another type of design review, such as the just-mentioned scenario-based review. Here is one way of doing it:

1. Perform a scenario-based design review, as previously described.

2. Compare what the presenter says to the team to what is on the page in terms of steps, their order, language, instructions, questions, and details. Also, make note of significant design elements on the page that the presenter doesn't bother to mention and that aren't used in the scenario.

3. If there are any significant differences, ask why. Chances are you have found a problem.

A communication review applies a core *UI is Communication* principle: **What we say in person tends to be the right explanation, so if the design is different, it is probably wrong.** To simulate this technique, suppose a designer presents the page in Figure 5.25 during a design walkthrough.

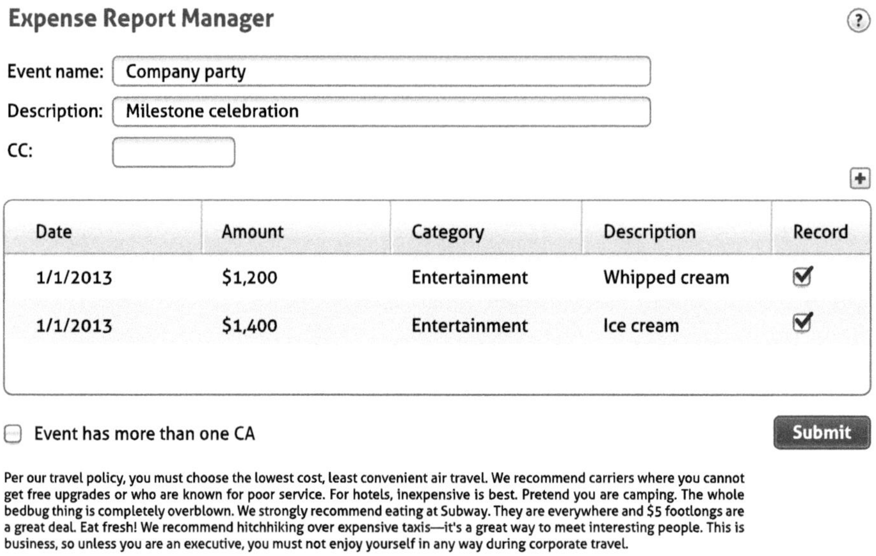

Expense Report Manager ⑦

Event name: [Company party]

Description: [Milestone celebration]

CC: [ ]

⊕

Date	Amount	Category	Description	Record
1/1/2013	$1,200	Entertainment	Whipped cream	☑
1/1/2013	$1,400	Entertainment	Ice cream	☑

☐ Event has more than one CA   [**Submit**]

Per our travel policy, you must choose the lowest cost, least convenient air travel. We recommend carriers where you cannot get free upgrades or who are known for poor service. For hotels, inexpensive is best. Pretend you are camping. The whole bedbug thing is completely overblown. We strongly recommend eating at Subway. They are everywhere and $5 footlongs are a great deal. Eat fresh! We recommend hitchhiking over expensive taxis—it's a great way to meet interesting people. This is business, so unless you are an executive, you must not enjoy yourself in any way during corporate travel.

FIGURE 5.25

An expense report page presented in a design walkthrough.

Further, let's say that the designer describes the page as follows:

On this page, employees create expense reports, which must be filed within 30 days. First the employee needs give the name of the trip, its purpose, and the cost center to charge the expenses to. Then the employee needs to enter each expense item, including the category, date, and amount. Expenses over $100 require a receipt. The employee also needs to give a justification for entertainment expenses. When done, the employee submits the report to his or her manager for approval.

Based on this description, some good feedback might be:

• The page title is "Expense Report Manager," yet you didn't describe any of these activities as management. Can we use a more useful, less technical title?

• The first thing you mentioned is that expenses must be filed within 30 days, yet that isn't anywhere in the UI. Seems important. Shouldn't we mention that? If we don't, how are users going to know?

- You described this as a "Trip," yet the UI says "Event," which is rather vague. Are most expenses for travel? If so, can we be more specific?

- You mentioned that each expense report needs a purpose, yet the UI says "Description." Isn't asking for the purpose more clear?

- You mentioned that all travel expenses need a justification. How do users know that?

- You mentioned "cost center," yet the UI has CC as well as CA for "cost assignment." Do all our employees know what CC and CA mean? Can we spell them out?

- You mentioned that some expenses require receipts, yet the UI says "Record." Receipt sounds more natural ... should we change this?

- When done, it sounds like the employee is really submitting the expenses for approval, yet the button just says "Submit." Should we make that clear?

- The page has a large block of text that explains corporate travel policy, yet you didn't mention any of that. It doesn't appear to be very important and it is really hard to read. Can we remove or simplify it?

All good questions. This technique is remarkably effective for finding communication problems quickly.

Communication reviews evaluate how well a design communicates, and you can do them easily while performing other types of design reviews.

Highlighter reviews

A *highlighter review* **evaluates the integrity of a page as well as its effective use of layout and screen space.** Here is the process:

1. Choose a scenario.

2. Make a printout of every page used in the scenario.

3. Perform the scenario, highlighting everything that is potentially useful along the way.

4. (Optional) Repeat for other scenarios, using a different highlight color.

5. Evaluate the results.

In evaluating the results, here are some things to look for:

- How much of the page is highlighted? What didn't get highlighted, and why is it there?

- Where are the most important screen elements placed? Is the prime screen real estate used appropriately?

- How much of the page is dedicated to the most important screen elements? Is the star of the show getting top billing?

- Are screen elements truncated or do they require scrolling to see?

- Are there large blocks of unused screen space?

To show an example, Figure 5.26 shows a screen for a travel reservation app. The scenario is to check the status of my next flight to make sure everything is according to schedule.

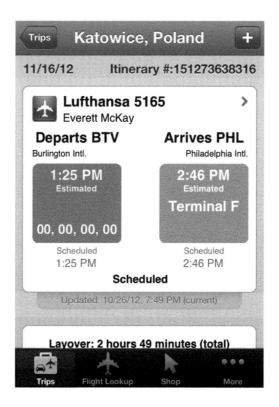

FIGURE 5.26

A screen to evaluate with a highlighter review.

OK, what do you think at this point? The results of the highlighter review are shown in Figure 5.27.

FIGURE 5.27
The screen after a highlighter review.

The highlighter review shows that this screen did well, because I highlighted most of its content. Still, not everything was highlighted, so applying the process suggests these questions:

- I didn't highlight the itinerary number because it doesn't mean anything to me or the airline. According to the iOS guidelines, the top of the screen is considered the most valuable, so why is this information there? Does it really have to be at the top of the screen?

- I didn't highlight the generic airplane icon because it tells me nothing that isn't obvious. It might have value if there were other types of reservations, but could this icon be more useful, perhaps using the Lufthansa logo instead?

- I didn't highlight my name or the updated time stamp, but they don't take much space. Let's assume that these might be useful in other scenarios.

- Notice how much screen space didn't get highlighted. Although generous whitespace is a good thing, is there a more space-efficient layout that might work better on a smartphone?

These are all good questions and suggest room for improvement, and they are all easier to identify with the highlighter test.

Highlighter reviews are a simple way to evaluate the integrity of a page as well as its effective use of layout and screen space.

Scanning reviews

A *scanning review* evaluates how scannable a page is by reading it according to three sets of rules: immersive reading rules, scanning rules, and "Ginger" rules. Remember from Chapter 3 that users don't read, they scan—so you should design pages specifically for scanning.

Immersive reading is for comprehension. Here are the rules for an immersive read:

- Read all text on the page in a left-to-right, top-to-bottom order.

- Read standard icons. For example, read a warning icon as "Warning!"

- Ignore anything that requires interaction, such as tooltips or flyouts.

In applying these rules, the text should make sense, should be well written and not redundant, and it shouldn't sound silly or feel tedious. After all, that is the text that is there, so reading all of it should be a good experience.

Scanning is for finding things quickly. Here are the scanning rules:

- Read generally from left to right, top to bottom, but let your eye gravitate to things that demand attention.

- Read all prominent text, but only the first line.

- Read all interactive control labels.

- Read error and warning icons and red text, but only if they stand out.

- Ignore everything else.

In applying these rules, it should be clear what to do. If not, the page isn't scannable.

The "Ginger" rules are like the scanning rules but more extreme. Ginger is a dog in a famous Gary Larson cartoon called *What we say to dogs vs. what they hear.* (see Figure 5.28) Unfortunately, I can't show you the cartoon, but the joke is that the only thing that Ginger hears is her name. It turns out that when quickly scanning a UI, users behave very much like Ginger.

FIGURE 5.28
What we say to users vs. what they hear.

Here are the "Ginger" rules:

- If there is a heading, read the first seven words or so.

- Read all interactive control labels.

- Read anything that the heading or interactive controls indicate that you should read.

- Read anything that demands attention.

- Ignore everything else.

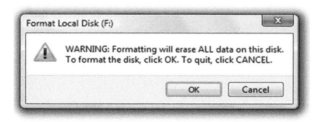

FIGURE 5.29
Format Local Disk confirmation from Windows.

In applying these rules, it should still be clear what to do. If it's not, the page isn't scannable for users who are barely paying attention.

For example, here is the Format Local Disk confirmation from Windows.

If you apply the immersive reading rules, you will read all the text in the confirmation in a left-to-right, top-to-bottom order. Note that the warning icon is read twice. Does this feel well written? Not redundant? Does it sound silly or feel tedious?

Now let's apply the scanning rules. In Figure 5.30 I have removed what you wouldn't read based on these rules.

FIGURE 5.30
A scanning read of the same confirmation.

FIGURE 5.31
What Ginger sees.

Is it clear what to do?

Now, here is the Ginger read (see Figure 5.31).

You might think the warning icon would show up here, but that's not my experience. Rather, users often click OK to immediately dismiss the dialog box, realize that it had a warning icon, and regret not reading it more carefully before dismissing it. Often all the warning icon does is lead to regret.

Is it still clear what to do? Of course not! Ginger (like everyone else) will click OK without reading anything. This UI is not designed for scanning. Fortunately, the fix is simple, as shown in Figure 5.32.

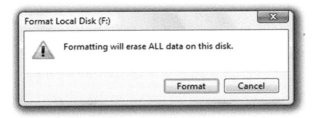

FIGURE 5.32
The final result: This confirmation is designed for scanning.

This technique is remarkably effective in identifying scanning problems.

> Scanning reviews evaluate how scannable a page is by reading it according to three sets of rules.

Five-second tests

A *five-second test* **evaluates the scannability and memorability of a page simply by having users view it for five seconds and then answer a few basic questions about the purpose of the page and important design details, such as the call to action.** If users can't answer those questions, that strongly suggests that you need to redesign the page to make it more scannable and make those key details stand out more.

Five seconds is a very brief period of time, but this amount of time is used to capture users' immediate impression rather than their analysis.

Here is the process:

1. Determine your goals for the study.

2. Chose the pages to evaluate.

3. Design a small number of questions to ask users to achieve your goals.

4. Run the test with a variety of users:

    a. Show a page for five seconds.

    b. Remove the page from view.

    c. Ask the questions.

5. Look for trends across the responses to identify areas for improvement.

To simulate a typical study, review the page in Figure 5.33 for exactly five seconds (no cheating!).

FIGURE 5.33
Please look at this page for only five seconds.

Now answer the following questions:

- What product or service does this page promote?
- Why should you consider buying or using it?
- What is its price?
- How do you buy it or try it?
- Describe what you remember seeing on the page.

Were you able to answer these basic questions? If not, what does this tell you about the design?

> Five-second tests evaluate the scannability and memorability of a page simply by having users view the page for five seconds and answer a few basic questions about its purpose.

GIVING AND RECEIVING FEEDBACK

The ability to give and receive effective design feedback is crucial for teams to do their best work. I have noticed that these are not natural skills, so I would like to share some tips on each. When giving feedback:

- Give feedback at the right level. If the goal is to get high-level, big-picture feedback, don't give feedback on fonts and colors—even if you are the boss.

- Avoid feedback based on personal opinion. Instead, frame feedback in terms of scenarios, personas, value, and design principles.

- Give feedback that is specific and actionable. Saying that a UI isn't intuitive is vague and not actionable. Saying that a UI needs better feedback is.

- Be supportive and encouraging. Remember that you are working together as a team. And be balanced by starting with positive feedback; it doesn't have to all be negative.

When receiving feedback:

- Welcome the feedback. Smile and say thank you. Remember that this is the price you have to pay to do your best work.

- Don't take the feedback personally. Remember that the goal is to improve the product, not to criticize you—even if the feedback isn't delivered diplomatically.

- Take the feedback seriously and encourage more.

Regarding giving feedback at the right level, I have noticed a phenomenon that I call *manager feedback inversion***, where managers tend to give feedback at exactly the wrong level.** Here is what might be going on:

- **Early in the process.** Here, you present rough wireframes to get high-level, big-picture feedback. Unfortunately, managers perceive the roughness to mean that the design isn't yet worthy of serious attention, so they give feedback on what they easily notice—usually the details!

- **Late in the process.** Here, you present higher-fidelity mockups to get lower-level, detailed feedback. Now managers perceive that the design is getting real, so they start to pay serious attention by noticing high-level, big-picture problems that they should have noticed much earlier in the process.

The best solution to manager feedback inversion is to set design review rules and enforce them—even for managers.

WHAT ABOUT AGILE DEVELOPMENT?

It's important for any UI design process to be compatible with agile development. Many development teams have either adapted an agile development process or are working on it.

Chances are, your team has, too. The design community is still working on how best to integrate UI design into an agile process.

In case you are unfamiliar with the term, *agile* **refers to lightweight software development methods** based on rapid, iterative, adaptive development, where working software is delivered in regular time-limited phases, requirements and solutions evolve through collaboration and evolutionary development, and rapid and flexible response to change is encouraged. This is in contrast to the traditional heavyweight *waterfall model*, where the process steps are sequential and relatively inflexible, and the resulting product isn't evaluated or fully debugged until the end of the process—once the work is mostly complete.

Agile methods are based on the *Manifesto for Agile Software Development*, which is quite simple. In fact, here it is:

> We are uncovering better ways of developing software by doing it and helping others do it. Through this work we have come to value:

- **Individuals and interactions** over processes and tools
- **Working software** over comprehensive documentation
- **Customer collaboration** over contract negotiation
- **Responding to change** over following a plan

> That is, while there is value in the items on the right, we value the items on the left more.

Though the concept of agile development is simple, there is plenty of room for interpretation. My interpretation is that traditional software methods are too heavy, time consuming, and inflexible and often fail to produce good results. As a result, we shouldn't waste time on planning, documentation, and process *that aren't effective* but instead get immediate feedback to make sure we are on track and respond accordingly.

Not everyone shares this interpretation. Many people interpret *agile* to mean that most planning, design, and documentation are wasteful, that we don't know what users want without constant feedback and iteration, and so the best thing to do is start coding right away. They believe that writing code is the best measure of progress. For example, here is an excerpt from *Getting Real: The Smarter, Faster, Easier Way to Build a Successful Web Application,* by 37signals:

> Get something real up and running quickly. Running software is the best way to build momentum, rally your team, and flush out ideas that don't work. It should be your number one priority from day one ... Stories, wireframes, and even HTML mockups are just approximations. Running software is real.

> With real, running software everyone gets closer to true understanding and agreement. You avoid heated arguments over sketches and paragraphs that wind up turning out not to matter anyway.

Although I'm sure this approach works well for 37signals (a very small, very agile team), I believe this is poor advice generally. **For larger, less agile teams developing complex systems with dependencies, writing production code is the worst way to make most UI design decisions.**

The communication-driven design process that I have described in this chapter clearly requires up-front planning and design work. Many agile teams are loath to do such up-front planning, especially with short sprint cycles. But UI design, ultimately, *is* planning.

To make the case for this investment, I would like to modestly propose a *Manifesto for Communication-Driven UI Design*:

- **Effective UI design decisions require effective team communication.** Effective communication is focused on clear goals: communicating the right information to the right people at the right time. We shouldn't waste time communicating when there is no clear need—just because the process says so.

- **Lighter forms of communication are better.** Generally, use the lightest-weight form of communication that does the job well. Lighter forms of communication are easier to create and change, and they allow for faster iteration. There is little investment, so it's easier to look at alternatives or even start over. They also encourage more and better feedback because they are focused on high-level issues and perceived as unfinished and easily changeable. Agile methods prefer face-to-face communication, but it's hard to communicate significant UI design ideas this way.

  For communicating design ideas generally, sketching works best during ideation, wireframes work best for interaction design, and tools such as Photoshop and Illustrator work best for pixel-level visual design. Large, overly detailed documents that nobody reads are never a good choice.

- **Production code is commitment.** Yes, production code is real, so it involves real effort, real investment, and therefore real commitment. During the design phase, discovering better, completely different designs should be good news, but it won't be if there is already a significant code investment in the old design. No matter how agile the team, nobody wants to throw away working production code. By contrast, nobody gets emotional when a sketch or rough paper prototype is thrown away.

- **Effective UI design planning is practical.** The trick is to be focused and principled—which ineffective planning often fails to do. Customer collaboration, no matter how close and frequent, accomplishes little if nobody knows what to do or what a good UI design looks like. Focusing your design planning on effective human communication is an excellent way to stay focused and principled.

- **Efficient UI design planning is an excellent investment.** If done properly, efficient UI design planning is lightweight and entirely compatible with the agile goals of rapid iteration, collaboration, and being flexible and responsive to change.

Efficient UI design planning enables teams to make good decisions quickly and confidently *by design* instead of stumbling across them by accident. For a communication-driven process to work, teams have to accept this manifesto to be willing to make the modest up-front investment and perhaps use longer sprints to accommodate the extra work required.

The payback is to make the overall process more efficient. The ultimate measure of progress is the number of good decisions made and the least time wasted. By contrast, UI design by coding trial and error is a long, rough slog. Wasting time incrementally improving a poor, hastily "designed" UI is never agile.

SUMMARY

If you remember only 12 things:

1. **Although there is no single best design process, a communication-driven approach works well for most situations** and it allows you to leverage everyday interpersonal communication skills. If you can explain how to perform a task in person in a way that's clear and concise, this process will help you map that explanation into the language of UI—in a way that is naturally user and user-goal centered.

2. **A good user interface must go well beyond mechanically enabling a task.** Enabling a task is the first step, not the last. You need to do some work to map what the technology wants into a UI that users can understand and use easily and that meets their goals.

3. **Design is making creative decisions on behalf of target users to create a product that satisfies their goals.** A good design process incorporates the essential ingredients of this definition. The rational decision-making process is a good foundation for making important, potentially risky decisions.

4. **Watch out for the classic process mistakes, which are those process-related design mistakes that everyone tends to make.** Doing so will help you understand why intelligent, capable, well-motivated teams with the best of intentions so often fail to create good designs. Many fundamental product design blunders can be traced back to some basic process mistake.

5. **Define your product's (or feature's) value proposition**—the reason your target users will want to use it—and ensure that the design delivers it by maximizing its benefits, minimizing its costs, and making its value obvious. Value motivates people, so if your product or feature doesn't deliver clear value, little else matters.

6. **Use scenarios to understand your product from the customers' point of view.** Great design requires clear targets and scenarios provide those targets. If your product supports many scenarios, identify the top scenarios and focus on them. You can't design well by having random people doing random things for random reasons in random contexts.

7. **Define personas to better understand your target users.** Instead of long day-in-the-life stories, use short user models with relevant details that are focused on the design task at hand. Every decision you make should be consistent with the relevant persona. Discrepancies reveal design problems.

8. **Start the design phase by sketching out the conversations**—what the UI needs to communicate to determine how you would explain the task in person. Traditionally, many people start the design phase by exploring the UI's physical presentation, which tends to miss the communication angle. Once you understand what to communicate, you are then better able to explore the physical presentation of that communication through sketching.

9. **Use sketching during brainstorming to express and explore many ideas quickly.** Choose the strongest ideas based on the scenarios, personas, and value propositions you developed during the planning phase. Then develop those strongest ideas by prototyping.

10. **Generally, the lowest-fidelity prototype that achieves your goals is best.** Low-fidelity prototypes are great for determining task flows, rough page layouts, and basic interaction, whereas high-fidelity prototypes are great for getting pixel-level visual details such as fonts, colors, and exact layout plus high-level visual goals such as visual appearance and appeal, scannability, and personality.

11. **Effective design evaluations are crucial for your team to do its best work.** Use scenarios to drive the refinement process to evaluate the design from the user's point of view. Communication-driven evaluation techniques such as communication reviews, highlighter reviews, scanning reviews, and five-second tests are quick, easy to do, and very effective in finding communication problems.

12. **The communication-driven UI design approach requires modest up-front planning and designing to make the overall process more efficient.** Doing so enables you to make the right decisions quickly and confidently by design, making it compatible with agile processes. However, agile teams are under pressure to deliver working code right away and are reluctant to make such investments. To make it work, teams have to trust the process and be willing to make those investments and adjust the process to accommodate the need for up-front UI design planning.

EXERCISES

To improve your ability to use the design process, try the following exercises. *Assume that anything is possible. Don't let concerns over development costs or current technology limitations inhibit your thinking.*

1. **Adapting the design process.** Think of a design challenge that requires an innovative solution. Devise a design process to help you find such innovative solutions quickly and confidently. How important is a working prototype (or code, if software) in this process?

2. **Design is effective human communication.** Find an example of a good design that doesn't communicate well on a human level. What does the design do to compensate? Alternatively, find an example of a poor design that communicates poorly. How can you improve the design by improving its communication?

3. **Don't design like a programmer.** Find a UI that looks as though it were designed by a programmer (you shouldn't have to look too hard!). Why specifically does the design feel that way? Propose an alternative design that feels less technical and more user focused.

4. **Bad design CSI.** Find a product that is potentially useful but suffers from poor design. Review the classic process mistakes and choose the top three that most likely explain why it failed. Now suppose that you were managing the team that created the product. What could you do to prevent or correct those process mistakes?

5. **Value propositions.** Find a product that you really love and write its value proposition. Now do the same for a product that you thought you would love but don't. In both cases, what does value proposition tell you about the product's design? Now assume that you wrote those value propositions before the products were developed. Do you think you could accurately predict the products' success?

6. **Scenarios.** Take a feature that you are working on and design a UI based on that feature description alone. Evaluate the results. Now think about the tasks the feature is used for and improve your design based on supporting those tasks. Evaluate the results again. Now define the top scenarios for that feature and improve your design based on the scenarios. Be sure to put a lot of thought into the user's context. Evaluate the results again. Do you see an improvement over your original feature-based design?

7. **Personas.** Design a set of three personas for a project you are working on. Now define a persona for yourself and for your team. Compare. Do you have any insight into how you differ from your users?

8. **Brainstorming.** Think of a design challenge that requires an innovative solution. Think this problem through on your own and propose a strong solution. Now get a group of people together, have a brainstorming session, break up into teams, and have each team present its solution.

   Now take your original solution plus all the new ideas from the brainstorming and propose another design iteration. How much better is it than your original design? Do you think you could have created that new design working alone?

9. **Focus on the communication.** Think of a design challenge for a complex task. Get a group of people together and form two teams. Have Team A focus their effort purely on the UI. Have Team B initially focus on explaining the task to someone in person (without knowing they are designing a UI), then after that have them design the UI. Use the same, fixed amount of time for both teams. Did Team A sketch a pile of features? Did Team B focus on effective communication? Which team's design is better?

10. **Prototyping.** Think of a design challenge for a complex task. Get a group of people together and brainstorm the problem as a group. Now break into two teams and give each team the same fixed amount of time. Have Team A develop a single high-fidelity, detailed prototype. Have Team B develop as many high-level prototypes as they can using rough, low-fidelity prototypes including paper. Evaluate the results. Which team has the better design ideas?

11. **Innovation.** Think of a design challenge for a complex task. Get a group of people together and form two teams. Have Team A focus on creating a radically innovative solution, and have Team B focus on creating a familiar approach based on established design patterns. Which design is better? Which is easier to use and understand?

12. **Communication design reviews.** Find a multipage task that has room for improvement. Quickly perform a communication review, a highlighter review, a scanning review, and a five-second test. What problems did you find? Which design review technique was the most useful? Which was the most effective at finding problems quickly?

UI Design Examples

All the proof of a pudding is in the eating.

—WILLIAM CAMDEN

At this point, we understand what it means for a design to be intuitive, how to design for effective human communication (both interaction and visually), plus how to design on a human level. We also have a communication-focused design process. **It's time to put everything together by working through realistic design problems in detail.**

For the design challenge, I would like to design an airline travel application as both a desktop site and a mobile app. Here is a summary of the challenge:

> To design an app that enables users to quickly and easily perform airline travel-related activities, such as booking, changing, and reviewing reservations, plus any related tasks to help users prepare or complete the trip.

I chose this example because it is familiar enough to not require much explanation, challenging enough to be relevant for someone designing a typical site or business application, yet difficult enough to show the benefits a communication-focused approach provides over more traditional design approaches.

My goal for this chapter is to illustrate how focusing on effective communication drives the design process, leads to designs that are intuitive and user centered, and helps you make the right decisions quickly and confidently.

AN OVERVIEW OF COMMON ALTERNATIVE DESIGN APPROACHES

To get an appreciation for the benefits of a communication-focused design process, let's start by comparing the way we might approach the design challenge using the most common alternatives. In this section, I have outlined some common alternative design techniques that many software professionals use, along with their pros and cons. Some of these techniques work well; others, not so much.

I am assuming that a communication-focused design process is a new technique for you and that you might need some convincing. But if you are already on board and don't need further convincing, feel free to skip ahead to Design Challenge 1.

Before continuing, you might want to stop and think about how you would ordinarily approach this design problem:

- What process steps would you use?

- How would you make design decisions?

- What would the design look like?

- How would you evaluate the results?

- How good do you think the results will be?

Designing like a programmer

Chapter 5 presented the idea of designing like a programmer—where programmers have a tendency to enable tasks mechanically and let features and technology drive design decisions.

Many programmers would tackle an airline travel app by first designing the backend database to support searching for flights in a way that meets requirements such as handling flight segments and different types of tickets. (Of course, determining those requirements is a significant part of the design challenge.) During this process, they might design a data structure for searching for flights that looks like this:

```
struct FlightOptions {

    int        FlightSegments;

    String     DepartureAirportCodes[maxFightSegments];

    String     ArrivalAirportCodes[maxFightSegments];

    Date       FightDates[maxFlightSegments];

    int        Travelers;

    int        TravelersAges[maxTravelers];

    TicketClass    TheTicketClass;

    Bool       NonstopOnly;

    Bool       RefundableOnly;

};
```

FIGURE 6.1
A data structure for flight searches.

Then design a UI that directly exposes this data structure directly to users, as shown in Figure 6.2.

A Web Page

http://dk-travel.com

Flight Options

Flight 1: Departure airport:

Airport code

Arrival airport:

Airport code

Travelers: 1

Traveler ages: 0 0 0 0 0

Ticket class:

All

Departing:

mm/dd/yy

Segments: 1

Non-stop only
Refundable only

Search

Designed for robots

FIGURE 6.2
An "obvious" UI for finding a flight that closely mirrors the underlying technology. Users will get this, right? Talk about form following function.

If you are a programmer, admit it: you do this, right?

Pros: It's easy to design, write, and test the code because the UI is a thin layer that presents the technology to users.

Cons: The UI isn't necessarily usable because people don't work the way code works. In this case, the underlying technology handles flight segments and traveler ages in a way that doesn't mirror how users think about them.

My expectations: At best, this approach enables tasks mechanically—resulting in a functional but not necessarily usable solution. At worst, the results are unusable because users don't think or behave the way the code works. It also often results in extreme complexity because developers are tempted to expose everything—all in one screen. In this case, most flights are round trip to a single destination, most reservations are for coach, most users don't know airport codes, and so on, but code-focused UIs often overlook these details by essentially assuming that all flight reservations are equally likely.

Sketching

Many designers would tackle this problem by creating a list of features and sketching a variety of ways to present them. In fact, the Apple iOS Human Interface Guidelines recommend a variation on this approach.

For an airline travel app, a designer might start with a list of airline travel-related features, as shown in Figure 6.3. Then the designer might sketch out different ways to present those features, along the way hoping to discover what works best, as shown in Figure 6.4.

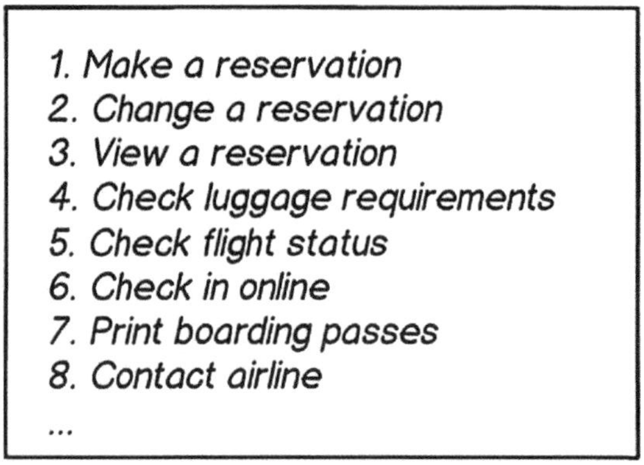

1. Make a reservation
2. Change a reservation
3. View a reservation
4. Check luggage requirements
5. Check flight status
6. Check in online
7. Print boarding passes
8. Contact airline
...

FIGURE 6.3

Starting the design with a list of features.

A Web Page
http://dk-travel.com
DK-Travel--Always the best deal!
Sign in
Flights
Search
Travel specials
Your travel info
View a reservation
Flight status
Check in
Print boarding passes
Hot travel destinations!
no where in particular

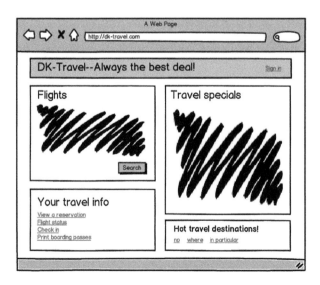

FIGURE 6.4

A sketch of an airline travel homepage.

Pros: As I mentioned in Chapter 5, sketching has many advantages because it is a simple, efficient way to visualize and explore design ideas—either by yourself or with your team.

Cons: Sketching often focuses the design effort on the *physical presentation* of the UI. If good UI design is about effective human communication, how can we determine the best way to present that communication physically when we don't even know what it is yet?

For example, review my sketch in Figure 6.4. What insight does it give us about the problem, how to make the tasks intuitive or simple, and how to best achieve the user's goals? Using this approach, all too often our attention will be completely focused on the layout.

My expectation: Sketching without any preliminary design analysis focuses on visual design elements, control selection, and the elements' physical presentation details, such as size, location, and flow. It focuses on making sure that everything is there and physically fits on the page. Sketching helps us visualize design ideas and variations quickly, but any insights beyond the physical presentation are often more accidental rather than deliberate.

Not that there is anything wrong with that—it's just not the best first step.

Designing with user research data

Designers on teams with user researcher support (which, unfortunately, isn't very common) would tackle this problem by starting with user research to answer some basic questions, such as:

- Who are our target users? What are their goals?

- What problems do they have with existing solutions?

- What improvements would they like to see?

They might also do some usability lab studies of competing solutions to get objective data on how well they perform and where they could be improved.

FIGURE 6.5
Designing with user research.

Pros: A great start to any project. Why speculate when we can gather real data?

Cons: The only cons are cost and time involved plus the potential for using the research data as a substitute for thinking. Research data should be used to support the design decisions, not make them for us. Unfortunately, that is often what happens.

My expectation: A design team that depends too heavily on user research data is vulnerable to making small, incremental improvements to existing solutions because that is what the data is most likely to reveal. That's not bad if that's your goal. But courageous design sometimes requires interpreting and challenging the user research data, which many data-driven teams are reluctant to do.

Designing by formal requirements

Here a user researcher or business analyst performs user and stakeholder research to understand what users need to satisfy their goals, and this data is boiled down into a set of requirements that the product design must satisfy.

Here are some possible requirements for an airline travel app system:

- Must support flight search for one-way, round-trip, and multiple-destination (up to five) flights.

- Must respond to one-way and round-trip domestic flight searches within 10 seconds, domestic multiple-destination searches with 15 seconds, and international flights within 25 seconds.

- After users click the Search for Flights button, will display a progress feedback page within 2 seconds.

- Initially, the flight search UI displays a "City or airport" placeholder in the airport text box; after a search (successful or not), the last input city or airport is the default for each airport text box.

- ...

Pros: If well done, the requirements can make an excellent decision-making framework based on real customer data. A requirements document provides a contract for acceptance criteria for the stakeholders.

Cons: This approach presumes that users know what they want and that meeting requirements results in a usable, desirable product. This process doesn't work well if the non-user stakeholders (such as project managers) fail to represent the target users. The process encourages long requirements lists, which are hard to understand and may make sense individually but not necessarily cumulatively. Also, it's easy for development teams to focus on designing solutions that technically meet the requirements and do nothing more—even if doing so fails to achieve the underlying user goals that led to the requirements in the first place. This approach potentially stifles design thinking if going beyond the requirements isn't encouraged or rewarded.

My expectations: Sometimes "requirements" turn out not to be true target user requirements but stealth UI specs. For example, does making a flight reservation really need a separate progress feedback page? Does it really need to be displayed within 2 seconds? Because they are considered requirements, we will never know, because nobody will bother to ask these questions.

Designing with user stories

User stories **are one or more sentences in concise, plain language that capture a user's goal or task as part of his or her role in using a product. These stories are often used in place of formal requirements in agile development methods.** User stories typically use this format:

As a *<user role>*, I want to *<do something supported by the program>* so that I *<can achieve something of value>*.

Here are some possible user stories for an airline travel app:

- As a traveler, I want to search for flights based on cities, airport names, and airport codes so that I can find flights using the information I already know.

- As a traveler, I want to be able to choose my seats and avoid undesirable seats. Whenever I have a tight connection, I want a seat up front so that I can avoid missing flights.

- As a business traveler, I want the site to remember and apply my travel preferences so that I can book travel conveniently.

- As a business traveler, I need to balance convenience and flexibility with cost savings.

- As a business traveler, I need to get my reservations approved before I can purchase them so that I can comply with my company's travel policies.

- As a business traveler, the meeting I am flying to has been postponed, so I need to change both my flight and rental car.

- As a frequent business traveler, I want to travel with my preferred carriers so that I can get frequent-flyer points and preferred seating.

- As a frequent business traveler, I want travel based on convenience and flexibility more than cost savings.

- As a leisure traveler, I want to choose from the least expensive flights, even at the cost of minor inconvenience.

- …

Pros: Compared to formal requirements, user stories are much simpler, more user centered, and more goal focused. Providing a specific role and possibly a context provides more credibility and insight than formal requirements, which typically lack this information. The resulting designs are more likely to be focused on users and the value the product gives users than is feature-focused design.

Perhaps most important, user stories are less likely to be stealth UI specs. Stealth specs like the following are obviously suspicious:

As a traveler, after clicking the Search for Flights button, I want the site to display a progress feedback page within 2 seconds.

Who says that's what travelers want?

Cons: Like requirements, user stories tend to be granular, so they may make sense individually but not necessarily cumulatively. Worse, the specific design targets aren't very clear. Who are the target users? What are they trying to do? What are their goals beyond the individual story? What is their larger context or environment? An actual user profile and scenario might span several user stories. To answer these questions, we may have to synthesize many user stories to get the full picture—assuming that we bother to do this in the first place. Most people don't.

My expectations: As with formal requirements, it's easy for development teams to focus on designing solutions that technically meet the user stories and do nothing more—even if doing so fails to achieve the underlying target user goals that led to the user stories in the first place. In fact, the tight release cycles used in agile processes encourage "closing" the user stories and nothing more. This approach potentially stifles design thinking if going beyond the user stories isn't encouraged or rewarded.

Designing by committee

Teams that lack strong design talent often resort to the classic "design by committee" approach (even if they won't admit it), where the UI design is "owned" by the team (and therefore not owned by anyone) and important decisions are made by consensus. The logic behind this approach seems sound: If the team lacks design expertise, it's better to take advantage of everyone's input to make better design decisions.

Pros: Design by committee has the potential to fully engage the team by leveraging everyone's skills and input. Important decisions reached through consensus are better, right?

Cons: Successful team members quickly learn that this isn't a design process but a political process. Better to propose safe, conventional, easy-to-implement solutions to get quick consensus than to propose anything daring. Often, such "design by committee" decisions aren't better, they're just safer.

Another challenge is that committee members feel obligated to make their contribution any way they can, and they often do so by wrangling over minutiae while completely ignore the critical, big-picture issues.

FIGURE 6.6
Design execution by committee—the old fashioned way. Everybody takes a shot, but nobody has any responsibility or gets any blame.

My expectation: Design by committee often leads to designs that do the job but are otherwise lacking, without any design courage. After all, the art of politics is to obtain something that nobody wants but everybody can accept. But designing by committee makes bosses happy—especially when the consensus opinion matches theirs—which somehow happens surprisingly often.

As Sir Alec Issigonis once noted, "a camel is a horse designed by committee." He's not a fan, either.

FIGURE 6.7

"A camel is a horse designed by committee." —Sir Alec Issigonis

Designing by copy or by design pattern

Here designers might tackle this problem by researching competing products (in this case, other travel sites) to see how they work as well as looking at unrelated products that have similar functionality for design patterns and trends.

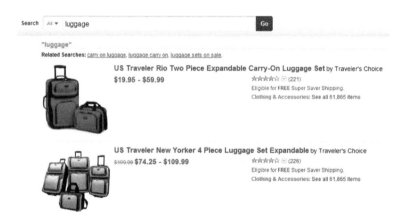

FIGURE 6.8

Although Amazon isn't designed for reserving flights, it might serve as a good design model. Featuring customer ratings for airlines and matching flights is an interesting idea.

Pros: A quick, easy way to determine and leverage good design solutions and communicate complex design ideas.

Cons: Has the potential for limiting thinking to existing solutions and propagating bad design. Individual design elements might work well individually but not work together harmoniously.

My expectation: This is an excellent technique to inspire new design ideas based on existing solutions. Mindless copying of other designs (without considering the target users, their goals, and so on) is less likely to be successful. Unfortunately, mindless design-by-copy is quite popular.

Summary

In Chapter 5, I made the case that there is no single best UI design process. **All the design process approaches that we just reviewed have merits (some more so than others), but they lack a way to make good user-centered design decisions quickly and confidently. A communication-focused design process will help us achieve this goal.**

Let's see how in the next section.

All the design approaches described in this section have merits, but they lack a way to make the right user-centered design decisions quickly and confidently.

DESIGN CHALLENGE 1: AN AIRLINE TRAVEL DESKTOP SITE

To show the benefit of a communication-focused design process, let's work through designing an airline travel site for desktop UI using the design process described in Chapter 5. Most of the steps will be described in some detail. The time and space available forbids a complete solution, but you should get a strong idea of how a communication-focused design process works by the end of the challenge.

Planning step 1: Start with a solid product concept

Let's start the planning phase by defining the concept for this product:

Dunner Kruger is a global travel agency that wants to move its services online. Dunner Kruger's focus is business travelers as well as vacationers looking for great deals. Their new airline travel site, dk-travel.com, needs to reflect these strengths by helping business and leisure travelers buy the right tickets at the best price, with minimal effort. The site is free to users; Dunner Kruger makes a commission from their carriers when customers buy a ticket.

Now we know the business objective. The target audience is fairly broad, but note that it excludes travel agencies and corporate travel offices. Dunner Kruger's focus is individual travelers.

Planning step 2: Provide clear value through the value proposition

Let's now define a value proposition that will provide the reasons that the target users will want to use the site. There is a lot of competition for air travel sites, so merely enabling customers to book flights isn't enough to be successful—we must deliver clear value compared to the competition.

For business travelers, dk-travel.com makes it is easy to book flights according to travel preferences and business policies with minimal effort. For leisure travelers, dk-travel.com makes it easy to find great travel deals, especially for families with some flexibility when traveling to popular destinations. In both cases, comparison shopping and booking repeated flights are especially easy, particularly compared to competing travel sites.

Delivering this value proposition is crucial because value is what motivates people. If dk-travel.com fails to deliver value compared to the alternative solutions, nothing else about the design is going to matter. So, to be successful, *dk-travel.com* must maximize these benefits (quickly finding the right flight for the right price), minimize the cost of using the site (the user's time and effort), and make the site's value immediately obvious, especially compared to the competition.

Planning step 3: Model the target users through personas

For user-centered design, we need clear target users. **Let's now define three personas to characterize three classes of users for dk-travel.com:**

Michele, the occasional business traveler:

- Travels on business a few times per year.
- Must get approval for travel, and flights must conform to corporate travel policies.
- Can spend more for flexibility and convenience as long as the trip conforms to corporate travel policies.
- Doesn't know major airports, airport codes, or aircraft types.
- Most travel is domestic.

Filipe, the frequent business traveler:

- Travels on business at least once per month on average.
- Travels to some destinations repeatedly and knows most of their airport codes. For efficiency, prefers searching for frequent destinations using airport codes instead of city names.
- Given the amount of travel, needs flexibility and convenience and has permission to spend more for flexible flights.
- Enrolled in many frequent-flyer programs but prefers to use his top two carriers to receive the most benefits and maintain elite status.
- Prefers flying business class on larger planes.
- Travel is both domestic and foreign, some intercontinental. Filipe has permission to fly business class for intercontinental flights.
- With so much travel it's hard to keep things straight, so Filipe wants to be able to check flight information and status quickly from anywhere using his smartphone.

Marie, the leisure travel bargain hunter:

- Travels only a few times a year either to popular vacation destinations or to visit family.
- Usually travels with spouse and child, so is very price sensitive and motivated to save money.
- To save money, motivated to comparison shop for different travel days, carriers, and airports.
- Willing to trade convenience and flexibility for lower prices. For example, willing to fly to nearby airports and drive to destination if that will save money.
- Taxes and baggage fees add up quickly, so Marie needs to be aware of the total cost when choosing flights. Marie wants the baggage fees to be obvious and will pack accordingly. She never wants to be surprised at the airport.
- Enrolled in only a couple frequent-flyer programs and typically won't qualify for preferred boarding or free upgrades. She prefers familiar carriers but isn't motivated to choose a carrier based on a frequent-flyer program—ticket cost is more important.
- Doesn't know which cities have major airports, airport codes, or aircraft types. Needs assistance with this information.
- Most travel is domestic.

With these personas, we now have a much better understanding of the target users and their goals. For example, knowing that frequent business travelers are very motivated to fly with their preferred carriers gives us an insight that we might otherwise miss.

Note that we don't need long, detailed documents to do this. We don't need to know the details of each persona's life story—the kids, the coffee, the cars, the cats, etc.—because they aren't relevant to the design task at hand. Instead, it's better to keep the personas simple by focusing on details that drive design decisions.

For most teams, these personas would be based on a combination of known facts and some assumptions to fill in the blanks. Of course, the personas are stronger if they're based on user research, and having research could make details more accurate and any numeric data more precise.

Planning step 5: Understanding what users will do through top scenarios

Let's now define the top scenarios: those contextual tasks that users are most likely to do and will delight users when done especially well. These scenarios will then drive many design decisions.

We need to choose these top scenarios carefully. The challenge is that an airline travel app, like many business applications, could support dozens of scenarios. Some complex business applications may support possibly hundreds of scenarios. But we can't realistically design for hundreds of scenarios, so we have to choose a small number of top scenarios that are especially important.

Here are three good top scenarios for dk-travel.com:

Michele, an occasional business traveler, needs to travel from her office in Los Angeles, California, to mid-town Manhattan for a three-day industry conference. Her company is strongly encouraging its employees to keep travel expenses under control. She wants to be away from her family for the least amount of time, so she would be willing to take a "red-eye" flight. The JFK, La Guardia, and Newark airports are all equally acceptable to her, but she doesn't travel often and isn't aware that Newark is close by her destination.

Filipe, a frequent business traveler, needs to travel from his office in Chicago, Illinois, to Shanghai, China, to help his team close a business deal. He needs to be there for a five-day work week, but he wants to arrive a couple days early to recover from the flight. He has permission to fly business class as long as the round-trip flight is under $6,000. Being from Chicago, he has a strong preference for flying with United or United partners such as Asiana.

Marie, a leisure travel bargain hunter, wants to take her husband Chip and their young daughter to Fort Lauderdale, Florida, from their home in Montreal, Quebec Canada, to visit family over winter break. Given its popularity, that route tends to be very expensive, so she wants the best deal and can be flexible with travel dates. She is enrolled in the Air Canada frequent-flyer program, but that doesn't influence her decisions much. She will rent a car, so flying to Miami is also an option. Given the young age of her child, she wants to avoid long flights and long layovers as well as very short layovers where they might be too rushed or miss a connection. Of course, getting seats together is crucial. Finally, for all their gear she will have to check in at least two bags, so she is worried about check-in baggage costs.

To compare to task-based design, note that the task in each of these scenarios is essentially the same: Somebody needs to book a flight. It's everything else about each scenario—the specific user, their specific goals, and the specific context they are in—that makes the scenarios useful design tools. Often I find that the task itself is often the least interesting part of a good scenario.

To compare to user stories, note how user stories are much more granular, so we don't have a complete picture of the user's goals and context. Also, user stories are usually role based (such as a "frequent business traveler"), so we don't have a complete picture of the target user, either.

Note how these three scenarios cover a wide range of user goals and contexts. Clearly, not all travelers have exactly these details, but these scenarios are representative of the types of airline travel concerns that many users are likely to have. If we design for these scenarios well, there's a good chance that our design will cover many other scenarios, too. In practice we might have more than three top scenarios—two or three per target user is reasonable. But we want to have a small, practical number.

Realism is important here—having realistic user scenarios results in much better design decisions. These feel like real user-focused scenarios that address real goals and concerns, not made-up technology-focused scenarios to advertise the importance of a new feature or project objective. Many software teams essentially design for random people in random places doing random tasks for random reasons. That leads to random design decisions, so that approach isn't nearly as helpful.

Planning step 6: Determine the problems we need to solve

It's useful to be clear on what specific problems we are trying to solve—above and beyond providing value and supporting the top scenarios. Here are some airline reservation problems worth solving:

- To book a flight, travelers need to specify travel dates, times, and airports, but they may have significant flexibility here. Some flyers might not even know exactly what they want. (Example: Marie wants to travel to New York City sometime this summer.)

- Booking a flight is an iterative process. Even if users aren't comparison shopping, they aren't likely to specify all the information perfectly on the first try.

- The more flexibility travelers have, the more comparison shopping they are likely to do. Comparison shopping is very clumsy on most travel sites, where users have to improvise it on their own. Note that selecting a flight more likely means "I'm interested in this flight" than "I want to book this flight now." It might be better to build comparison shopping directly into the UI, requiring features such as the ability to save searches and print itineraries that haven't been purchased yet.

- Total costs (including baggage fees) and comparison shopping are very important for leisure travelers.

- Although total costs are an important factor, other factors such as convenience, flexibility, overall travel time, layover airports and times, and departure and arrival times affect traveler's choices as well.

- Preferred carriers and their partners, corporate travel policies, and upgrades are very important for business travelers.

- We can simplify finding good flights by taking full advantage of previous user input and some basic facts about how users make choices. Users shouldn't have to manually specify everything each time they do a search.

- Users might need help selecting airports because they are more aware of destination cities than airport names. They might be confused if a destination city is served by more than one airport.

Later, when we evaluate our design, we need to make sure that these problems are actually solved.

Design step 1: Defining conversations to focus on effective human communication

With the planning phase done, let's start the design phase. As I suggested earlier in this chapter, many designers would start by identifying a set of useful features, then sketching how those features could be presented, but these sketches tend to focus on the physical presentation of the UI and not go beyond that. So instead, let's put some thought into effective communication to help us better understand what we need to present in the UI.

To establish a baseline, let's temporarily do the opposite and outline what the airline reservation task might look like from a purely mechanical point of view. Here are the task steps and user input required to get the task done mechanically:

1. Sign in or create an account

   - User signs in or creates a new account, providing a username and password.

2. Gather flight info (starting from a blank form, requires specific airports and dates for each segment and the number of travelers)

   - User enters all flight criteria, clicks Search.

   - If any problems with input data, site gives an error message.

3. Present matching flights (unfiltered, sorted based on departure time)

   - User reviews flight options, makes a choice.

4. Confirm flight

   - User reviews details, agrees to terms, clicks Continue.

5. Select travelers

   - User enters traveler information required to issue tickets. Presented option to choose seats.

6. Select seats

   - If user choses option, selects seats for each traveler for each segment.

7. Gather payment info

  • User enters credit card information, clicks Purchase.

8. Final confirmation

  • User saves or prints flight information.

Although this task sequence gets the job done mechanically, there are some problems:

• The task starts by requiring users to sign in. Users typically want to shop first, then buy once they find what they are looking for. Requiring sign-in is an unnecessary hurdle that discourages shopping.

• Starting with a blank form requires users to provide the same information over and over, especially when comparison shopping. Chances are that the next search will be very similar to the previous one.

• Users have to know exactly what they want to fill out the form. They may have flexible dates, times, or even airports, so they might not even know this information.

• There is no user assistance in making choices beyond responding to error messages.

• Presenting all matching flights might be overwhelming for popular routes, especially if certain flight combinations make no sense compared to the alternatives.

• Displaying the matching flights based only on departure time makes it difficult to find flights based on other criteria.

• There's no opportunity to refine the search while viewing the matching flights. Users are better able to specify certain options and filters while viewing the results rather than when making the search initially.

• The travelers for this flight are likely to be travelers from previous flights. User shouldn't have to reenter all the traveler information.

• Credit card information might be the same as last time. Users should have a secure way to save it.

To improve the task, let's now think through how we might perform the task in person, where a traveler is making a reservation with a human travel agent. I call these interactions *conversations.*

FIGURE 6.9

The task should feel like a human conversation, so let's characterize that conversation.

Here are conversations that outline the first two steps to reserve an airline ticket. First, I outline the questions the travel agent would ask, the choices that are available, and the default values the agent would normally assume. To help translate the conversation to UI, I then outline important details for the interaction: the action the user would take, the feedback the user would receive, any notable details to get it right, plus what a successful interaction looks like from the user's point of view.

The goal behind the conversations is to help determine good design decisions, so I'm not making any firm UI decisions here—it's too early. Rather, the goal is to just get a feel for what a good human conversation would look like. At this point, anything that looks like a UI decision is only a suggestion.

Where would you like to fly?

Travel agent: Asks the traveler for the following information, providing suitable defaults whenever possible.

What type of flight are you making?

- Choices: Round-trip, one-way, or multi-city flight
- Default: Round-trip (most common)

Where are you leaving from? Is the departure city flexible? Do you need help finding it?

- Choices: Cities, airports, airport codes
- Default: Last departure city (most likely), otherwise need to ask

Where are you flying to? Is the destination city flexible? Do you need help finding it?

- Choices: Cities, airports, airport codes
- Default: Last destination city (most likely), otherwise need to ask

When would you like to leave? Is this date flexible?

- Choices: Specific date (if flexible, date range), time or time range
- Default: Last departure date, otherwise need to ask

When would you like to return? Is this date flexible?

- Choices: Specific date (if flexible, date range), time or time range
- Default: Last return date (if valid) or same day as departure date

Who is flying?

- Choices: Adults, children (with ages), seniors
- Default: The current user if known, last number of people and ages, or one adult

What fare class would you like?

- Choices: Economy, business, first class
- Default: Last class chosen or economy

Supporting UI:

- **User action:** User provides the flight criteria, then clicks **Find flights.**
- **Feedback:** Engaging, accurate progress indicator to show search progress.
- **Input:** For efficiency and forgiveness, users shouldn't have to reenter recently input information, even when handling errors, clicking Back, or changing the number of flight segments. Provide a date picker and airport picker to make these selections easy and error proof. Both pickers should make it easy to choose recent selections.
- **Success criteria:** Users should be able to make each selection with confidence, without assistance or error. Error messages are rare because controls are constrained to valid values.

Choose your flight to your destination

Travel agent: Here are the flights (one segment at a time) that meet your criteria, lowest price first. To help you choose, each flight shows:

- Price (including taxes)
- Airline
- Flight information for each segment (departure and arrival information cities and times, duration, actual carrier)

- Overall duration, plus layovers
- Meals
- Baggage fee information
- Seat preview
- Type of aircraft

Would you like to sort the results to help you make a selection?

- Choices: Sort by price, departure time, arrival time, stops, duration
- Default: Sort by price

Would you like to filter the results to help you make a selection?

- Choices: Filter by airline, number of stops, flight times, fare class
- Default: Show all results (no filtering)

Would you like to modify your flight search criteria?

- Provide user ability to change anything from step 1 without starting over. Make it especially easy to change dates and airports, since those are most likely.

Supporting UI:

- **User action:** User chooses each segment in order, typically by reviewing the results by scrolling, sorting, and filtering. Clicks **Continue** when done with all segments.
- **Feedback:** Text at top of page makes flight segment being chosen and any previously selected segments obvious. Each new selection updates lowest price possible based on current selections.
- **Visual details:** The following information should be obvious at a glance:
  - Best flights with lowest fares
  - Offerings of preferred carriers and their partners
  - Nearby airports and a sample of their best offerings
  - Flights with especially tight connections
- **Shopping:** Can use a matrix to show prices for multiple date searches. To keep the results list manageable, filter out unlikely choices. If there are still many reasonable choices, display the most likely by default and allow users to access all by clicking **Show all flights.**
- **Success criteria:** Users should be able to find the segments they want quickly. The most desirable choices should stand out visually. There should be few options that users would never choose. Users should rarely have to return to the first **Where would you like to fly?** step to make changes unless they are starting completely over.

Though I call these conversations, I am not limiting myself to the metaphor; these are not presented as literal conversations between two people. But they summarize the information that would be exchanged in an actual human conversation, plus they give details on what the UI needs to support that conversation, in terms of both interaction and visual design, to make it work on a human level. Note that the raw data structure in Figure 6.1 fails to provide us with any guidance beyond the mechanical.

After completing these conversations for the remaining steps, we can then evaluate the design by applying the scenarios, personas, and value propositions that we defined in the planning phase. Some questions to ask:

- Does it feel like a natural, friendly conversation? That is, does the conversation feel like what you would actually do and say in person? Does anything feel unnatural, mechanical, or inefficient?

- Are the scenarios fully supported? What changes can we make to better support the scenarios?

- Are the details right for the target personas? Will each persona like a solution that follows this conversation?

- Are we delivering value by helping users find the right flights with minimal effort, especially for comparison shopping and repeat bookings? Will that value be obvious to first-time users?

Sketching the physical presentation isn't necessary to answer these questions—we can answer them without thinking about pages, controls, layout, color, graphics, and the like. We can then quickly refine the conversations as necessary to fix any shortcomings. For example, reviewing our scenarios shows that we need to make sure the site works well with frequent-flyer information, corporate travel policies, and showing hidden costs. So, there's more work we can do here. When we start by sketching, at best we discover accidentally what the conversations show us deliberately.

Although we haven't designed the solution yet, we have documented what needs to happen in the conversation. This gives an overall guide for the design, but there is still a tremendous amount of flexibility in the interaction and visual design. This is not a spec, nor is it requirements. We now know what to do, but we don't know how best to do it.

Let's now design some task flows and pages. We are ready to start sketching!

Design step 2: Designing the task flow

Now that we know what we need to communicate, let's sketch out a high-level task flow. If we are thinking about the task of booking a flight mechanically, we might sketch out steps that look like those in Figure 6.10. The goal here is to determine the pages, roughly what goes on them, and how to navigate between them.

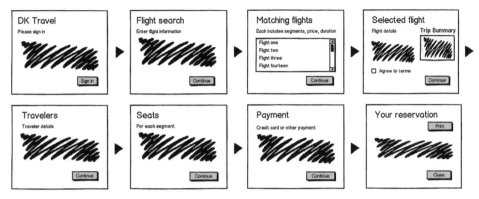

FIGURE 6.10

An initial sketch of the task flow.

If you are familiar with storyboards, note that this sketch is similar to a storyboard, but the focus is on the steps and their communication rather than visualizing the user performing the task steps and the interaction details. This difference makes these task flows easier to create, more focused on optimizing the task flow, and easier to draw for people without artistic skills.

Now that we have a task flow sketched out, we want to ensure that:

- **All steps are here and are necessary**—that we haven't missed any important steps. It's fairly common to realize that you have missed a step late in the process, so this is important. But on the other hand, make sure the steps are really necessary, and can't be done automatically.

- **The steps have the right order.** A different task order might make the task flow more logical and efficient to users. By delaying optional steps, we can possibly make the task feel more efficient, even if the total work required is the same.

- **The steps have the right grouping.** We can make the task flow more logical and efficient by combining steps that might work well together or separating steps that don't. Again, the right grouping might change the user's perception of the task, even if the total work is unchanged.

- **The steps feel natural and efficient.** Take a step back and make sure it feels like the way you would do the task in person. If not, there might be room for improvement.

- **The steps *sound* natural and user centered.** Do the steps sound like a natural, friendly conversation—or are they focused on the mechanics and the code? Is the purpose of each step clear from the user's point of view? Adding a verb to the step description helps make the steps clearer and more user centered because it focuses on what the user is doing instead of what the code needs.

By going through this evaluation, we can make some improvements. We will realize that we should make signing in optional, that choosing seats should be optional, that we can rephrase the steps and the commit buttons to be more user centered and purposeful, and that the point at which users are making the purchase should be obvious, as shown in Figure 6.11.

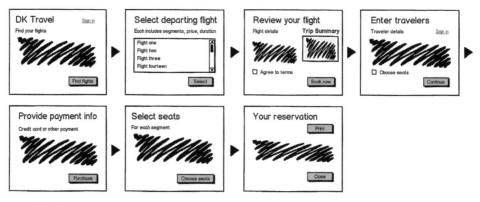

FIGURE 6.11
An improved sketch of the task flow.

Although the task flow improvements in this example were modest, it's common to make significant improvements at this step. Here are some insights you are likely to find:

- **Phrasing matters.** If we phrase the steps in terms of nouns instead of verbs, the steps are often mechanical and code centric. Rephrasing the steps and using clear verbs can reveal that the task flow needs significant improvement or even a complete overhaul. If one of your steps is called "Travel Manager," you have more work to do. Don't skip this step!

- **Perception matters.** Users don't want to do steps like signing in, providing payment information, or selecting travelers until it is necessary. Delaying such steps or making them optional reduces the perception of effort, even if ultimately the amount of work ends up being the same once the task is completed.

- **We might be doing too much on a page.** Developers are especially inclined to try to do as much as possible on a single page, resulting in very complex task steps. Better to split the steps or separate optional steps.

- **More than one task flow might work.** We might discover that several task flows work well and we can't decide between them based on effective communication and our scenarios, personas, and so on. If that's the case, consider usability lab studies to help make the decision.

This is about as much as we can do without specific page designs, so let's now sketch some pages!

Design step 3: Designing the pages

Let's sketch the first two pages for booking a flight. For this task, I will use the following process:

1. Start with main instruction for each page (even if implicit)—in this case, *Find your flights* and *Select your flight segments*. Main instructions were explained in detail in Chapter 1.

2. Choose the right controls for the user input—generally, the simplest, lightest-weight, most constrained controls. Choosing the right controls was explained in detail in Chapter 2.

3. Add labels and instructions to make it clear what the user is supposed to do. We explored well-designed labels and instructions in Chapter 2.

4. Layout the static page so that it has a logical flow and is easy to scan. We looked at the attributes of effective layout and scanning in Chapter 3.

5. Design the dynamic behavior. We explored how to present UI elements dynamically in an intuitive way in Chapter 2.

6. Optimize, make efficient, provide good feedback, and have a good personality. We explored how to communicate well on a human level in Chapter 4.

And here are the resulting designs (see Figure 6.12).

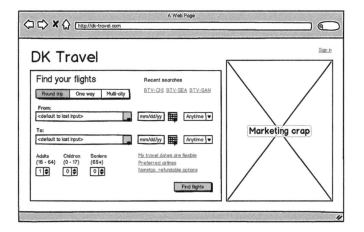

FIGURE 6.12

The "Find your flights" page

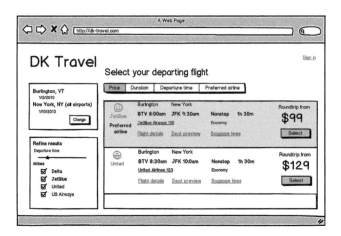

FIGURE 6.13

The "Select your flight segments" page.

Before moving on, I want to make sure that:

- It's clear what the user is supposed to do on each page. Check!

- Everything on the page is clearly related to the main instruction (even if the main instruction is implicit). Check!

- It feels like a natural, friendly conversation—what I would actually say in person. Check!

Design step 4: Getting the details right

Once all the pages are designed, it pays to take a step back and make sure the details are right before we move on to the refinement phase. Of course, the goal of the refinement phase is to identify and correct such details, but we can make the refinement phase more productive by fixing any obvious problems now.

To get the details right, here are some things to review:

- **Value proposition.** Does the design really deliver benefits, reduce costs, and make the value obvious?

- **Scenarios and persons.** Have we got the details right to fully support the scenarios? Are the user goals being achieved? Is the design consistent with the persona attributes? Does the design work well in the user's environment and context?

- **Conversations.** Does the design address the details we identified in the conversations?

- **Problems solved.** Does the design solve the problems we identified during the planning phase?

- **Simplicity and optimization.** What can be removed? What should be hidden by default? What can we optimize? Is there any unnecessary effort?

By performing this analysis for the airline reservation site, I want to make sure that:

- Users don't have to sign in. If they do sign in, the site remembers them.

- Users can quickly find what they are looking for with confidence, even if they have significant flexibility or don't know exactly what they want.

- Users rarely have to reenter previously provided information, even if they change airports and flight segments.

- Users can quickly narrow down the search results to their preferred flights.

- The flights that users choose most often are the easiest to find.

- Comparison shopping and booking repeated flights are easy to do.

- Frequent flyer programs and corporate travel policies are easy to accommodate.

- There are no obvious usability glitches.

For more ideas on design details to check, review "Getting the details right" in Chapter 5. Once we have a good story for these details, we are good to go.

Design step 5: Making a choice and getting real

We still have a few design details that we still need to resolve, but at this point we have one design direction that we are pursuing. That isn't always the case—we might have several competing designs and need to make a choice between them. Ideally our decision-making framework will help us make that decision with confidence, but if not, we might have to carry over more than one design direction into the refinement phase.

To advance to the refinement phase, we will need something more concrete to evaluate. We can start the refinement phase with anything from working code to an interactive prototype to a detailed paper prototype. Agile practitioners prefer working code at this point (as well as every other point). Personally, I prefer to use the lightest-weight approach that will get the job done well, and that is often a paper prototype. We reviewed the different prototyping approaches in Chapter 5. For more information on paper proto-typing, I recommend *Paper Prototyping: The Fast and Easy Way to Design and Refine User Interfaces,* by Carolyn Snyder and *Paper Prototyping Training Video* by Nielsen Norman Group.

Let's assume that we have a detailed paper prototype, so we'll move on to the Refinement phase.

Refinement step 1: Expert evaluation

I describe a variety of evaluation techniques in Chapter 5 and pointed out that expert evaluation has the benefit of being quick, inexpensive, and focused. So let's start there.

Most teams start with a team-based design review. This will allow us to get feedback from the full team and allow everyone to contribute. But as I mentioned in Chapter 5, such team-based design reviews tend to be ineffective, primarily because they focus on the wrong things, give mostly personal or unimportant feedback, and don't use the limited design review time effectively.

I recommend using scenario-based design reviews so that we can evaluate the design from the user's point of view instead of our own personal perspective. Thus, a simple design review walks through each of the top scenarios that we defined in the planning phase and evaluates the proposed design from that perspective.

To make these reviews effective, I recommend setting some ground rules. Here are my favorites:

- **Everyone participates!** If you have helpful, relevant, productive feedback, please share it. Don't be shy!

- **Stay on topic.** The design team sets the objectives for the design review, and everyone else on the team must follow them. If details such as colors, fonts, icons, and text are off the table, don't bring them up!

- **Focus on finding *potential* problems.** The design team will determine whether any issues raised are actual problems or whether there are good solutions to them later; we won't do that during the review.

- **No defending, designing, or debating!** Let's use the limited time we have effectively. Since we are finding potential problems, let's not waste time defending the current design, trying to figure out solutions, or having debates over minor issues. These tasks are more appropriately and more effectively done elsewhere. During the review, make your point and move on—don't dwell.

- **Avoid personal opinion.** Instead, phrase your feedback in terms of the scenarios, personas, design principles, and research data. For example, instead of saying, "I don't like the way users select the airport," consider saying, "I don't think the Marie persona will be able to select the airport correctly with this design." If you can't phrase your feedback in terms of the scenarios, personas, design principles, or research data, it probably is just personal opinion—and therefore better kept to yourself.

- **Give specific, actionable feedback.** Put some thought into how you phrase your feedback so that the team can actually do something with it. For example, don't say, "I find the flight search feature unintuitive." Instead, say specifically what the problem is, such as "Seat selection has poor feedback" or "The sign-in command isn't discoverable."

- **Win as one.** We are a team, so let's act like one. The review process should be a positive experience; the design team should feel good about the feedback. Let's find the problems, but let's also mention what is good about the design. Let's be considerate when delivering the feedback. Focus your feedback on the design, not on the competency of its designers. A design review shouldn't be a cruel bash-fest. You are not Steve Jobs, so don't act like him!

In addition to design reviews, I recommend using the other expert evaluation techniques that I mentioned in Chapter 5, especially communication, highlighter, and scanning reviews.

Refinement step 2: Usability lab studies

We will never know for sure whether our design is good until we test with real users. A *usability lab study* evaluates a design by having actual target users perform realistic tasks and determining whether they can complete them successfully. This is the ultimate measure of usability and user behavior (pre-deployment), and it always trumps expert-based evaluation, speculation, and personal opinion. As a result, usability lab studies are considered the gold standard of design evaluation. For more information, I recommend *Usability Engineering,* by Jakob Nielsen, and *Rocket Surgery Made Easy,* by Steve Krug.

Wrap-up

Could we have come up with a similar design using other techniques such as task- or feature-based design? Perhaps. But the drivers here are personas, scenarios, value, and effective communication. When features and technology are the drivers, these other objectives tend to get lost. Focusing on creating user scenarios, having effective communication, and delivering clear value is a great way to get a competitive edge in a crowded field.

> A communication-centered design approach, driven by user scenarios and effective communication, helps you and your team make solid user-centered design decisions quickly and confidently.

DESIGN CHALLENGE 2: AN AIRLINE TRAVEL MOBILE APP

One characteristic of our Filipe persona, the frequent business traveler, is that he needs to be able to check flight information and status quickly from anywhere using his smartphone. Since our users need mobile apps, let's apply the same communication-focused process to design one.

Good mobile apps take full advantage of what mobile devices are uniquely great at by:

- Focusing on doing "one thing" quickly and efficiently

- Optimizing for small screens and touch-based interaction

- Taking full advantage of device capabilities, such as Internet connectivity and location awareness

Consequently, well-designed mobile apps aren't just small desktop apps or sites. Rather, they focus on mobile scenarios and take full advantage of the mobile device capabilities. As a result, they may provide only a subset of the full desktop or Website functionality, or even completely different functionality.

Communicates
poorly

FIGURE 6.14

Well-designed mobile apps aren't just small desktop apps or sites.

Let's design a mobile app for dk-travel and see how it differs from the desktop Website.

Planning step 1: Start with a solid product concept

Let's start the planning phase by defining the concept for this product:

The dk-travel mobile app provides customers with all the trip-related information and services they need while traveling. Itineraries, flight status, check in, boarding passes, connections, changing reservations—it's all there. Travelers can get the important trip information they need in real time without having to check the full site, call customer service, or wait in line.

This concept has four important details:

- **The mobile app is optimized for scenarios you need while traveling.** Changing an existing reservation is an important mobile scenario, but booking a new reservation—the top desktop scenario—is not.

- **The mobile app needs to provide *important* information**—not all conceivable information. Users may have to refer to the full site for less important information.

- **The mobile app needs to provide timely information.** Stale flight status info has little value when your flight has just been canceled and your travel plans are in jeopardy.

- **We consider the app a success if users don't need to use the full site** or call customer service while traveling to get important information and services.

This approach will make the dk-travel mobile app a complement to the full Website, not a replacement for it.

Planning step 2: Provide clear value through the value proposition

Let's now define a value proposition, which will provide the reasons that users will want to use the site.

The dk-travel mobile app is the fastest, simplest way to get timely flight status, check in, get boarding passes, check connections, and change reservations.

Delivering on this value proposition is crucial because value is what motivates people. If the dk-travel mobile app fails to deliver value compared to the alternative solutions, nothing else about the design is going to matter. So to be successful, the dk-travel mobile app must make the top scenarios as fast and simple as possible. It's all about speed and simplicity. After all, if the alternatives were faster and easier, why bother?

Planning step 3: Model the target users through personas

We can use the same personas as the desktop site because they describe the classes of users that we are interested in. Still, we can supplement the original personas with characteristics about their mobile app usage for travel information. **Let's now enhance our three personas to characterize their use of the dk-travel mobile app.**

Michele, the occasional business traveler:

- Has a smartphone, carries it in her pocket or purse while traveling.
- Occasionally checks her smartphone while boarding and unboarding a plane and while waiting in the terminal.
- Most likely to check itineraries, flight and connection status.
- Knows the common touch gestures.
- May also bring a tablet or laptop.

Filipe, the frequent business traveler:

- Has a smartphone, carries it while traveling—often in his hand.
- Constantly checks his smartphone while boarding and unboarding a plane and while waiting in the terminal. Prefers doing so with a single hand.
- Most likely to check flight and connection status but will take advantage of any other features as long as they are quick and easy to use.
- Knows most touch gestures.
- May also bring a tablet or laptop.

Marie, the leisure travel bargain hunter:

- Has a smartphone, carries it in her purse while traveling.
- Occasionally checks her smartphone while boarding and unboarding a plane and while waiting in the terminal.
- Far more likely to check email and messaging than the dk-travel mobile app.
- May check flight and connection status but more likely to have her mind on other things.
- Knows only the basic touch gestures. She doesn't use double-tap, touch and hold, swipe, or multitouch.
- Will not bring a tablet or laptop while traveling, so if she can't do a task with her smartphone she will have to call the airline. (On occasion, people use their smartphones to make phone calls.)

With these mobile personas, we now have a much better understanding of the target users and their goals. For example, knowing that leisure travelers are more likely to monitor their messages and email than the mobile app suggests that they might prefer to opt into travel-related messages than to use the app itself.

As before, we don't need long, detailed documents to do this design. We can keep it quick and simple. These personas should be based on research data instead of speculation, but do the best you can.

Planning step 5: Understanding what users will do through top scenarios

Let's now define the top scenarios: those contextual tasks that users are most likely to do and that will delight users when done especially well. These scenarios will then drive many design decisions.

Here are some good top scenarios for the dk-travel mobile app:

1. Filipe travels so frequently that he has trouble remembering his next flight and its details, including departure times, carriers, confirmation codes, flight numbers, and durations. He would even appreciate a reminder of the trip a day before, just in case.

2. Michele and Filipe want to check the status of their next flight or connection using the mobile app. Marie would prefer to receive an email or text message if a flight is delayed or cancelled.

3. Michele and Filipe would like to check in the day before departure and use their smartphones to show their boarding passes. Marie has to check baggage, so she is more likely to check in at the airport.

4. If they miss a connection, Michele and Filipe would like to book another connection quickly using the mobile app. Marie might do that, too, but she also might see a gate agent.

5. Filipe occasionally needs to change flights (usually to delay the return) when things don't go as planned. He would like to see all the reasonably priced alternative flights, along with the total cost of making the change.

6. Michele and Filipe need easy access to the total ticket and baggage costs to help fill out their expense reports.

7. Michele and Filipe would like an easy way to make sure they receive credit for their frequent-flyer programs and to claim credit if they don't.

These scenarios will be much easier to do on a well-designed mobile app than on the full Website. We are now ready to start designing!

Design step 1: Defining conversations to focus on effective human communication

Let's put some thought into conversations to help us better understand what we need to present in the UI. **Here is a conversation for accessing travel information:**

Access travel information Traveler

I need to know the details for an upcoming flight. I especially need to know if anything has changed since the original reservation. To start my trip, I need the following:

- The next flight
- The flight destination
- The fight date

Travel agent: Based on that information, here is the information for your upcoming flight:

- Final destination and trip dates (to identify the trip)
- For each segment (with any changes clearly identified)
  - Departure and arrival date and time, plus duration
  - Carrier, flight number, and confirmation code
  - Departure and arrival airports
  - Gates
  - Seats
  - A timestamp to show when the information was last updated.

Would you like me to remind you the day before the flight?

- Choices: No, yes, by alarm, email, or text message.
- Default: Alarm

Supporting UI:

- **User action:** User reviews the flight information, finds information they are looking for plus any changes, opts in for flight reminder. Optional: If there is a flight change that is unacceptable, make it easy for user to review alternatives.
- **Input:** User should only have to select the desired flight from a list. No other input or knowledge required.
- **Visual details:** Any changed flight information should be obvious at a glance.
- **Success criteria:** Users should be able to make each selection with confidence, without assistance or error. Users should be able to determine any flight changes and the timeliness of the information at a glance.

   Although we haven't designed a solution yet, we have documented what needs to happen in the conversation. And though this gives an overall guide for the design, there is still a tremendous amount of flexibility in the interaction and visual design. This is not a spec, nor is it requirements. We now know what to do, but we don't know how to do it yet.

Design step 2: Designing the task flow

Now that we know what we need to communicate, let's sketch out a high-level task flow. The task flow for accessing travel information is straightforward (see Figure 6.15). The goal here is to determine the screens, roughly what goes on them, and how to navigate between them.

FIGURE 6.15
A sketch of the task flow.

What's most notable about this task flow is what isn't there: no sign-in (no CAPTCHA!) and most notably, no homepage. A well-designed mobile app gets right down to business without any unnecessary hurdles. Desktop UIs need homepages; mobile apps don't.

Design step 3: Designing the screens

We now have enough information to sketch all the screens in the task flow for accessing flight information. They are shown in Figures 6.16 and 6.17.

FIGURE 6.16
A sketch of the screens for the flight information task (iPhone version).

FIGURE 6.17
A sketch of the screens for the flight information task (Android version).

Note that these are just sketches, not a full-blown design using the entire smartphone screen. At this point, we need to focus on the flow and the communication, not the details. We can get a lot of design work done just with this information. Designing the full screens would be the next step.

Designing for small touch screens means larger, easy-to-touch controls, fewer UI elements on the screen, and a top-down screen flow. It's especially important to make every UI element count.

Chapter 1 described *inductive UI*, **where task steps are designed to be self-explanatory (and therefore more intuitive) by having explicit main instructions that describe the purpose of the screen.** Few mobile apps use main instructions, primarily because screen space is limited and the top of the screen is so valuable.

However, mobile apps can use an alternative technique. Given that mobile apps are focused on doing "one thing" well and their screens are focused on single steps, users should be able to easily predict what they are supposed to do on a screen based on the context (the action that led to the screen) plus the top portion of the screen. Consider displaying a full main instruction only if it's not clear what to do based on the top portion of the screen. Using this technique forces you to design from the top of the screen down.

FIGURE 6.18
Can you predict what you are supposed to do on these screens based on this information alone?

I call this *mobile inductive UI*. **This concept is important enough that we should evaluate the task flow predictability as part of the design evaluation process.** If users can't accurately predict what they are supposed to do at a glance on each screen, we need to improve the task flow communication.

Design step 4: Getting the details right

Once all the screens are designed, it pays to take a step back and make sure we've got the details right before we move on to the refinement phase. For a mobile app, I like to review the following:

- **Mobile character.** Does it feel like a mobile app? Does it do "one thing" extremely well, focus on mobile scenarios, and take full advantage of the mobile device capabilities? Does it comply with the platform's guidelines? (BTW: The iOS Human Interface Guidelines, Android Design Guidelines, and Windows Phone Guidelines are all excellent.)

- **Value proposition.** Does the design really deliver benefits, reduce costs, and make its value obvious?

- **Scenarios and persons.** Have we got the details right to fully support the scenarios? Are the user goals being achieved? Is the design consistent with the mobile persona attributes? Does the design work well in the user's environment and context?

- **Conversations.** Does the design address the details we identified when we created the conversations?

- **Problems solved.** Does the design solve the problems we identified during the planning phase?

- **Simplicity and optimization.** What can be removed? If we can't remove something completely, can we hide it by default? What can we optimize? Is there any unnecessary effort?

By performing this analysis for the mobile app, I want to make sure that:

- The app already knows all the user's booked flights, so getting travel information and changing flights require minimal interaction. Users should select but rarely have to type.

- The flight information is updated in a timely manner, and the timeliness is accurate and obvious.

- It is easy to make flight changes to the same destination. Only the most desirable flights are displayed by default, and the listings provide enough information to make an informed choice with confidence.

Once we make sure that we have a good story for these details, we are good to go.

Design step 5: Making a choice and getting real

At this point, we can complete the process for the mobile app by performing the steps as described in Chapter 5. Again, we need something concrete to evaluate. As always, I prefer to use the lightest-weight approach that will get job done well, and for me that is usually a paper prototype.

Let's assume that we have a detailed paper prototype and move on to the Refinement phase.

Refinement phase

You can apply all the techniques I described in the Refinement phase in Chapter 5 to mobile apps. I especially recommend scenario-based reviews, communication reviews, highlighter reviews, scanning reviews, and five-second tests, since they all work well for mobile apps.

You might want to consider doing what I call a *one-handed review*, where you try to perform the top scenarios using a single hand. Some tasks require using two hands, and that's fine, but use this test to make sure that any tasks that don't require both hands can be done reasonably well with a single hand.

Well-designed mobile apps aren't just a small version of a desktop app or site. Rather, they focus on mobile scenarios and take full advantage of the mobile device capabilities. As a result, they may provide only a subset of the full desktop or Website functionality, or even completely different functionality.

SUMMARY

If you remember only six things:

1. **A communication-driven approach works well for most situations and it allows you to leverage everyday interpersonal communication skills.** If you can explain how to perform a complex task in person in a way that's clear and concise, this process will help you map that explanation into the language of UI—in a way that is naturally user and user-goal centered.

2. **A good user interface must go well beyond mechanically enabling a task.** Enabling a task is the first step, not the last. You need to do some work to map what the technology wants into a UI that users can understand and use easily and that meets their goals.

3. **There is value in good planning.** Tools such as scenarios, personas, value propositions, and user research data create a decision-making framework to help you make the right decision quickly and confidently.

4. **Sketching is a simple, efficient way to visualize and explore design ideas, but it focuses mostly on the *physical presentation* of the UI, and the evaluation is mostly visual.** Your sketches will be more productive if you put some thought into what you need to communicate first.

5. **Consider starting the design phase by defining conversations**, which summarize what the UI needs to communicate about the task in terms of steps and user input, which in turn mirrors how you would explain the task in person.

6. **Well-designed mobile apps aren't just small desktop apps or sites.** Rather, they focus on mobile scenarios and take full advantage of the mobile device capabilities. As a result, they may provide only a subset of the full desktop or Website functionality, or even completely different functionality.

EXERCISES

To improve your ability to use a communication-focused design process, try the following exercises. *Assume that anything is possible. Don't let concerns about development costs or current technology limitations inhibit your thinking.*

1. **Setting clock times.** Choose an everyday product that has a built-in clock (such as a car, coffee maker, security system). Design a UI that enables users to change the time correctly on the first try, without experimentation or mistakes. Perform some usability testing to validate your design.

2. **Setting radio stations and alarm times.** Design a clock radio for a hotel room that enables travelers to choose radio stations and set wakeup times efficiently and without error. How does the hotel room context change the design? How does having good feedback improve the design?

3. **Forgiving calculator.** Design a calculator that prevents common mistakes and makes it easy for users to correct them. Characterize what common mistakes can be prevented, easily corrected, or not easily corrected. For serious mistakes, is there an alternative to starting completely over? How important is having good feedback?

4. **Car rental GPS.** Design a GPS navigation system specifically for rental cars. How does the car rental context change the design? How are the car rental GPS scenarios different? How are the users different? Consider privacy concerns as well.

5. **Microwave oven control panel.** Design a control panel for a microwave oven. Use carefully crafted scenarios and personas to drive your design decisions. Can users perform the top scenarios quickly and conveniently—without making mistakes? Is the design forgiving when users do make mistakes?

6. **Microwave oven app.** Now suppose that the microwave oven doesn't have a control panel but is controlled wirelessly by a mobile device. Redesign the previous UI for a mobile experience. How does the design differ? Do the scenarios change?

7. **Subway ticket kiosk.** Design a subway ticket kiosk for first-time users, experienced commuters, and families traveling together. Assume that the fare depends on the final destination, one-way versus round-trip, and the time of day (rush hour costs more). Consider the various problems users are likely to have or mistakes they are likely to make and either prevent them or help users recover easily.

8. **Exercise equipment control panel.** Design a control panel for a piece of exercise equipment, such as a treadmill or stair climber. Design it for first-time users, families, and health clubs. Allow users to start their preferred exercise quickly and conveniently—without making mistakes—but to also adjust the workout in progress. Give good feedback as users perform their exercise, and present it in a way that's fun, motivating, and informative.

9. **Car key fob.** Design a key fob for an automobile so that users can use it correctly without looking. Assume the fob is in usually in the user's pocket. Provide a Panic button, but design it so that users are unlikely to press it by accident and can stop it on the first try if they do. Now compare your design to your own key fob. How is it better?

10. **Design a site to book a conference room.** Consider the factors required to choose an appropriate room. Support both fixed and flexible requirements. What information do you need to provide so that users are confident that they have chosen the right room?

Conclusion

User interfaces are everywhere. When you encounter a new product, pay special attention to its design. If you like it and can figure out how to use it immediately, try to understand specifically why the design works well. If you dislike it or find it difficult to use, try to understand why and determine what you could do to fix the problem.

Although there are many roads to poor design, my bet is that most poor designs you find boil down to some form of ineffective human communication. The product was hard to use—not because you made mistakes as a user but because the product's designers failed to understand what you were doing with the product and how to communicate those tasks to you effectively. Instead, the designers probably thought that solving the problem mechanically was good enough and that you wouldn't mind investing the time and effort required to figure out how it works.

Over time, you will learn how to design intuitive, user-centered interfaces by focusing on effective communication. UI is communication!

Recommended Reading

Here are my "desert island" selections:

Buxton, B. (2007). *Sketching User Experiences: Getting the Design Right and the Right Design*. San Francisco, CA: Morgan Kaufmann. Reason: A beautiful exploration of the creative side of design.

Cooper, A., Reimann, R., & Cronin, D. (2007). *About Face 3: The Essentials of Interaction Design*. Indianapolis. In: Wiley. Reason: Seminal thinking on interaction design with good behavior for actual people and their goals instead of focusing on features and technology.

Goodwin, K. (2009). *Designing for the Digital Age: How to Create Human-Centered Products and Services*. Indianapolis. In: Wiley. Reason: An encyclopedic coverage of the UX design process. A great resource for answering design process questions.

Heath, C., & Heath, D. (2007). *Made to Stick: Why Some Ideas Survive and Others Die*. New York, NY: Random House. Reason: Not a UI book—rather, it's about effective human communication of ideas. While a different domain, the concepts are surprisingly similar to *UI Is Communication*.

Johnson, J. (2010). *Designing with the Mind in Mind: Simple Guide to Understanding User Interface Design Rules*. Burlington, MA: Morgan Kaufmann. Reason: An approachable summary of the human psychology behind design principles.

Krug, S. (2005). *Don't Make Me Think: A Common Sense Approach to Web Usability* (2nd ed.). Berkeley, CA: New Riders. Reason: An approachable introduction to UI design that presents many useful UI design principles.

Nielsen, J. (1993). *Usability Engineering*. Chestnut Hill, MA: Academic Press. Reason: The "bible" of usability engineering. Required reading for anyone doing usability studies, plus the foundation of usability heuristics.

Norman, D. (2002). *The Design of Everyday Things*. New York, NY: Basic Books. Reason: Now my second-favorite UI book recommendation. It's well named—Norman explores intuitive UI design by understanding the design of everyday things.

Redish, J. (2012). *Letting Go of the Words: Writing Web Content That Works* (2nd ed.). San Francisco, CA: Morgan Kaufmann. Reason: An excellent, communication-focused approach to writing for the Web. Required reading for anyone working with UI text.

Wroblewski, L. (2008). *Web Form Design: Filling in the Blanks*. Brooklyn, NY: Rosenfeld Media. Reason: An excellent, focused treatment of an important subject with a strong communication angle. LukeW came dangerously close to saying "Forms are communication."

Glossary

Above the fold   The area of a surface that is visible without scrolling. Originally this term referred to the part of a folded newspaper that (when piled in a stack) can be seen without picking it up.

Accessibility   Software is accessible when it can be used by the widest range of users, including those who have disabilities and impairments.

Access key   A key combination used to perform a command using the keyboard. Access keys are used primarily for accessibility. They usually can't be assigned consistently, so they aren't memorized but instead are documented in the program. By contrast, *shortcut keys* are for efficiency.

Acknowledgment   Feedback that shows that a command has been completed. Typically used when completion is important to users and there is no other obvious feedback.

Activity indicator   Feedback that shows a long-running task is being performed but without showing its progress. By contrast, a *progress indicator* indicates progress.

Affordance   Visual properties of a UI element that indicate how to perform an interaction. For example, push-button controls look like real-world buttons that can be pushed. If affordance is successful, users don't have to experiment or deduce how to perform the interaction.

Alignment   To arrange in a straight line. UI elements are often arranged horizontally so that their left edges align to an invisible vertical alignment grid. UI elements are also often arranged vertically so that text baselines align for a smooth reading line.

Antialias   A smoothing technique used to reduce the perception of a jagged appearance, such as subpixel rendering. Modern fonts use antialiasing to appear to have smooth shapes.

Animation   Used to give the appearance of motion or change over time. Use animations to give feedback, preview the effect of an action, show the relationship between objects, draw attention to change, or explain a task visually.

Attitude   The personality conveyed by a program. Software attitude mirrors human attitude.

Aspect ratio   The ratio of the width of an object and its height. For example, high-definition television uses a 16:9 aspect ratio.

Balance   Even spatial distribution of content on a surface. Surfaces with good layout feel balanced, whereas unbalanced layouts are often left-heavy.

Banner   Content displayed in a contrasting rectangular region on the screen, typically used to emphasize the content.

Banner blindness   The user tendency to ignore content presented on banners. Ironically, this often means that content intended to draw attention attracts it the least. The user's desire to avoid advertisements (which are typically displayed in banners) partially explains this phenomenon, but users also avoid looking at headings on banners, which clearly aren't ads.

Bar   A narrow pane on the side of a surface, typically used for commands or status information. Menu bars, toolbars, tab bars, navigation bars, and status bars are typical examples.

Below the fold   The area of a surface that requires scrolling to see. *Above the fold* originally referred to the part of a folded newspaper that (when piled in a stack) can be seen without picking it up.

Body language   The presentation of a UI element that suggests how it is used—beyond the purpose of the control. For example, the size of a text box indicates the typical maximum size of the expected text.

Brainstorming   An interactive group process for generating many ideas rapidly in order to discover creative, unobvious solutions to a challenging problem. Compare with *ideation*.

Branding   The expectations and positioning of a product and company (to differentiate from the competition) by its customers.

Button   A control with which the user's primary interaction is clicking or tapping.

Caret   A flashing vertical bar that shows the input position within a text box.

Check box   A control used to toggle an option on or off.

Chevron   An arrow-shaped glyph that indicates that there are more items available for display. Users click the arrow to show or hide the items.

Classic UI   Old-fashioned user interface conventions and styles that trace back to the original WIMP (windows, icons, menus, and pointer) style used by desktop UIs.

Color   The appearance of light as perceived by the eye. Color is often defined in terms of hue (shade), saturation (purity versus dullness), and luminosity (brightness).

Combo box   A control that is a combination of a text box and a drop-down list.

Command   An action provided by a program.

Command button   A control used to perform a command for which the primary user interaction is clicking or tapping. Same as a *push button*.

Commit button   A push button that performs the main purpose of a surface, proceeds to the next step in a task, or cancels the task. OK, Continue, Close, Done, Back, Next, and Cancel are common commit buttons. For example, Send might be the commit button on a page for which the purpose is to send emails.

Commit point   The point in a task flow where the user commits to the action. After the commit point, user actions might be difficult to reverse. A good task flow makes the commit point obvious. For example, in purchasing a product, Next commands aren't commitments, but Purchase is.

Confirmation   A message that verifies that the user would like to proceed with an action. Effective confirmations are used with risky actions and offer a good reason not to proceed. If there is no such reason, don't give a confirmation.

Consistency   Conformity of appearance and behavior within a program or across programs. Consistency helps make programs easier to use (allowing users to leverage existing knowledge) and intuitive (by making interactions discoverable and predictable).

Context   The user's current circumstances. Context is an important part of scenarios and a great way to enable simplicity.

Context menu   A menu that displays only the commands and options relevant to the user's current context.

Contrast   The luminosity difference between the foreground and background. Strong contrast for text and glyphs makes them easier to read. Current accessibility guidelines require at least a 5:1 contrast ratio between text and its background.

Control   An interactive UI element.

Conversation   The dialogue between a program and users to perform a task; analogous to the conversation between two people.

Conversation pattern   The dialogue between a program and users to perform a task; analogous to the conversation patterns between two people.

Courageous design   A willingness to take intelligent risks to create a great user experience, such as doing the right thing without asking. Playing it safe often results in designs that are complex, annoying, and not enjoyable to use.

Cursor   An image that shows the current point of interaction on the screen and tracks the location of the mouse or similar input device. Also called a *pointer*.

Deductive UI   A task flow that isn't self-explanatory, requiring users to figure it out using thought and experimentation.

Default value   A value that is selected by default, typically determined by either the program or the user's previous selection.

Delayed effect   The effect of an action takes place later (when a commit button is pressed) instead of immediately.

Design   A process to make creative decisions on behalf of target users to create a product that satisfies their goals.

Design model   The designer's intention for the way a product is supposed to work. By contrast, a *user model* is the user's interpretation of how the design works. A design is intuitive when the design model and the user model are essentially the same.

Design thinking   A way of thinking about product design that truly understands and values great user experiences and takes the steps necessary to make them happen. In contrast to *design talking*.

Designing like a programmer   The mistaken belief that a good UI mechanically enables a task. Such UIs often directly expose whatever the underlying technology needs from users to perform a task, without thinking about the target user's goals, knowledge, or context.

Desktop UI   Refers to UIs designed primarily for desktop and laptop computers, as opposed to mobile devices.

Dialog box   A window that allows users to perform a command or answer questions or that provides users with information or feedback. Lightboxes are typically used instead for Web UI, to avoid pop-up blockers. Sheets are modal dialog boxes attached to specific documents in Macintosh.

Dialogue   A two-way conversation pattern where users control the conversation. By contrast, a *monologue* is a one-way conversation pattern.

Direct manipulation   An action that users perform directly on a UI element as opposed to indirectly through a command, menu, or dialog box.

Disabled   A UI element that temporarily prevents interaction. A disabled state is shown visually by replacing the element's affordances, usually with something simple, gray, and flat.

Discoverability   The ability for users to find a UI element quickly—when and where they need it.

Display   Another term for *screen*.

Drag and drop   A direct manipulation to perform an action by physically moving a UI element.

Drag   A touch gesture used to move an object, reorder a list, or pan or scroll a view. Contrast with *flick* and *swipe*.

Drop-down list   A list control that is normally collapsed, showing only the currently selected item. Has a drop button to reveal the list of choices.

Dynamic UI   A UI element that is displayed dynamically, either on demand or as a side effect of an interaction with another UI element.

Dynamic sizing   Where controls are visible statically but their sizes change dynamically based on the current context. For example, if the user clicks on one control, it will enlarge and make neighboring controls smaller.

Elastic user   A target user that hasn't been specifically defined, so they have whatever attributes each team member wants them to have at the moment.

Ellipsis   Three dots (...) to indicate incompleteness. Typically used to indicate (1) that a command requires additional information to execute, (2) that a task is in progress, or (3) truncated text.

Emotional intelligence   An experience that has functionality and details that connect to users on an emotional level.

Error message   A message that states a problem that has already occurred. By contrast, a *warning* describes a condition that might cause a problem in the future.

Expert evaluation   A type of design evaluation that involves "experts" (instead of real users) applying techniques or rules to evaluate the design on the behalf of real users. Contrast with *usability lab study* and *user research*.

Feature   A capability provided by a program.

Feedback   An indication that an action is being performed or has completed successfully or unsuccessfully.

Field   A control that users type into; usually a text box.

Flick   A touch gesture that is a quick, straight stroke of a finger, typically used to pan or scroll a view quickly. Contrast with *drag* and *swipe*.

Flow   A mental state in which users are fully absorbed in activity and during which they lose their sense of time and have feelings of great satisfaction. Term coined by Mihály Csíkszentmihályi.

Flyout   A slide-out pane that temporarily shows more information.

Focal point   The place where the user's eye looks first on a surface, typically the strongest UI element.

Font   A set of attributes for text characters, consisting of typeface, size, weight, italic, etc.

Forgiveness   The ability to let users easily recover from mistakes or to prevent mistakes from happening in the first place.

Gesture   A touch-based movement on the screen used to issue a command.

Glyph   A symbol used to label a command. Glyphs are flat (2-D without shading), monochrome shapes. By contrast, *icons* are 3-D, shaded, full-color pictures.

Goal   At the highest level, the reason that people use a product or feature.

Graphic design   The visual design of a product—how it looks. Compare with *interaction design* and *information architecture*.

Grouping   An organization that shows relationships of UI elements.

Guideline   A rule, based on experience and convention, which makes a design easy to use and understand and have familiar, consistent appearance and behavior. Contrast with design *principle*.

Gutenberg diagram   A scanning pattern whereby users scan a page using an arching pattern, starting in the upper-left corner and ending in the lower right. Along the way, they might notice the upper-right corner (the strong fallow area) but see the lower-left corner (the weak fallow area) last.

Heat map   A visualization that shows where users are spending their time, by following either users' eyes (eye tracking) or the computer's pointer (mouse tracking).

HiPPO   An acronym for the *Highest-Paid Person's Opinion*; often someone with strong personal opinions that are counter to what target users really want. Not *your* boss, of course.

Hue   The shade of a color. The other color components are *saturation* and *luminosity*.

Hover   Holding the pointer over a single screen location, which can result in displaying dynamic UI elements. Hover isn't supported by touch-based devices.

Icon   A small picture—often rendered using 3-D, full color, and shading—used to label a command, option, or object. By contrast, *glyphs* are flat (2-D without shading), monochrome symbols or shapes.

Icon overlay A small overlay placed on top of an icon to provide status-related information.

Ideation A process for generating many ideas rapidly in order to discover creative, unobvious solutions to a challenging problem. Term derived from *idea generation*. In contrast to *brainstorming*, ideation isn't necessarily an interactive group activity.

Immediate effect When the effect of an action takes place immediately instead of later (when a commit button is pressed).

Immersive read A comprehensive reading mode in which users read almost everything in a left-to-right, top-to-bottom order (in Western cultures). By contrast, users *scan* to find things quickly.

Inductive UI A self-explanatory task flow that users easily understand without thinking or experimentation.

Information architecture The design of the organization, labeling, searching, and navigating of information within a product so that things are easy to find. Compare with *interaction design* and *visual design*.

Instruction Text that explains what users are supposed to do with a surface or control.

Interaction design The interaction design of a product—how it "feels." Compare with *information architecture* and *visual design*.

Intuitive A UI is intuitive when target users understand its behavior and effect without use of reason, memorization, experimentation, assistance, or training.

Inverted pyramid A presentation style in which the most important information is placed first and details follow according to their importance. Using this style, users can stop reading at any time once they have the information they need.

Invisible An interaction that has no visual clues on the screen. For example, shortcut keys, gestures, and most drag-and-drop interactions are invisible. Alternatively, a UI is described as invisible when its mechanics are so smooth and natural that users are completely focused on their work and don't even notice the UI itself. Compare with *flow*.

Label UI text associated with a control.

Layout The placement, sizing, spacing, and emphasis of UI elements and content within a page.

Layout grid An invisible alignment system used to give a page a coordinated, orderly appearance.

Lightbox A pane that displays a step in a task without using a separate page. Used in Web pages. Similar to dialog boxes used in other desktop UI but avoids pop-up blockers.

Link A control used to navigate to another page or initiate a command.

List box A list control that always displays a portion of its contents. By contrast, a *drop-down list* is normally collapsed, showing only the currently selected item.

Luminosity The brightness of a color. The other color components are *hue* and *saturation*.

Main instruction An instruction that explains the purpose of a surface.

Manager feedback inversion   The tendency of managers to give feedback at exactly the wrong level.

Marking menu   A cascading menu system in which commands are chosen from segmented circles instead of linear lists. The benefits of this approach are that it doesn't require precise selection and that command selection patterns are like gestures. Both benefits are important in touch-based UI.

Mechanical design   An approach to design that focuses on performing a task mechanically, playing little attention to usability. See *Designing like a programmer.*

Menu   A list of available commands or options. A context menu displays only those commands and options relevant to the user's current context.

Menu bar   A bar used to display a comprehensive set of menus. By contrast, a *toolbar* displays the most frequently used commands.

Menu button   A button used to display a single menu. Compare with *split button.*

Message box   A window (often modal) that displays information about a particular condition, such as an error message.

Metaphor   When an object with similar behaviors or properties is used as a substitute. For example, the desktop used by Windows and Macintosh is a metaphor for a workplace. Compare with *metonym* and *synecdoche.*

Metonym   When a completely different but related object is used as a substitute. For example, Hollywood is a metonym of the U.S. cinema industry. Compare with *metaphor* and *synecdoche.*

Mobile UI   Refers to UIs designed for easily portable, touch-based smartphones and tablets, as opposed to desktop and laptop computers. Compare with *desktop UI.*

Modal   A state with specific or limited capability due to operating in a mode. Users must exit the mode or switch to another mode to access other capabilities.

Modern UI   Modern user interface conventions and styles that take advantage of modern UI technologies (that are rich, composite, and contextual), Internet connectivity, animations and transitions, intelligence, and responsiveness. Compare with *classic UI.*

Monologue   A one-way conversation pattern in which users have very little control over the conversation. By contrast, a dialogue is a two-way conversation pattern.

Natural conversation   An experience that feels like a real, in-person conversation between two people—without any unnecessary references to technology.

Natural mapping   An interaction in which there is a clear relationship between what the user wants to do and how to do it. For example, setting the time on an analog watch has natural mapping, whereas digital watches typically have unnatural mapping.

Navigation   Describes the interaction in which users find their way through a program to access information or a feature or to perform a multistep task.

Notification   Information that is useful and relevant but not critical. Notifications don't require the user's attention—they are ignorable.

One-handed review   An evaluation technique whereby users try to perform the top scenarios with a mobile device using a single hand.

Opt in   The ability for users to select optional features explicitly. Less intrusive to users than opt-out, especially for privacy and marketing-related features, because there is no presumption of the user's wishes.

Opt out   The ability for users to remove optional features they don't want. More intrusive to users than opt-in, especially for privacy and marketing-related features, because there is an assumption of the user's wishes.

Option   A choice available to users for customizing a program or feature. Same as a *setting*.

Page   A unit of presentation for an application, such as a Web-based app hosted in a browser. Classic UI typically uses windows instead of pages. Mobile UI uses *screens* instead of pages because mobile apps usually fill the entire screen. *Surfaces* refers to pages, windows, and screens generically.

Page flow   A multistep task with unconstrained navigation—users can choose the order of the steps. Contrast with a *wizard*, which has constrained navigation.

Palette   A movable window that displays a set of related commands. Essentially an undocked toolbar.

Pane   A rectangular region within a surface, typically used for secondary information or commands. For example, most browsers expose their Find feature through a pane.

Persona   A fake person constructed with user research data to represent a class of real target users. Personas are the actors in scenarios.

Personality   The characteristics of a product that connect emotionally with users. All software has a personality—whether intentional or not—so it is better to have a personality that is carefully designed than one that is accidental.

Pixel   An individual physical point in an image, with red, green, and blue subelements. Term derived from *picture element*. Contrast to *point* and *subpixel*.

Placeholder   A label for a text box placed as temporary, uneditable text within the control itself, instead of an external label.

Platform   An environment for using and developing software. Windows, Macintosh, iOS, Android, and HTML5 are current platforms.

Point   An individual virtual point used to lay out and size UI elements, which may consist of more than one pixel. For example, Apple's Retina Display has four pixels for each point (two pixels in each dimension). Contrast to *point* and *subpixel*.

Pointer   An image that shows the current point of interaction on the screen, controlled by a mouse or similar input device. Also called a *cursor*.

Principle   A high-level concept, based on experience, that helps designers recognize good design. Contrast with *guideline*.

Progress indicator   Feedback that shows the rough progress of a long-running task. By contrast, an *activity indicator* just shows that the task is being performed. Despite the name, an indeterminate progress bar is an activity indicator, not a progress bar.

Progressive disclosure   A technique of displaying the most commonly used controls and information by default, but users can display more on demand.

Property   An attribute or setting for an object.

Prototype   An interface mockup that demonstrates how a program or features is going to look or behave. Used to communicate, improve, and test established design ideas, whereas *sketching* is used to conceive, visualize, and explore the ideas in the first place.

Purposeful   Instructions that explain what users are supposed to do, focusing on the objective and tying them to the user's goals and motivation—instead of the basic mechanics of the interaction. *Mechanical instructions* explain what to do physically, whereas *purposeful instructions* explain how and why.

Push button   A control used to perform a command for which the user's primary interaction is clicking or tapping. Same as a *command button*.

Pyramid   An academic presentation style whereby baseline facts are placed first, ultimately concluding with the most important information. Using this style, users must read the entire presentation to benefit. Contrast with *inverted pyramid*.

Radio button   A control used to select from a mutually exclusive set of options.

Required input   Input that users must provide, typically with either a text box or a list without a default value.

Respect   When a UI recognizes that there is an impatient, emotional human being at the other end of the interaction by valuing the user's time, paying attention and remembering user input, and behaving with an appropriate etiquette—like a good assistant.

Responsive   When an interface allows users to perform productive work as quickly as possible. For productivity, responsiveness is more important than overall speed.

Ribbon   A command bar that organizes a program's commands and options into a series of tabs at the top of a surface.

Robot   A nonhuman user who only cares about solving problems mechanically and is unemotional, is extremely patient, doesn't get distracted or bored, and never makes mistakes. Of course, there are no nonhuman users—hence the problem with designing for robots.

Sans-serif font   A font without serif strokes, used to make the letters more legible.

Saturation   The purity or dullness of a color. The other color components are *hue* and *luminosity*.

Scan   A mode of reading in which users try to find things quickly. By contrast, users read *immersively* to read everything for comprehension.

Scan path   The path the user's eye generally follows when scanning a surface.

Scenario   Describes a specific target user trying to achieve a specific goal or perform a specific task in a specific context. Scenario-based design is better than task- or feature-based design because it focuses on the user's perspective on the task instead of just the mechanical details.

Screen   Usually refers to the entire display but may be used to refer to a window or page. For example, the *sign-in screen* for a Website is actually a page.

Scroll   To move the content of a surface to change its visible portion.

Sentence capitalization   A capitalization style that capitalizes the first word of a new sentence. Compare with *title capitalization*.

Serif font   A font with small turns that often finish the strokes of letters, used to make the letters more readable.

Setting   A choice available to users for customizing a program or feature. Same as an *option*.

Shortcut key   A key combination used to perform commands quickly using the keyboard. They usually aren't documented directly in the UI, so they are memorized (by advanced users) and therefore must be assigned consistently within an app and across different apps. By contrast, access keys are primarily for accessibility.

Simplicity   The reduction or elimination of design elements that target users are aware of and consider unessential.

Sketch   A quick way to conceive of, suggest, and explore design ideas with your team during the activity of ideation, usually on paper or whiteboards. Sketching is used to explore design directions in the first place, whereas *prototyping* is used to communicate, improve, and test established ideas.

Skeuomorphism   A derivative design that retains ornamental design details from the original design. For example, a note-taking app might have a spiral wire binder graphic to suggest a bound notebook, even though that detail serves no practical purpose.

Slider   A control used to select from a range of values, where the desired value isn't exactly known or the exact value isn't meaningful. For example, the numeric value of a volume slider usually isn't meaningful to users—making a slider an appropriate choice.

Split button   A push button combined with a drop-down menu accessed by clicking on a down arrow on the side of the push button. Clicking the main push button performs a frequently used default command, whereas the drop-down menu has related but less frequently used commands. Compare with a *menu button*.

Static UI   A UI element that isn't interactive, or a UI element that is always displayed. Contrast with *dynamic UI* and *control*.

Step   An individual unit of activity in a multistep task. A task achieves a user goal, whereas a step alone may not. Simple tasks may have only one step.

Storyboard   A conceptual visual description of a use case, illustrating the interactions between the user and the software.

Subpixel rendering   A way to increase the apparent resolution of a display by taking advantage of the red, green, and blue subelements to smooth out fonts and drawings.

Surface   A UI element used to present content such as a screen, window, or page. Surfaces have different weights, are fixed or floating, and may or may not be modal.

Swipe   A touch gesture that is straight across an object, typically used to reveal commands or more information. Contrast with *drag* and *flick*.

Synecdoche   When a part represents the whole. For example, using a fork on a map to represent a restaurant is a synecdoche. Compare with *metaphor* and *metonym*.

Tab   A control used to display different information or different views of the same information within a single pane.

Target user   A user of a product or feature on whose behalf you need to make design decisions. The key insight: Target users aren't you. Or your mom ... or your boss ... or your boss's mom.

Task   A unit of activity that achieves a user goal, which may consist of several steps. A task achieves a user goal, whereas a step alone may not. Simple tasks may have only one step.

Task flow   The presentation of a multistep task across pages or within a single page.

Termination point   The place where the user's eye stops when scanning across a surface.

Text box   A control used to input unconstrained text, such as names and addresses. Because they are unconstrained, text boxes require more knowledge and are more error prone than other controls.

Title capitalization   A capitalization style that capitalizes all nouns, verbs, adverbs, adjectives, and pronouns but not articles, conjunctions, or prepositions. However, this style capitalizes the first and last words, regardless of their parts of speech. Compare with *sentence capitalization*.

Tone   The attitude a UI conveys to the user. Tone is an important part of software personality. For most software, the best tone is professional yet friendly.

Top scenario   Among the most important scenarios used to drive the design process—one that users are most likely to do and that will delight users when done especially well.

Toolbar   A docked bar that displays the most frequently used commands and options. An undocked toolbar is often called a *palette*. By contrast, a *menu bar* displays a comprehensive set of commands and options.

Tooltip   A small pop-up pane that labels or explains the control being pointed to.

Touch   Direct interaction with a display using a finger. Multitouch uses more than one finger.

Training   The time, effort, and money required to learn how to use an unintuitive product. Nobody wants to spend money on training.

Transition   A type of animation used to keep users oriented during state changes and object manipulations. Good transitions give the illusion of interacting with real-world objects.

Typeface   The visual style of a font. A font consists of a typeface, size, weight, italics, etc.

Value proposition   The reason users will want to buy and use a product or feature. It evaluates the benefits and costs of using a product or feature as well as its differentiation with alternative solutions. A good value proposition motivates users, whereas a weak value proposition means that they won't care.

Visible   A command that has visual clues on the screen.

Visual design   The visual design of a product—how it looks. Compare with *interaction design* and *information architecture*.

Visual hierarchy   A presentation format that emphasizes the most important information and is easily scannable. Surfaces are harder to scan and read if all UI elements appear uniformly.

Unintuitive   A UI that requires thought, memorization, experimentation, assistance, or training to use. Not immediately self-explanatory.

Usability lab study   A user research technique to evaluate and find improvements to a design by testing it with real users performing real tasks, often in a usability laboratory. Contrast with *expert evaluation*.

Use case   A list of steps that define the interaction between a user and a program to achieve a goal.

User-centered design   A design philosophy and process focused on satisfying the needs of target users for a product.

User experience (UX)   Encompasses the entire experience users have with a product. That experience includes the user interface, but it also transcends the UI to include the internals that users don't interact with directly as well as the externals, such as the purchasing process, the initial product experience (often called the *out-of-box* experience), customer and technical support, product branding, etc.

User manual   A document that explains why a UI isn't intuitive.

User model   The user's interpretation of the way a design works. By contrast, the *design model* is the designer's intention of how a product is supposed to work. A design is intuitive when the design model and the user model are essentially the same.

User interface (UI)   What connects users to the product's underlying technology. It is what users see and feel directly when using the product. Contrast with *user experience*.

User research   Refers to a variety of techniques used to gain insight into user needs and behaviors. Includes usability lab studies, user interviews, contextual inquiries, focus groups, surveys, A/B tests, and data mining.

User story   One or more sentences in concise, plain language that capture a user's goal or task as part of his or her role in using a product. Although agile development methods employ *user stories*, this book recommends using *scenarios* for UI design instead.

UI is Communication   The concept that a user interface is essentially a conversation between users and a product to perform tasks that achieve users' goals, so well-designed UIs require effective human communication.

UI Tetris   A design technique that focuses on solving a design problem mechanically—placing controls because they fit, not because they belong. Like a game of Tetris—one you eventually lose.

Warning   A message that describes a condition that might cause a problem in the future. By contrast, an *error message* states that a problem has occurred.

Web navigation   A task navigation model that has clear means to advance to the next step, a consistent way to go back to the previous step, a consistent way to get home or cancel the task, and if helpful, a consistent way to search.

Window   A rectangular surface on which programs and content appear and that typically can be moved, resized, or minimized. Web UI typically uses pages instead of windows. Mobile UI uses screens instead of windows because mobile apps fill the entire screen.

Wireframe   A prototype with content and functionality represented by rough controls, rectangles, lines, text, and simple glyphs. Layout and element sizes are rough, and details such as colors, backgrounds, fonts, graphics, and icons are often omitted.

Wizard   A multistep task with constrained navigation—steps have a fixed order. Contrast with a *page flow,* which has unconstrained navigation.

Index

Note: Page numbers with "*f*" denote figures, "*t*" denote tables and "*b*" denote boxes.